Traditional Islam in the Modern World

This book seeks to distinguish clearly between traditional Islam and both modernism and the ''fundamentalist'' or resurgent forms of Islam which are often confused with traditional Islam. The author, who speaks from the traditional point of view, delineates clearly how traditional Islam, as rooted in the Quran and the prophetic *Sunnah*, and as lived over the centuries by Muslims, differs from both the modernist and the ''fundamentalist'' schools in so many domains ranging from art and science to politics. He then discusses the encounter of traditional Islam with the challenges which face it in the modern world in general, as well as in the specific realms of education, science, philosophy and architecture and urbanism which are of central concern to the contemporary Muslim world.

The book also devotes a section to some of the leading Western interpreters of Islam who in one way or another have appreciated and made known some aspects of traditional Islam to the West and who represent another dimension of the encounter between traditional Islam and the modern world. Finally, the existing tendencies of thought in the Islamic world are described. The author considers how these tendencies may develop in the future and looks at the trends which are most likely to dominate the Islamic world in the years to come.

The Author

S.H. Nasr was born in Iran. He studied in America where he received his BS in physics from M.I.T. and his MA and PhD in the history of science and learning with concentration in Islamic Science, from Harvard. From 1958-79 he was professor of philosophy at Tehran University. In 1979 he became Professor of Islamic Studies at Temple University and is now University Professor of Islamic Studies at George Washington University.

Dedicated to Sayyidī
Abū Bakr Sirāj al-Dīn
al-Shādhilī al-ʻAlawī
al-Maryamī

Other works by Seyyed Hossein Nasr in European languages

Three Muslim Sages
Ideals and Realities of Islam
An Introduction to Islamic Cosmological Doctrines
Science and Civilization in Islam
Sufi Essays (also as Living Sufism)
An Annotated Bibliography of Islamic Science
Man and Nature: The Spiritual Crisis of Modern Man
Islam and the Plight of Modern Man
Islamic Science: An Illustrated Study
The Transcendent Theosophy of Ṣadr al-Dīn Shīrāzī
Islamic Life and Thought
Knowledge and the Sacred
Islamic Art and Spirituality
Need for a Sacred Science
The Islamic Philosophy of Science

Traditional Islam in the Modern World

Seyyed Hossein Nasr

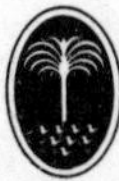

KEGAN PAUL INTERNATIONAL
London and New York

First published in 1987 by
Kegan Paul International Ltd
PO Box 256, London WC1B 3SW, England

First paperback edition 1990. Reprinted 1994

Distributed by
John Wiley & Sons Ltd
Southern Cross Trading Estate
1 Oldlands Way, Bognor Regis
West Sussex, PO22 9SA, England

Columbia University Press
562 West 113th Street
New York, NY 10025, USA

Printed in Great Britain

ISBN 0 7103 0332 7

British Library Cataloguing in Publication Data
Nasr, Seyyed Hossein, 1933–
Traditional Islam in the modern world.
1. Islam
I. Title
297

ISBN 0 7103 0332 7

US Library of Congress Cataloging in Publication Data
A catalog record for this book is available from the Library of Congress

Contents

In the Name of God, Most Merciful, Most Compassionate

Preface

The extensive interest in Islam displayed in recent years in many Western circles, far from helping to make the various aspects of Islam better known, has often caused confusion. Distortions have also resulted from the passion which the subject arouses and from the vested interest that numerous parties have in the kind of treatment that Islam is given.

A few decades ago, Muslims could justly complain of the distortions present in studies by orientalists and Islamicists; also of the lack of interest on the part of the general Western public in matters Islamic. Today, thanks to genuine attempts by certain sections of the Islamic world to reassert their Islamic character and to seek to preserve the Islamic tradition, but also as a result of the unfortunate use of Islam by all kinds of political forces, apathy towards subjects of an Islamic nature has certainly diminished. A number of new misinterpretations have, however, arisen to supplement those of the more classical orientalists. There now exists a substantial body of journalistic treatments of Islamic subjects perpetrated in the name of scholarship [or masquerading as scholarship]; a leftist and often explicitly Marxist treatment of Islam, which has now moved out of the specifically identified Communist sphere to the West and even to certain parts of the Islamic world; and, finally, a new so-called resurgent or 'fundamentalist' Islam, which currently produces a quantitatively substantial literature in the European languages and plays no small role, in both words and deeds, in forming the image of Islam in the West.

As a result of the appearance of these and other contemporary interpretations of Islam, the task of understanding Islam as it has been lived and viewed traditionally over the centuries becomes ever more difficult. One knows who speaks for Western interpretations of Islam, who for the modernists within the Islamic world and who for that whole spectrum of thought and action usually called fundamentalism. But then, who speaks for traditional Islam: the Islam lived for centuries by theologians and jurists, by philosophers and scientists, by artists and poets, by Sufis and simple people of faith throughout the Islamic world during the fourteen centuries of Islamic history – the Islam which is in fact still followed by the vast majority of Muslims, from the Atlantic to the Pacific?

It is as a response to the pressing need to expound traditional Islam that this and all our other works on Islam have been written. Almost every day an issue arises in which the view of Islam is sought and usually either some modernistic or 'fundamentalist' response from quarters bearing Islamic credentials is provided – if not simply a scholarly answer by a Western Islamicist, who may in fact occasionally provide a more balanced one precisely because he is not personally entangled in the present-day intellectual tensions that beset the Islamic world. Whenever possible, we have sought to make a humble contribution to the knowledge of Islam in the West by presenting the traditional Islamic point of view precisely on such themes as are currently under debate.

In some of our earlier books, especially *Islam and the Plight of Modern Man* and *Islamic Life and Thought*, we have already provided studies of a number of traditional Islamic views that are in confrontation with the modern world. In the present volume, we continue this task by concentrating at the same time more fully upon the contrast between traditional Islam and its revivalist and 'fundamentalist' manifestations, and dealing with issues of particular significance to the Islamic world and to the Western understanding of Islam, beginning with a study of the nature of traditional Islam itself in the Prologue.

The first section then turns to some of the basic facets of the Islamic tradition which are being widely discussed today, beginning with the meaning of *jihād*, a term that has become almost a household word in the West but is widely misunderstood and often maliciously misinterpreted. A study is then made of work ethics as described in traditional Islamic sources and found within traditional Islamic society itself; we distinguish between the two and seek to bring out the permanent value of traditional Islamic work ethics and its continuing validity. In the next essay, attention is turned to the critical question of the relationship between the male and the female in both its inner as well as its social aspects. Without simply surrendering to current fads, yet accepting the challenges posed to Islam concerning the role and position of women, we have sought to provide knowledge of the metaphysical and psychological foundations in Islam of the male/female relationship, upon the basis of which all the social aspects of the relationship are founded. Finally in the first section, we have sought to provide some knowledge of Shi'ism as it developed in Safavid Persia as the state religion, thereby making available an in-depth theological and historical background necessary for an understanding of the role of Shi'ism in present-day Iran, and indeed in the whole of the Middle East.

The second section delves directly into the question of the confrontation of traditional Islam with modernism, beginning with an overall study of Islam in the present-day Islamic world and the relation between traditional, 'fundamentalist' and modernist elements and forces. There then follow some reflections upon the relationship between the intellectual aspects of traditional Islam and modern thought, and the impact of the tradition upon current intellectual life among Muslims. The section concludes with a chapter on an issue that is central to the struggle between various forces within the Islamic world, namely the meaning of 'development' in the context of Islamic values.

The third and longest section of this work is devoted to the study of the tensions between traditional Islam and modernism in various cultural contexts. Here we have dealt first and foremost with education, which is such a central issue in almost every Islamic country; then with philosophy, the study and teaching of which is closely related to education, on the one hand, and to the whole intellectual tension between tradition and modernism, on the other. Finally, we have turned to architecture and city planning, two closely related disciplines which again have together become a major arena of contention within the Islamic world, arousing much passion and debate, and also having a great impact upon the religious and cultural life of the whole community.

The final section of this work turns to the study of three exceptional Western interpreters of Islam, from the point of view of their contributions to Islamic studies, the first being a Catholic, the second a Protestant and the third a Muslim. This section not only seeks to bring out the value of the works of these scholars, but also demonstrates that traditional Islam, in contrast to the modernism and 'fundamentalism', bases its judgement of Western scholarship on truth and not merely on geography. While critical of what is distorted in orientalist scholarship, the traditional perspective does not allow itself to explode into vituperative statements simply because the author of a statement happens to be a Westerner; nor does its praise of any piece of scholarship on Islam simply arise out of an inferiority complex because that work is produced in a Western language and uses all the paraphernalia of modern scholarship. These essays hope to make clear what Western scholarship on Islam can do towards bringing about a better understanding when based upon sympathy and love, without having to compromise either the rigour of scholarship or (of even greater importance) the demands of the truth.

Although the future, according to the Islamic perspective, belongs to God and He alone has knowledge of it, there is today so much interest in the future of the Islamic world and in making projections from present-day trends, that we felt it necessary to give some attention to this burning issue. The final essay therefore seeks to deal with present tendencies in the Islamic world and how these trends are likely to develop in the near future. We have made this study in full awareness that all human knowledge and science fails to comprehend the exact stages of the unfolding of God's Will in human history and have therefore been careful to add that in such matters God knows best.

In preparing this manuscript for publication, we wish to express our profound gratitude to Katherine O'Brien, whose aid has been indispensable. We hope that this collection of essays will be a humble step towards bringing about better understanding in the West of the views of traditional Islam and also make the teachings of the Islamic tradition more easily accessible to those Muslims whose upbringing and training make this type of exposition more comprehensible to them than truths expressed in a traditional language. At the present moment, any step taken towards bringing about better understanding of Islam in the West cannot but be of mutual benefit to both the Islamic world and to the West: two worlds whose destinies are inter-related in ways that are not always perceptible but which embrace spiritual, artistic and intellectual life, as well as activities in the political and economic arenas – or all that constitutes both the tapestry of the inner life and that of human history as it unfolds in the matrices of time and space.

wa mā tawfīqī illā bi'Llāh

12 Ramaḍān, 1385 (A.H.)

June 1, 1985 (A.D.)

Prologue

What is Traditional Islam?

Two centuries ago, if a Westerner, or for that matter a Chinese Confucian or a Hindu from India, were to study Islam, he would have encountered but a single Islamic tradition. Such a person could have detected numerous schools of thought, juridical and theological interpretations and even sects which remained separated from the main body of the community. He would moreover have encountered both orthodoxy and heterodoxy in belief as well as in practice. But all that he could have observed, from the esoteric utterances of a Sufi saint to the juridical injunctions of an *'ālim*, from the strict theological views of a Ḥanbalite doctor from Damascus to the unbalanced assertions of some extreme form of Shi'ism, would have belonged in one degree or another to the Islamic tradition: that is, to that single tree of Divine Origin whose roots are the Quran and the *Ḥadīth*, and whose trunk and branches constitute that body of tradition that has grown from those roots over some fourteen centuries in nearly every inhabited quarter of the globe.

Then, some two hundred years ago, the waves of modernism began to reach the shores of *dār al-islām*, and with the passage of time gradually inundated them. One could detect the influence of modernist ideas and movements from the late 12th/18th and early 13th/19th centuries onwards in certain fields, such as military science, astronomy and medicine, in some parts of the Islamic world. Soon there were modernist trends in education, socio-political thought, law and, somewhat later, in philosophy and art; finally, such trends could be found in religion itself. For anyone who understood the essence of modernism based on and originating in the secularizing and humanistic tendencies of the European Renaissance, it was easy to detect the confrontation between traditional and modern elements in the Islamic world.

Only during the past few decades has a new phenomenon appeared which necessitates distinguishing rigorously between traditional Islam and, not only modernism, but also that spectrum of feeling, action and occasionally thought that has been identified by Western scholarship and journalism as 'fundamentalist' or revivalist Islam. There were, needless to say, revivalist movements going back to the 12th/18th century. But this earlier 'fundamentalism' associated with, let us say, Wahhabism or the Deoband school of India, was more a truncated form of traditional Islam, in opposition to many aspects of the Islamic tradition and highly exoteric but still orthodox, rather than a deviation from the traditional norm. Despite the fact that in the name of reform such movements did much to weaken and impoverish traditional Islam, they could still be understood in terms of the dichotomy between the traditional and the modern, although their importance has been much overemphasized in Western scholarship at the expense of the truly traditional revivers of Islam. There is much more written in European languages on such figures as Jamāl al-Dīn Astrābādī, known as al-Afghānī, or Muḥammad 'Abd al-Wahhāb than, let us say, on a Shaykh al-'Alawī, or 'Abd al-Qādir al-Jazā'irī seen in his religious and esoteric aspects and not simply as a political leader.[1]

Today, however, there is not only the modernist trend standing against the traditional but also a whole series of movements which speak of reviving Islam in opposition to modernism and that very Western civilization which, for several centuries, served as the soil in which modernism grew and was nurtured. It is precisely at this moment of history that it is crucial to distinguish these movements which have come to be called the 'new fundamentalism', or simply 'Islamic fundamentalism', from traditional Islam, with which they are often confused; although anyone who has read works of a traditional nature on Islam[2] and compared them to those championed by the current 'fundamentalists' can immediately discern the basic differences existing between them, not only in content but also in the whole 'climate' in which they breathe. Needless to say, that which is branded as 'fundamentalism' includes a wide spectrum, parts of which are close to the traditional interpretation of Islam. But the main thrust of that type of politico-religious movement now called 'fundamentalism' is different in such a basic manner from traditional Islam as to warrant the sharp distinction drawn between them here, despite the existence of certain areas where some types of 'fundamentalism' and certain dimensions of traditional Islam are in accord.

Before bringing out these basic differences, it is necessary to say a word about the term 'tradition' as used here and in all of our other writings. As used by the 'traditionalists', the term implies both the sacred as revealed to man through revelation and the unfolding and development of that sacred message in the history of the particular humanity for which it was destined in a manner that implies both horizontal continuity with the Origin and a vertical nexus which relates each movement of the life of the tradition in question to the meta-historical Transcendent Reality. Tradition is at once *al-dīn* in the vastest sense of the word, which embraces all aspects of religion and its ramifications, *al-sunnah*, or that which, based upon sacred models, has become tradition as this word is usually understood, and *al-silsilah*, or the chain which relates each period, episode or stage of life and thought in the traditional world to the Origin, as one sees so clearly in Sufism. Tradition, therefore, is like a tree, the roots of which are sunk through revelation in the Divine Nature and from which the trunk and branches have grown over the ages. At the heart of the tree of tradition resides religion, and its sap consists of that grace or *barakah* which, originating with the revelation, makes possible the continuity of the life of the tree. Tradition implies the sacred, the eternal, the immutable Truth; the perennial wisdom, as well as the continuous application of its immutable principles to various conditions of space and time.[3] The earthly life of a tradition can come to an end – and traditional civilizations do decay. But that decay, as well as the presence of contending schools of thought, which have always existed in traditional civilizations, are still within the framework of tradition. What is directly opposed to tradition is counter-tradition, to which we shall turn later, and of course modernism, without whose existence there would in fact be no need for the usage of such a term as 'tradition'. If traditionalists insist on the complete opposition between tradition and modernism, it is precisely because the very nature of modernism creates in the religious and metaphysical realms a blurred image within which half truths appear as the truth itself and the integrity of all that tradition represents is thereby compromised.

The significance of traditional Islam can also be understood in the light of its attitude towards various facets of Islam itself. It accepts, of course, the Noble Quran as the Word of God in both content and form: as the earthly embodiment of God's Eternal Word, uncreated and without temporal origin. It also accepts the traditional commentaries upon the Quran, ranging from the linguistic and historical to the sapiental and metaphysical. In fact, it interprets the Sacred Text, not on the basis of the literal and external meaning of the words alone, but on the basis of the long tradition of hermeneutics going back to the Blessed Prophet himself and relying upon oral transmission as well as upon written commentaries. The latter range from the works of Ḥasan al-Baṣrī and Imām Ja'far al-Ṣādiq to those composed by traditional authorities up to the present day.[4]

As for *Ḥadīth*, again the traditional school accepts the orthodox collection of the six *Ṣiḥāḥ* of the Sunni world and the 'Four Books' of Shi'ism. It is willing to consider the criticism brought forth against spurious *ḥadīth* by modern critics. But it is not willing to accept unquestioningly the premises upon which modern criticism is based, namely the denial of the penetration of the Sacred into the temporal order through revelation, the reality of oral transmission and the possibility of knowledge by the Prophet on the basis of direct access to the Source of all knowledge rather than from purely human agents of transmission. Traditional Islam does not reject *Ḥadīth* because it does not accord with the modern world's conception of historical causality and the diluted meaning of revelation which has even penetrated into modern Western religious thought. It relies upon the critical methods of *Ḥadīth* scholarship as cultivated over the centuries, but also as based on the historical continuity of the tradition and the *barakah* which protects the truth within a tradition as long as that tradition is alive. It is also open to all critical appraisals of the *Ḥadīth* corpus, as long as the criticism is not based on the assumption that what has left no traces in written records does not exist. The traditional perspective always remembers the famous principle of Islamic philosophy, that *'adam al-wujdān lā yadallu 'alā 'adam al-wujūd*'; that is, 'the non-existence of knowledge of something is not proof of its non-existence'.

Traditional Islam defends the *Sharī'ah* completely as the Divine Law as it has been understood and interpreted over the centuries and as it has been crystallized in the classical schools (*madhāhib*) of Law. Moreover, it accepts the possibility of giving fresh views on the basis of legal principles (*ijtihād*), as well as making use of other means of applying the Law to newly-created situations, but always according to such traditional legal principles as *qiyās*, *ijmā'* and *istiḥsān*.[5] Moreover, for traditional Islam, all morality is derived from the Quran and *Ḥadīth* and, in a more concrete manner, from the *Sharī'ah*.

As far as Sufism or the *Ṭarīqah* is concerned, traditional Islam considers it as the inner dimension or heart of the Islamic revelation, without denying either the state of decadence into which certain orders have fallen over the centuries or the necessity of preserving the truths of Sufism only for those qualified to receive them. The attitude of traditional Islam to Sufism reflects that which was current during the centuries prior to the advent of puritanical and modernist movements in the 12th/18th century, namely that it is the means for the attainment of sanctity meant for those wishing to encounter their Creator here and now and not a teaching meant to be followed by all members of the community. Again, the defense of Sufism is based on the acceptance of its reality as manifested in various Sufi orders and on respect for the diversity existing within these orders, not on the identification of Sufism with a particular order or school. Nor does the traditional school overlook the opposition that has existed between certain representations of the exoteric and esoteric dimensions of Islam. In fact, this opposition is understood as being necessary in the light of the nature of the Islamic revelation and the condition of the humanity to which the revelation was addressed. The traditional school thereby reiterates the view of authorities such as al-Ghazzālī, in the Sunni world, and Shaykh Bahā' al-Dīn al-'Āmilī, in the Shi'ite world, who have been masters of both the exoteric and esoteric sciences, and who have defended both dimensions of Islam while explaining why the esoteric comprehends the exoteric but the exoteric excludes and does not comprehend the esoteric.[6]

Not every traditional scholar has been a master of all the traditional schools of thought nor accepted all their premises and teachings. Even in the traditional world, followers of one school of *kalām* opposed other schools of *kalām*, followers of *kalām* opposed philosophy, and philosophers of one school those of another. But all these oppositions were once again within the traditional universe. The traditionalists do not defend only one school at the expense of others but insist on the value of the whole intellectual tradition of Islam in all of its manifestations, every one of which has issued from the Islamic revelation. Moreover, the various traditional schools of Islamic theology, philosophy and science are evaluated in the light of the Islamic world-view. They are in fact seen as keys to the understanding of aspects of the intellectual universe of Islam, rather than as stages in the growth of this or that school of Western philosophy or science and hence seen to be of value by many scholars only because of the contribution they have made to modern Western thought.

As far as art is concerned, traditional Islam insists upon the Islamicity of Islamic art, its relation to the inner dimension of the Islamic revelation and its crystallization of the spiritual treasures of the religion in visible or audible forms. Traditionalists insist upon the fact that religion possesses, not only a truth, but also a presence and that the *barakah* emanating from Islamic art is as essential for the survival of the religion as the *Sharī'ah* itself. Again it is recognised that certain forms of Islamic art decayed in certain areas and that some types of traditional art are more central and essential than others, but under no condition can one be indifferent to the power of forms over the human soul. One cannot simply neglect the significance of Islamic art by insisting only upon the ethical aspects of the religion. From the Quranic revelation there issued, not only regulations for how human beings should act, but also the specific principles according to which they should make things. Islamic art is directly related to Islamic spirituality,[7] and the traditionalists remain the staunchest supporters of traditional art against all the ugliness which now invades the Islamic world, in the form of architecture, artifacts and the like, in the name of compassion for human beings and concern for the material welfare of society.

In no domain is the difference between the traditional and modernist as well as 'fundamentalist' views more evident than in the fields of politics, social life and economics. As far as social life is concerned, the traditional perspective insists upon Shari'ite institutions and units, such as the family, the village and local urban quarters, and generally upon a social fabric based on the bonds created by religion. In economics, realism is never sacrificed in favour of an unrealizable idealism, nor is it thought possible to inculcate the virtues of hard work, honesty and frugality simply by external force or pressure. Economics is always seen as married to morality in the light of a human situation which preserves personal human contacts and trust between individuals, as one sees in the traditional bazaar, rather than as related to impersonal and grandiose organizations, whose very size precludes the possibility of direct human relationships.[8]

In the political domain, the traditional perspective always insists upon realism based upon Islamic norms. In the Sunni world, it accepts the classical caliphate and, in its absence, the other political institutions, such as the sultanate, which developed over the centuries in the light of the teachings of the *Sharī'ah* and the needs of the community. Under no condition, however, does it seek to destroy what remains of traditional Islamic political institutions, which are controlled by traditional restraints, in the hope of installing another Abū Bakr or 'Umar but meanwhile settling for some form of dictatorship. Moreover, such dictatorships are usually outwardly based on the external forms of political institutions derived from the French Revolution and other upheavals of European history, even though they are presented as the authentic Islamic form of government. As for the Shi'ite world, the traditional perspective continues to insist that final authority belongs to the Twelfth Imam, in whose absence no form of government can be perfect. In both worlds, the traditional perspective remains always aware of the fall of the community from its original perfection, the danger of destroying traditional Islamic institutions and substituting those of modern, Western, origin, and the necessity of creating a more Islamic order and of reviving society from within by strengthening faith in the hearts of men and women rather than by external force. The traditional image of socio-political revival is that of the 'renewer' (*mujaddid*), identified over the centuries with great saints and sages, such as 'Abd al-Qādir al-Jīlānī, al-Ghazzālī,

Shaykh Abu'l-Hasan al-Shādhilī and Shaykh Aḥmad Sirhindī, and not the so-called 'reformers' who have appeared upon the scene since the 12th/18th century.

To understand traditional Islam better, these views must be compared and contrasted with those of both the so-called 'fundamentalists' and the modernists. It is essential to remember that, at this moment in human history, one must distinguish in all religions and civilizations, not only between the traditional and the modern, but also between authentic tradition and that pseudo-tradition which is also counter-traditional, but which also displays certain characteristics outwardly similar to the traditional. As far as the Islamic world is concerned, these distinctions appear clearly once one is able to distinguish between the traditional, as here defined, and that pseudo-traditional perspective which is often identified with one form or another of 'fundamentalism'. This, while claiming to restore Islam to its original purity, is in fact creating something very different from the traditional Islam which was brought by the Prophet and which has survived and grown like a living tree during the fourteen centuries since his migration to Madinah.[9]

These differences between the traditional and the counter- or pseudo-traditional in Islam become clearer once the traditional is compared to the so-called 'fundamentalist' in specific fields.[10] The traditionalist and the so-called 'fundamentalist' meet in their acceptance of the Quran and *Ḥadīth*, as well as in their emphasis upon the *Sharī'ah*, but even here the differences remain profound. As already mentioned, tradition always emphasizes the sapiental commentaries and the long tradition of Quranic hermeneutics in understanding the meaning of the verses of the Sacred Text; whereas so many of the 'fundamentalist' movements simply pull out a verse from the Quran and give it a meaning in accordance with their goals and aims, often reading into it a meaning alien to the whole tradition of Quranic commentary, or *tafsīr*. As for the *Sharī'ah*, tradition always emphasizes, in contrast to so much of current 'fundamentalism', faith, inner attachment to the *dicta* of the Divine Law and the traditional ambience of lenient judgment based upon the imperfections of human society,[11] rather than simply external coercion based on fear of some human authority other than God.

Outside of this domain, the differences between the traditional and the counter-traditional in Islam are even more blatant. Most of the current 'fundamentalist' movements, while denouncing modernism, accept some of the most basic aspects of modernism. This is clearly seen in their complete and open-armed acceptance of modern science and technology. Many of them even seek a Quranic basis for modern man's domination and destruction of nature by referring to the Quranic injunction to man to 'dominate' (*taskhīr*) the earth, as if the man addressed in the Quran were not the perfect servant of God (*'abdallāh*) and God's vice-gerent on earth (*khalīfatallāh*), but rather the modern consumer. They engage in lengthy arguments to demonstrate how Islamic science served as the necessary background for Western science and made possible the creation of this science despite Christianity, forgetting completely that the nature and character of Islamic science are entirely different from those of modern science.[12] Their attitude to science and technology is in fact nearly identical with that of the modernists, as seen on the practical plane in the attitude of Muslim countries with modern forms of government compared to those which claim to possess one form or another of Islamic government. There is hardly any difference in the manner in which they try to adopt modern Western technology, from computers to television, without any thought for the consequences of these inventions upon the mind and soul of Muslims.

This common attitude is in fact to be found in the domain of knowledge in general. The process of the secularization of knowledge that has occurred in the West since the Renaissance, against all traditional Islamic teachings concerning 'science', (*al-'ilm*), is not only taken for granted as a sign of progress by the modernists, but is also hardly even noticed by the so-called 'fundamentalists'. By simply equating modern forms of knowledge with *al-'ilm*, the latter claim to follow the injunctions of Islam in their espousal of modern science, rarely asking themselves what kind of *'ilm* it was that the Blessed Prophet instructed his followers to seek from the cradle to the grave. Nor do they pause to ponder what are the real implications of the famous saying, sometimes attributed to 'Alī ibn Abī Ṭālib, 'I become the slave of him who teaches me a single word.' Could this 'word' possibly be a term pulled out of a chemistry dictionary, or one drawn from some computer language?[13] The real nature of much so-called 'fundamentalist' thought in its relation to modernism is made evident in the whole question of the process of the secularization of knowledge in the West and the adoption of the fruit of this process in so many quarters of the contemporary Islamic world, not to speak of some of the solutions being offered to the problem of the Islamization of knowledge by followers of both the modernist and the 'fundamentalist' camps.

Another remarkable similarity between the modernist and 'fundamentalist' groups which is in complete contrast to the traditionalist position is to be found in their attitude towards art. As already mentioned, traditional Islamic civilization is marked by its emphasis upon beauty being wedded to every aspect of human life, from the chanting of the Quran to the making of pots and pans. The traditional Islamic ambience, both the plastic and the sonoral, have always been beautiful, for traditional Islam sees beauty as a complement of the Truth. According to the well-known *ḥadīth*, God, who is also the Truth *(al-Ḥaqq)*, is beautiful and loves beauty. Moreover, the norms of Islamic art are inwardly related to the Islamic revelation and the spirituality which emanates from it.[14] Beauty represents the aspect of presence in religion, as doctrine represents the truth. Yet, how insignificant do the greatest masterpieces of Islamic art appear to both the modernists and 'fundamentalists', and how nearly identical is their view concerning the spiritual significance of Islamic art. If one camp now produces mosques which look like factories except for a pesudo-minaret or dome added superficially merely to signal the building's function, the other is known to have declared that it makes no difference whether Muslims pray in the most beautiful Mogul or Ottoman Mosque or in a modern factory, as if all Muslims were already saints and not in need of the external support of those forms which act as vehicles for the flow of Muḥammadan *barakah* to the individual and the community. The attitude towards art in its vastest sense should in fact be in itself sufficient to reveal the true nature of so-called revivalist or 'fundamentalist' Islam in relation to both modernism and traditional Islam as it always has been and will continue to be to the end of time.

Nowhere, however, does the veneer of Islamicity that covers so many movements claiming a revival of Islam wear more thinly than in the field of politics. Here, while calls are made to return to the origin of Islam, to the pure message of the Quran and to the teachings of the Prophet, and to reject all that is modern and Western, one ends up by adopting all the most extreme political ideas that have arisen in Europe since the French Revolution, but always portraying them as Islamic ideas of the purest and most unadulterated kind. One therefore defends revolution, republicanism, ideology and even class struggle in the name of a supposedly pure Islam prior to its early adulteration by the Umayyads, but rarely bothers to inquire whether the Quran or *Ḥadīth* ever used those terms or even why a movement which claims Islamicity is so direly in need of them, or indeed why the attack against traditional Muslim political institutions coincides so 'accidentally' with those of the left in the modern world?

The case of ideology is very telling as far as the adaptation of modern notions in the name of religion is concerned. Nearly every Muslim language now uses this term and many in fact insist that Islam is an ideology. If this be so, then why was there no word to express it in Arabic, Persian and other languages of the Islamic peoples? Is *'aqīdah* or *uṣūl al-'aqā'id*, by which it is sometimes translated, at all related to ideology? If Islam is a complete way of life, then why does it have to adopt a 19th century European concept to express its nature, not only to the West but even to its own adherents? The truth of the matter is in fact that traditional Islam refuses ever to accept Islam as an ideology and it is only when the traditional order succumbs to the modern world that the understanding of religion as ideology comes to the fore,[15] with momentous consequences for religion itself, not to speak of the society which is ruled in the name of religious ideology rather than according to the *dicta* of the *Sharī'ah*, as traditionally understood. To fail to distinguish between these two modes is to fail to grasp the most manifest distinction between traditional Islam and the 'fundamentalist'; in fact, it marks the failure to comprehend the nature of the forces at play in the Islamic world today.

A great deal more could be said concerning traditional Islam in contrast to both the modernist and 'fundamentalist' interpretations, although among the latter there are some groups which are closer to the traditional camp, while others are diametrically opposed to it and represent the counter-traditional. In conclusion, it is sufficient to add that the traditional school opposes the gaining of worldly power and any surrender to worldliness in the name of Islam, never forgetting the Quranic injunction that, 'The other world is better for you than this world.' While accepting the fact that Islam does not separate the religious from the 'secular' domain, traditional Islam refuses to sacrifice the means for the end and does not accept as legitimate the use of any and every possible political machination appropriated from completely anti-Islamic sources in order to gain power in the name of Islam. Moreover, traditional Islam does not condone intoxication fomented by hatred and anger any more than it does one caused by alcohol; nor does it see such a self-righteous and intoxicating hatred as a legitimate substitute for the need to solve the intellectual, moral and social problems which the Islamic world faces today.

Despite both modernism and this latter-day 'fundamentalism', traditional Islam still survives, not only in its past artistic and intellectual movements, but in the present-day lives of those scholars and saints who still follow the path of the Prophet, in those craftsmen and artists who continue to recreate those visual and audible forms that are vehicles for the grace of the Quranic revelation, and in that vast majority of Muslims whose hearts, minds and bodies still reverberate to the traditional teachings of Islam. One can even say that there has been a certain revival of traditional Islam in the spiritual, intellectual and artistic domains during the past few decades: a revival that has gone largely unnoticed because of the sensationalism of most of the news media and the lack of comprehension of many scholars concerned with the contemporary Islamic world. Traditional Islam will in fact endure to the end of history, for it is none other than that tree whose roots are sunk in the Quranic revelation and whose trunk and branches have constituted all that Islam has been over the centuries, before the aberrations and deviations of modern times came to cause many to confuse this authentic tradition with, not only the anti-traditional but also the counter-traditional, whose nature is more difficult to detect precisely because 'Satan is the ape of God.' But no matter how great the confusion, truth protects itself because it is none other than reality; on the contrary, that which apes it while at the same time denying it finally vanishes like the darkness of the early morn before the luminous rays of the sun.

Notes

1. This lacuna is now being gradually filled thanks to the pioneering works of such men as M. Lings, whose *A Sufi Saint of the Twentieth Century*, Berkeley, 1973, has become a classic; and M. Chodkiewicz, who has made several basic studies of Amīr 'Abd al-Qādir, for example, *Emir Abd el-Kader: Ecrits spirituels*, Paris, 1982.
2. There is now a fairly extensive literature in European languages, especially in English and French, devoted to traditional Islam or to aspects of the Islamic tradition, especially Sufism. These works include F. Schuon, *Understanding Islam*, trans. D.M. Matheson, London, 1979; *ibid.*, *Dimensions of Islam*, trans. P.N. Townsend, London, 1970; *ibid.*, *Islam and the Perennial Philosophy*, trans. P. Hobson, London, 1976; M. Lings, *What is Sufism*?, Berkeley, 1977; T. Burckhardt, *Introduction to Sufi Doctrine*, trans. D.M. Matheson, Northamptonshire, 1976; *ibid.*, *Fes, Stadt des Islam*, Otten, 1960; *ibid.*, *Moorish Culture in Spain*, trans. A. Jaffa, London, 1972; W. Stoddart, *Sufism, The Mystical Doctrines and Methods of Islam*, Northamptonshire, 1982; R. Dupaquier, *Découverte de l'Islam*, Paris, 1984; G. Eaton, *Islam and the Destiny of Man*, Albany, 1986; V. Danner, 'Religious Revivalism in Islam: Past and Present', C. Pullapilly, *Islam in the Contemporary World*, Notre Dame, 1980, pp. 21–43; *ibid.*, *The Islamic Tradition*, Warwick (N.Y.), 1986; and A.K. Brohi, *Islam in the Modern World*, Lahore, 1975. See also S.H. Nasr, *Ideals and Realities of Islam*, London, 1975; and *ibid*, *Islam and the Plight of Modern Man*, London, 1975.

   In Pakistan there is a journal entitled *Riwāyat* (edited by Suhayl Umar and published in Lahore) dedicated completely to tradition in general and traditional Islam in particular.

   There are works by well-known traditional Muslim authorities such as 'Abd al-Ḥalīm Maḥmūd, Javād Nourbakhsh and 'Allāmah Ṭabāṭabā'ī, which have been translated into English. It is of interest to note that the writings of the well-known writer Maryam Jameelah, which have always been strongly anti-modern, were close to the new 'fundamentalist' perspective in many ways but that more recently she has come to embrace the traditional point of view as seen in some of her extensive book reviews of the past two or three years.

   There is a great need in fact for a complete bibliography of works on Islam which are of a traditional character. Such a compilation would allow those who wish to pursue the subject to be guided in the maze of publications on Islam which have appeared during the past few years.
3. On the meaning of tradition see our *Knowledge and the Sacred*, New York, 1981, pp. 65ff. Concerning tradition, Schuon has written, 'Tradition is not a childish and outmoded mythology but a science that is terribly real.' From the foreword to *Understanding Islam*.

4. The vast commentary of 'Allāmah Ṭabāṭabā'ī, *al-Mīzān*, is an outstanding example of a contemporary traditional commentary to be clearly distinguished from those in which modern ideas appear either directly or in the guise of 'Islamic ideology' with an outwardly anti-Western color but inwardly in many ways akin to the anti-traditional ideas which have emanated from the West since the Renaissance.
5. There have of course been differences among traditional authorities themselves concerning these principles. But these differences have always existed within the traditional world-view and not against it. These differences cannot therefore be used as a pretext for the rejection of this world-view, which embraces all these differences without identifying itself with only one school or denying the possibility of error and deviation in the traditional world.
6. On this crucial question as treated in a universal context see F. Schuon, *Esoterism, as Principle and as Way*, trans. W. Stoddart, Bedford (U.K.), 1981; and Schuon, *Sufism, Veil and Quintessence*, trans. W. Stoddart, Bloomington (Indiana), 1981.
7. On this question see T. Burckhardt, *The Art of Islam*, London, 1976; and Nasr, *Islamic Art and Spirituality*, London, 1986.
8. It is remarkable how close are the views of the modernists and 'fundamentalists' concerning the rapid mechanization of means of production and the computerization of every section of the economy to the greatest extent possible without any concern for their religious and human implications.
9. As an example one can cite the case of women's dress and comportment. Traditional Islam insisted upon women dressing modestly and usually wearing some kind of veil or head-dress which would cover their hair. The result was an array of female dresses from Morocco to Malaysia, most of these dresses being of much beauty and reflecting femininity in accordance with the ethos of Islam, which insists upon conformity to the nature of things and therefore the masculinity of the male and femininity of the female. Then came the modernist changes which caused women to remove the veil, uncover their hair and wear Western dress, at least in many parts of the Islamic world. Now there appears that 'fundamentalism' or revivalism, which in some areas has placed a handkerchief on the head of women and a machine-gun in their hands with total disregard for the beauty of the rest of their dress as a reflection of their female nature as always envisaged by Islam. One wonders which is more pleasing to the eyes of God, the Western-clad Muslim woman who goes home and says her prayers, or a gun-wielding revolutionary whose Islamicity is summarized in a handkerchief to hide her hair while the fire of hatred hides all the gentleness and generosity that Islam has traditionally identified with womanhood and which burns even if she performs her prayers in public.
10. In this comparison attention is paid especially to recent forms of 'fundamentalism', not those of the 13th/19th and early 14th/20th centuries, which were a form of extreme exotericism and puritanism and

therefore a truncated form of tradition, not properly speaking anti-traditional or counter-traditional, although, in impoverishing the intellectual, cultural and artistic life of parts of the Islamic world, they played a rôle in facilitating the advent of modernism and its aftermath in the form of counter-traditional movements.

11. This is seen especially in Islamic penal codes, which traditionally have taken into account such factors so that they have been applied, but not only blindly and without consideration of all the moral factors involved.
12. See our *Science and Civilization in Islam*, Cambridge (Mass.), 1968, and our *Knowledge and the Sacred*, pp. 130 ff. See also T. Burckhardt, *The Mirror of the Intellect*, trans. W. Stoddart, Warwick (N.Y.), 1987, part I. Recently there has been greater attention paid among a number of Muslim scholars to the problems of confronting the already secularized knowledge which emanates from the Western world and which has affected Muslims in many fields since the 13th/19th century. See S.M. Naquib al-Attas, *Islam and Secularism*, Kuala Lumpur, 1978.
13. No knowledge can be Islamically worthwhile unless it is related to a higher plane and ultimately to God who, being *al-Ḥaqq* or the Truth, is the source of all veritable knowledge.
14. See T. Burckhardt, *The Art of Islam*; as well as his *Sacred Art East and West*, trans. Lord Northbourne, London, 1967, pp. 101–119.
15. See D. Shayegan, *Qu'est-ce qu'une révolution religieuse*? Paris, 1982, which contains a profound analysis of this subject, although his treatment of the traditional point of view is not that of the traditionalists themselves.

Part One
Facets of the Islamic Tradition

Chapter One

The Spiritual Significance of *Jihād*

'And those who perform jihād *for Us, We shall certainly guide them in Our ways, and God is surely with the doers of good.'*
(Quran XXXIX; 69)

'You have returned from the lesser jihād *to the greater* jihād.*'*
(Ḥadīth)

Perhaps today no issue concerning Islam is as sensitive and as often debated as that of *jihād*. Discussed in the mass media as well as in scholarly books, the various meanings given to the term are not only based on the divergent views of Western interpreters but also reflect the profound differences which exist between the traditionalists and 'fundamentalists' in their interpretation of this crucial concept. At the present moment, when the image of Islam in the West depends so much upon the understanding of the meaning of *jihād*, it is of the utmost importance to comprehend the way traditional Islam has envisaged this key idea over the ages and the manner in which it is related to Islamic spirituality.

The Arabic term *jihād*, usually translated into European languages as 'holy war', rather more on the basis of its juridical usage in Islam than on its much more universal meaning in the Quran and

Ḥadīth, is derived from the root *jhd*, whose primary meaning is 'to strive' or 'to exert oneself'. Its translation into 'holy war', combined with the erroneous notion of Islam prevalent in the West as the 'religion of the sword', has helped to eclipse its inner and spiritual significance and to distort its connotation. Nor has the appearance upon the stage of history during the last century, and especially during the past few years, of an array of mostly 'fundamentalist' or revolutionary movements within the Islamic world which often oppose each other and use the term *jihād* or one of its derivative forms, helped to make known the full import of its traditional meaning, which alone is of concern to us here. Instead, recent distortions and even total reversal of the meaning of *jihād* as understood over the ages by Muslims have made it more difficult than ever before to gain insight into this key religious and spiritual concept.

To comprehend the spiritual significance of *jihād* and its wide application to nearly every aspect of human life as understood by Islam, it is necessary to remember that Islam bases itself upon the idea of establishing equilibrium within the being of man, as well as in the human society where he functions and fulfils the goals of his earthly life. This equilibrium, which is the terrestrial reflection of Divine Justice and the necessary condition for peace in the human domain, is the basis upon which the soul takes flight towards that peace which, to use Christian terms, 'passeth all understanding'. If Christianity sees the aim of the spiritual life and its own morality as being based upon the vertical flight towards that perfection and ideal which is embodied in Christ, Islam sees it in the establishment of an equilibrium, both outward and inward, which is the necessary basis for this vertical ascent. The very stability of Islamic society over the centuries, the immutability of Islamic norms embodied in the *Sharīʿah*, and the timeless character of traditional Islamic civilization, which is the consequence of its permanent and immutable prototype, are all reflections of both the ideal of equilibrium and its realization. This equilibrium which is so evident in both the teachings of the *Sharīʿah* (or Divine Law) as well as in works of Islamic art, is inseparable from the very name of *islām* as being related to *salām* or peace.

The preservation of equilibrium in this world, however, does not mean simply a static or inactive passivity, since life by nature implies movement. In the face of the contingencies of the world of change, of the withering effect of time, of the vicissitudes of terrestrial existence, to remain in equilibrium requires continuous exertion. It means carrying out *jihād* at every stage of life. Human nature being what it is, given to forgetfulness and suffering from the conquest of our immortal soul by the carnal soul or passions, the very process of life in both the individual and the human collectivity implies the ever-present danger of loss of equilibrium; in fact, of falling into the state of disequilibrium which, if allowed to continue, cannot but lead to disintegration on the individual level and chaos on the scale of community life. To avoid this tragic end and to fulfil the entelechy of the human state, which is the realization of unity (*al-tawḥīd*) or total integration, Muslims both as individuals and members of Islamic society must carry out *jihād*; that is, they must exert themselves at all moments of life to fight a battle, at once both inward and outward, against those forces that, if not combated, will destroy that necessary equilibrium. This fact is especially true if society is seen as a collectivity which bears the imprint of the Divine Norm rather than an antheap of contending and opposing units and forces.

Man is at the same time both a spiritual and a corporeal being: a microcosm complete unto himself. Yet he is also the member of a society within which alone are certain aspects of his being developed and certain of his needs fulfilled. He possesses at once an intelligence, whose substance is ultimately of a divine character, and sentiments, which can either veil his intelligence or abet his quest for his own Origin. In him are found both love and hatred, generosity and covetousness, compassion and aggression. Moreover, there have existed until now not just one but several 'humanities', each with their own distinct religious and moral norms; also national, ethnic and racial groups with their own bonds of affiliation. As a result, the practice of *jihād*, as applied to the world of multiplicity and the vicissitudes of human existence in the external world, has come to acquire numerous ramifications in the fields of political and economic activity as well as in social life, and in consequence has come to partake, on the external level, of the complexity which characterizes the human world.

In its most outward sense, *jihād* came to signify the defence of *dār al-islām*, that is, the Islamic world, from invasion and intrusion by non-Islamic forces. The earliest wars of Islamic history, which threatened the very existence of the young community, came to be known as *jihād par excellence* in this outward sense of 'holy war'. But it was upon returning from one of these early wars, which was of paramount importance for the survival of the newly-established religious community and therefore of cosmic significance, that the Blessed Prophet nevertheless said to his companions that they had returned from the lesser holy war to the greater holy war: the inner battle against all the forces which would prevent man from living according to the theomorphic norm which is his primordial and God-given nature.

Throughout Islamic history, the call for the lesser holy war has echoed in the Islamic world when parts or the whole of that world have been threatened by forces from without or within. This call has been especially persistent since the 13th/19th century with the advent of colonialism and the threat that was posed to the very existence of the Islamic world. It must be remembered, however, that even in cases where the idea of *jihād* has been evoked in certain parts of the Islamic world, it has not usually been a question of religion simply sanctioning war but rather of the attempt of a society in which religion remains of central concern to protect itself from being conquered either by military and economic forces or by ideas of an alien nature. This does not mean, however, that in some cases, especially in recent times, religious sentiments have not been used or misused to intensify or legitimize a conflict. But to say the least, the Islamic world does not have a monopoly on this abuse, as the history of other civilizations, including even that of the secularized West, demonstrates so amply. Moreover, human nature being what it is, once religion ceases to be of central significance to a particular human collectivity, men then fight and kill each other for issues much less exalted than their heavenly faith. By including the question of war in its sacred legislation, Islam did not condone but rather sought to limit war and its consequences, as the history of the traditional Islamic world bears out. In any case, the idea of total war and the actual practice of the extermination of whole civilian populations did not grow out of a civilization whose dominant religion saw *jihād* in a positive light.

On the more external level, the lesser *jihād* also applies in the socio-economic domain. It implies the reassertion of justice in the external environment of human existence, starting with man himself. To defend one's rights and reputation, to defend the honor of oneself and one's family, is itself a *jihād* and a religious duty. So is the strengthening of all those social bonds, from the family to the whole of the Muslim people (*al-ummah*), which the *Sharī'ah* emphasizes. To seek social justice in accordance with the tenets of the Quran – but not of course in the modern secularist sense – is a way of re-establishing equilibrium in human society (that is, of performing *jihād*), as in the case of constructive economic enterprises, provided the well-being of the whole person is kept in mind and material welfare does not become an end in itself: provided, in fact, one does not lose sight of the already-quoted Quranic verse, 'The other world is better for you than this one.' To forget the proper relation between the two worlds would itself be instrumental in bringing about disequilibrium and would be a kind of *jihād* in reverse.

All of those external forms of *jihād* would remain incomplete and in fact contribute to an excessive externalization of human beings if they were not complemented by the greater or inner *jihād* which man should carry out continuously within himself; for the nobility of the human state resides in the constant tension between what we appear to be and what we really are, and also in the need to transcend ourselves throughout this journey of earthly life in order to become what we 'are'.

From the spiritual point of view, all the 'pillars' of Islam can be seen as being related to *jihād*. The fundamental witnesses (*shahādah*), 'There is no divinity but Allah' and 'Muḥammad is the messenger of Allah', through the utterance of which a person becomes a Muslim, are not only statements about the Truth as seen in the Islamic perspective but also weapons for the practice of inner *jihād*. The very form of the first letter of the first witness (*lā ilāha illa'Llāh* in Arabic), when written in Arabic calligraphy, is like a bent sword with which all otherness is removed from the Supreme Reality, while all that is positive in manifestation is returned to that Reality. The second witness is the blinding assertion of the powerful and majestic descent of all that in a positive manner constitutes the cosmos, man and revelation from that Supreme Reality. To invoke the two witnesses in the form of the sacred language in which they were revealed is to practice the inner *jihād* and to bring about awareness of who we are, from whence we come and where is our ultimate abode.

The daily prayers (*ṣalāt* or *namāz*), which constitute the heart of the Islamic rites, are again a never-ending *jihād* which punctuate human existence in a continuous rhythm in harmony with the rhythm of the cosmos. To perform the prayers with regularity and concentration requires the constant exertion of our will and an unending battle and striving against forgetfulness, dissipation and laziness. In short, it is itself a form of spiritual warfare.

Likewise, the fast of Ramaḍān, in which one wears the armour of inner purity and detachment against the passions and temptations of the outside world, requires an asceticism and inner discipline which cannot come about except through an inner holy war. Nor is the *ḥajj* to the center of the Islamic world in Makkah possible without long preparation, effort, often suffering and endurance of hardship. It requires great effort and exertion, so the Prophet could say, 'The *ḥajj* is the most excellent of all *jihāds*.' Like the knight in quest of the Holy Grail, the pilgrim to the house of the Beloved must engage in a spiritual warfare whose end makes all sacrifice and all hardship pale into insignificance; for the *ḥajj* to the House of God implies, for the person who practices the inner *jihād*, an encounter with the Master of the House, who also resides at the center of that other Ka'bah which is the heart.

Finally the giving of *zakāt* or religious tax is again a form of *jihād*, not only in that in departing from one's wealth man must fight against the covetousness and greed of his carnal soul, but also in that, through the payment of *zakāt* in its many forms, man contributes to the establishment of economic justice in human society. Although *jihād* is not one of the 'pillars of Islam', it in a sense resides within all the other 'pillars'. From the spiritual point of view in fact, all of the 'pillars' can be seen in the light of an inner *jihād*, which is essential to the life of man from the Islamic point of view and which does not oppose but rather complements contemplation and the peace which results from the contemplation of the One.

The great stations of perfection in the spiritual life can also be seen in the light of the inner *jihād*. To become detached from the impurities of the world in order to repose in the purity of the Divine Presence requires an intense *jihād*, for our soul has its roots sunk deeply in that transient world which fallen man mistakes for reality. To overcome the lethargy, passivity and indifference of the soul, qualities which have become second nature to it as a result of man's forgetting who he really is, constitutes likewise a constant *jihād*. To restrain the soul from dissipating itself outwardly as a result of its centrifugal tendencies and to bring it back to the center, wherein reside Divine Peace and all the beauty which the soul seeks in vain in the domain of multiplicity, this is again an inner *jihād*. To melt the hardened heart into a flowing stream of love which would embrace the whole of creation by virtue of love for God is to perform the alchemical process of *solve et coagula* inwardly: a 'work' which is none other than an inner battle against that which the soul has become, in order to transform it into that which it 'is' and has never ceased to be if only it were to become aware of its own nature. Finally, to realize that only the Absolute is absolute and that only the Self can ultimately utter 'I', is to perform the supreme *jihād* of awakening the soul from the dream of forgetfulness and enabling it to gain the supreme principial knowledge for the sake of which it was created. Inner *jihād* or warfare, seen spiritually and esoterically, can be considered therefore as at once the key to the understanding of the whole spiritual process and the path to the realization of the One that lies at the heart of the total Islamic message. The Islamic path towards perfection can be conceived in the light of the symbolism of the greater *jihād*, to which the Prophet of Islam, who founded this path on earth, himself referred.

In the same way that with every breath the principle of life, which functions in us irrespective of our will and as long as it is willed by Him who created us, exerts itself through *jihād* to vitalize our whole body, at every moment in our conscious life we should seek to perform *jihād* in, not only establishing equilibrium in the world about us, but also in awakening to that Divine Reality which is the very source of our consciousness. For the spiritual man, every breath is a reminder that he should continue the inner *jihād* until he awakens from all dreaming and until the very rhythm of his heart echoes that primordial sacred Name by which all things were made and through which all things return to their Origin. The Prophet said, 'Man is asleep and when he dies he awakens.' Through inner *jihād*, the spiritual man dies in this life in order to cease all dreaming, in order to awaken to that Reality which is the origin of all realities, in order to behold that Beauty of which all earthly beauty is but a pale reflection, in order to attain that Peace which all men seek but which can in fact be found only through this practice.

Chapter Two
Islamic Work Ethics

Work carried out in accordance with the *Sharī'ah* is a form of *jihād* and inseparable from the religious and spiritual significance associated with it. Moreover, in order to understand the ethical dimension of work from the traditional Islamic point of view, it is necessary to recall at the outset the fact that the term 'work' in Arabic is not distinguished from the word for 'action' in its most general sense and is treated by the Divine Law (*al-Sharī'ah*) under the same category. In fact if one were to look for the translation of the word 'work' in an English-Arabic dictionary, one would usually find the two terms *'amal* and *ṣun'* given as its equivalents. The first of these terms means 'action' in general as contrasted with 'knowledge' and the second 'making' or 'producing' something in the artistic and artisanal sense of the word.[1] Human beings perform two types of functions in relation to the world about them. They either act within or upon that world or else make things by molding and remolding materials and objects drawn from that world. Work ethics in Islam applies in principle to both categories: to both *'amal* and *ṣun'*, since the Divine Law covers the whole network of human actions. While the principles of the aesthetic aspect of *ṣun'*, or 'art', in the primordial meaning of the word, belong to the inner dimension of the Islamic revelation,[2] the ethical aspect of both *'amal* and *ṣun'*, or all that man does externally, is to be found in the injunctions and teachings of the *Sharī'ah*. It is true that for the purposes of a particular discussion, one may limit the meaning of work to its economic or social aspect, but to understand Islamic work ethics in universal terms it is necessary to remember this wider and more general concept of 'work', whereby it is in fact never fully differentiated from human action, including art in general and the ethical considerations contained in the *Sharī'ah* pertaining to the domain of human action as a whole.

The Quran (V; 1) states, 'O you who have attained to faith! Be faithful to your covenants [*'uqūd*]' (M. Asad translation). These covenants or *'uqūd*, according to traditional Islamic commentators, include the whole of man's relations to God, himself and the world, and are a 'commentary of rectitude' for observation of the moral dimension of all human life. As M. Asad states in his commentary upon this verse, 'The term *'aqd* ('covenant') denotes a solemn undertaking or engagement involving more than one party. According to Rāghib [one of the traditional commentators], the covenants referred to in this verse, "are of three kinds: the covenants between God and man [i.e., man's obligations towards God], between man and his own soul, and between the individual and his fellow men" – thus embracing the entire area of man's moral and social responsibilities.'[3]

In the world-view of the traditional Muslim, the *'uqūd* referred to in this Quranic verse range from the performance of daily prayers to digging a well or selling merchandise in the bazaar. The moral responsibility placed upon the shoulders of 'the believers' by this verse extends to work as well as worship, and encompasses the whole of human life in accordance with the *dicta* of the *Sharī'ah*, which concern man's dealings with God as well as with his neighbor and even himself. The basis of all work ethics in Islam is to be found in the inescapable moral character of all human action and the responsibility which a human being bears for his or her actions, not only before the employer or employee, but also in relation to the work itself, which must be executed with the utmost perfection of which the 'actor' or worker is capable.

Responsibility for the work exists also and above all before God, who is witness to all human action. This sense of responsibility before God for all action and hence work in the more limited economic sense passes even beyond the grave and concerns man's ultimate entelechy as an immortal being. As in the Judeo-Christian traditions, so in Islam man remains responsible for the moral consequences of his actions on the Day of Judgement, whose awesomeness and majesty are emphasized with such remarkable eloquence and power in the final chapters of the Quran. The unitary perspective of Islam, which refuses to distinguish between the sacred and the profane, goes even further in refusing to distinguish between religious acts and secular ones, or between prayer and work. The fear of God and the responsibility felt toward Him by the traditional Muslim embrace acts of worship as well as work in the usual sense of the word. In fact, according to a well-known *ḥadīth*, God forgives upon the repentance (*al-tawbah*) of His creature what man owes Him but not what man owes to God's other creatures. The sense of responsibility to fulfil the terms of a contract, to achieve a piece of work as well as possible, to satisfy the person for whom the work is being done, as well as to treat the person who does the work well and fairly, are very strong among traditional Muslims. Many verses of the Quran and numerous *ḥadīths*, which have also penetrated the literature of the Islamic peoples in the form of poems and parables, continue to remind the Muslim of the deeply religious nature of all work which is carried out in accordance with the *Sharī'ah* and the moral responsibility related to work in all its aspects, social and economic as well as artistic and aesthetic. Islamic work ethics is inseparable from the moral character of all that a Muslim should accomplish in his earthly journey in accordance with the guidance and injunctions of the Divine Law.

Work is closely associated with prayer and worship in all traditional societies and this link is preserved and accentuated in Islam. The daily call to prayer (*al-adhān*) in its Shī'ite form repeats this principial relationship five times a day by exclaiming, *hayy*[u] *'ala'l-salāh*, 'Come unto the prayers'; *ḥayy*[u] *'ala'l-falāḥ*, 'Come unto salvation'; and *ḥayy*[u] *'alā khayr al-'amal*, 'Come unto good works'. From prayer there flows salvation or felicity of soul and, from that state of salvation, correct action and good works, the word *'amal* itself appearing once again in this basic assertion. Although the third part of this formula is not repeated in the Sunni form of the *adhān*, there too the rapport between prayer, work and correct action is always emphasized. Such Quranic verses as 'By the afternoon! Surely Man is in the way of loss, save those who believe, and do righteous deeds' (CIII; 1–3), in which it is made clear that righteous deeds[4] follow from faith and attachment to the principles of religion, remind all Muslims, Sunni and Shi'ite alike, of the relation between prayer and work; and also of the prayerful nature of work itself, as long as it is performed in accordance with the *Sharī'ah*.

To understand Islamic work ethics, the intertwining of work, prayer and even what is known in the modern world as leisure, is of great importance. The rhythm of traditional Islamic life is such that the hours of work are punctuated by prayer and this is also true of even that which is considered as cultural activity and leisure today. The very architecture of the traditional city is such that spaces for worship, work, education and cultural activities are harmoniously interrelated and integrated into a unity. The very fact that a person moves from the space of the mosque to the place of work and breaks the hours of work regularly to perform the daily prayers, deeply colors the meaning of work itself. Both the space and the time within which work take place are transformed by the Islamic prayers and thereby work itself gains a religious complexion which determines its ethical meaning in the Islamic context.

The first element of Islamic work ethics which must be considered is the *Sharī'ite* injunction that the accomplishment of whatever work is necessary to support oneself and one's family is as worthy, in the eyes of God, as the performance of religious duties classified as obligatory (*wājib*). Every person must work to support himself and those who depend upon him for their livelihood, these persons usually including the members of his immediate family; sometimes also female members and old or incapacitated persons belonging to the extended family circle. This duty is usually incumbent upon the man of the family, but the women are also responsible when external necessity dictates their working outside the home, as can be seen very often in the agricultural sector of society. Whatever is necessary for the continuation of human life gains, according to Islamic teachings, a religious sanction as the very result of that necessity.

There is, however, no emphasis in Islam upon the virtue of work for the sake of work, as one finds in certain forms of Protestantism. In the Islamic perspective, work is considered a virtue in the light of the needs of man and the necessity to establish equilibrium in one's individual and social life. But this duty towards work, and provision for one's needs and for those of one's family, is always kept in check and prevented from becoming excessive by the emphasis that the Quran places upon the transience of life, the danger of greed and covetousness, and the importance of avoiding the excessive accumulation of wealth.[5]

Work, like everything else in life, must be seen and performed within the framework of the equilibrium which Islam seeks to establish in the life of each individual as well as of Islamic society as a whole. While the earliest Islamic community was still in Makkah, this nucleus of the future society, which consisted of a spiritual élite, was advised to spend much of the night in prayer and vigil; but in Madinah, when a complete social order was established, the Prophet emphasized the importance of the members of the new religious community in general devoting a third of their day to work, a third to sleep and rest and a third to prayer, leisure and family and social activities.[6] This prophetic example has set an ideal for later Islamic society, according to which, while the performance of work to support one's family is considered a religious duty, the exaggerated emphasis upon work for its own sake is opposed in as much as such an attitude destroys the equilibrium that is the Islamic goal of life. If in many present-day Middle Eastern cities a taxi driver is seen to work much longer hours than is specified by the traditional tripartite division of the day, and that he performs his difficult work as a religious duty to support an often large family, it is usually economic necessity which dictates such a prolonged working schedule and not the desire for work as an end in itself. There is no innate religious value connected with work in itself simply as a means of amassing wealth and outside of the patterns established by the prophetic *Sunnah* and the *Sharī'ah*.

According to Islamic Law, work itself, considered in its economic aspect, should be carried out following a contract based upon justice and responsibility on the side of the employer as well as the employee. The worker is responsible to both the employer and to God to carry out, to the best of his or her ability, the work which he or she has undertaken to accomplish on terms agreed by the two sides. Only then will the earnings from such a work be *ḥalāl* (that is, religiously speaking, legitimate). The conditions and terms include both the amount of work, whether it be the hours specified, the price to be paid or the quantity to be produced and the quality to be achieved. There is a very strong moral element present among traditional Muslims as far as 'eating *ḥalāl* bread' is concerned; that is, gaining an earning which one deserves in accordance with the accomplishment of an agreed piece of work. If the worker cheats the employer in either the quantity or quality of the work to be accomplished according to their contract, then the earning is not *ḥalāl* and the consequences of 'eating bread' that is not *ḥalāl* fall upon both the worker and all those who benefit from his earnings. There has developed, in fact, within Islamic society, an elaborate system of giving alms, donations, etc., to make earnings *ḥalāl* and to prevent the negative consequences of eating non-*ḥalāl* 'bread': consequences which for believers include the possibility of the wrath of God descending upon them in the form of illness, loss of property and other calamities.

The concepts of *ḥalāl* and *harām* ('forbidden' or 'prohibited') also affect the kind of work which the Muslim can undertake. Certain types of work, such as the making and selling of wine or pork products, are forbidden, while other activities, such as playing music for a public audience, is accepted by most jurists provided no remuneration is received. Of course all work related to acts which themselves are forbidden by the *Sharī'ah*, such as theft and adultery, are likewise *ḥarām* and must be avoided. Other types of work have been particularly encouraged by the *Sunnah* and *Ḥadīth*, among them being agriculture, which was practiced by many of the companions of the Prophet, including 'Alī,[7] and honest trade, which was the profession of the Prophet himself in his early life.

The responsibility of the worker before the employer and God in the performance of work which is *ḥalāl* and also performed in a *ḥalāl* manner must be reciprocated by the employer, who is also responsible before both God and the employee. The employer must fulfil the terms of his contract just as must the worker. Moreover, the employer must display kindness and generosity towards those who work for him. Also, according to a well-known *ḥadīth*, the worker should be paid his wages before the sweat dries from his forehead.

Altogether the various aspects of work concerning the relation between the worker and the employer is at once ethical and economic, the two never being separated in the Islamic perspective. A personal, human relation has been traditionally emphasized, which relates, not only the two sides to each other, but also stresses the witness of God and that He is aware of all our actions and demands justice in all human relations, including those in this very important domain. The whole question of work and work ethics is in fact never envisaged in traditional Islamic thought from merely an economic point of view but also includes an ethical one related to the general Islamic perspective in which economics and ethics are combined. Economic activity divorced from ethical considerations based on justice would be considered illegitimate.[8]

The qualitative aspect of Islamic work ethics cannot be fully appreciated unless one delves into the kinds of work in which men and women were usually engaged in traditional Islamic society. These types of work involved such activities as agriculture, nomadic pasturing of sheep and other animals, artisanal work, economic transactions associated with the bazaar, domestic work and employment in the juridical, bureaucratic and military branches of government. In all cases, a very human and personal relationship was emphasized in those cases where human beings were involved, otherwise, as in agricultural and artisanal work, a science and an art based upon metaphysical and cosmological principles related to the Quranic revelation[9] and a symbolic language inextricably wed to the Islamic religion[10] provided the matrix for work. Hence the very ambience, materials used, actions performed and relations created took place in a sacralized universe in which everything possessed a religious and also an ethical dimension, and in which there was no type of work that was 'secular' or without religious significance. The success of Islam in creating a unified civilization dominated completely by the 'Idea' and 'Presence' of the sacred provided a climate for work within which the ethical could not be divorced from the economic. Islamic society in fact developed numerous ways and means whereby the various types of work to which allusion has been made above were sacralized and both the quality of the work as well as the ethical responsibility of all parties were checked and guaranteed to the extent that the frailties of human nature permit in any collectivity.[11]

On the most external level, the ethical requirements of work, including both production and transaction, were traditionally guaranteed by the *muḥtasib* (controller), whose function it was to see that the weights and measures used in the purchase and sale of articles were carefully tested, that the quality of the material sold matched the standard claimed by the seller, etc. The constant observation of various phases of work by religious authorities and the intermingling of the life of the ateliers and bazaars with that of the mosque created also to some extent an external religious guarantee of the preservation of the ethical conditions required by the *Sharī'ah* for work as both *'amal* and *ṣun'*. But the most important guarantee in this case was and continues to remain to a large extent the conscience of the individual Muslim and the religious values inculcated in him.

There developed during later Islamic history more specific institutions which were directly concerned with the ethical aspects of work and which related organizations connected with specific economic activities with moral and spiritual qualities. These institutions consisted of various guilds, orders and brotherhoods called *aṣnāf*, *futuwwāt*, *ukhuwwāt*, the *akhī* movement etc., which, from the Seljuq period, spread throughout the cities and towns of the Islamic world on the basis of less formal organizations dating from earlier centuries.[12] These organizations, which still survive to some extent, were directly linked to Sufi orders and considered work itself to be an extension of spiritual discipline. A bond of a religious nature linked the members with each other as well as with the master, who was both the teacher of the craft or trade involved and a spiritual authority. A spirit of chivalry dominated the guilds and they were in fact connected with orders of chivalry (*futuwwah* in Arabic; *jawānmardī* in Persian) both in their morphological and structural resemblance and in their association with Islamic esoteric teachings. The founder of both types of associations is considered to be 'Alī ibn Abī Ṭālib, whose central role in the dissemination of the esoteric teachings of Islam is only too well known.

A code of honor, strict work ethics, responsibility for and devotion to the quality of work, pride in one's *métier*, generosity to others and aid to members of the guild, as well as many other ethical and spiritual precepts associated with work, developed through such organizations. These guilds and orders were at once the guardians of ethical concern for work and the means by which the ethical character of the work of their members was guaranteed; they also guaranteed their members protection from external pressures and oppression.

In this domain, the particular category of work associated with the making of things, namely the arts and crafts (which have in fact never been regarded as different forms of activity in Islam), needs to be particularly emphasized. All work which concerns the making of things or *ṣun'* possesses religious and spiritual significance when done according to traditional criteria: with one's own hands and by means of techniques which possess an eminently symbolic, and hence spiritual, significance.[13] The ethical aspect of work in this case embraces also the aesthetic,[14] for to produce a work of beauty and quality requires the love of the maker for that work and brings into play the virtue of goodness. Such a work ennobles the soul of the person who creates it and fulfils deep religious and spiritual needs, while transmitting to the person who obtains the work, not only an object which fulfils a certain external need, but also a joy which refreshes the soul and possesses a definite religious significance. It is enough to behold a genuine Persian or Anatolian carpet, woven with love and devotion rather than for simply the sake of economic gain, to realize how important and central is the question of the relation of man to his work in any consideration of the ethical dimension of work. A mechanical and impersonal manner of making things destroys a basic dimension of the ethical value of work, no matter how fair the wages and how physically favorable the working ambience. In Islamic art, the beauty of objects designed for everyday use, ranging from textiles and carpets to bowls and lamps, testifies to the extremely wide range of those fruits of human labor which reflect love, devotion, joy and peace. These elements are inseparable from the question of the ethical dimension of work in Islam. The traditional guilds, brotherhoods and orders not only made possible the production of these works and the creation of the material basis of Islamic civilization on the basis of beauty and harmony, but also provided a work ethic which embraced aesthetic considerations as well and which related the love of beauty to the moral conditions of work. It also placed the moral consequences of the making of things upon the soul of the maker, who in making objects according to the norms of traditional art also remolds his own inner being.[15]

If one were to study work ethics in Muslim society today, one would not discover all the qualities and characteristics that have been mentioned above among actual workers – at least not everywhere and not among all types and classes of workers. Even during the last generation, in many Islamic lands, many of the moral qualities of workers and the ethical dimension of work had declined or even disappeared, especially in larger urban areas. The thesis presented above represents the traditional Islamic view of work ethics based upon the foundation of the Quran and *Ḥadīth* as well as on centuries of elaboration through *Sharī'ite* institutions, Sufi orders, family training and the general culture of Islamic society. But traditional Islamic society is no longer completely intact and the attitudes and practices concerning work observable today represent the partial breakdown of the traditional norm before the onslaught of the various forces of modernism.

The worker in much of the Islamic world, especially in urban areas, is often cut off from his family and social matrix. His relation to the rhythms and norms of nature has become severed. In many cases, modes of production based upon the impersonal machine have replaced traditional modes based upon love and devotion to a craft. Alien laws have partially supplanted the Divine Law and destroyed the homogeneity of the *Sharī'ah* as applied to all facets of life. Traditional institutions, such as the guilds, have weakened or ceased to exist, and the all-important human example of a master craftsman, who was also a religious and ethical teacher, has become rare and, in certain alien forms of industry, non-existent. All this has happened while the market to which the Muslim worker is of necessity related becomes dominated ever more by forces blind to moral considerations.

All of these as well as other factors and forces have partially destroyed the traditional fabric within which Islamic work ethics was applied and practiced. Nevertheless, neither that work ethics nor the people who are still attached to it have ceased to exist. Much of that traditional work ethics survives, while in even modernized sectors of society there is great nostalgia among many uprooted workers for that wholeness which characterized the traditional mode of work. Islamic work ethics, therefore, deserves to be known and studied, not only because it is still to be found in some segments and areas of Islamic society, but also because it remains the ideal which many Muslim men and women seek to realize today. Despite the havoc caused within the Islamic world by the advent of modernism and reactions created against it, devout Muslims, which includes most of those who work in one way or another in Islamic society, never forget the content of the *ḥadīth*, 'Strange are the ways of a believer, for there is good in every affair of his hand.[16]' Men and women of faith know that, if they are really people of faith, they must conform their work to the norms established by God and be able to offer their work to Him by performing it in accordance with the ethical precepts contained in the sources of the Islamic revelation.

Notes

1. By extension the term *ṣinā'ah* or *ṣan'ah*, related to *ṣun'*, is now also used to mean 'industry' in the modern sense of the term.
2. On the relation of Islamic art to the Islamic revelation see Burckhardt, *The Art of Islam*, and Nasr, *Islamic Art and Spirituality*.
3. M. Asad, *The Message of the Qur'ān*, Gibraltar, 1980, p. 139, nt. 1.
4. *'Amal al-ṣāliḥ*, that is, righteous deed or good action, is interpreted by traditional commentators to mean first of all religious duties such as prayer and fasting and, by extension, work done in virtue and with honesty.
5. For example the verse, 'And covet not that by which Allah has made some of you excel others. For men is the benefit of what they earn. And for women is the benefit of what they earn.' (IV; 32 – Mawlānā Muḥammad'Alī translation).
6. The change of the rhythm of life of the community after migrating from Makkah to Madinah and the change from the exceptionally gifted original nucleus of a new social order to the actual founding of the first Islamic society is described with great perspicacity in M. Lings, *Muḥammad – His Life Based on the Earliest Sources*, London, 1983.
7. There are many *ḥadīths* which extol the virtue of agriculture, such as, 'Never a Muslim plants, or cultivates a land, and if out of that men eat, or animals eat, or anything else eats, but that becomes charity on his (the planter's) behalf', *Ṣaḥīḥ Muslim*, rendered into English by 'A.H. Siddiqi, New Delhi, 1978, vol. III, p. 818.
8. On Islamic economics in relation to ethics see M. Abdul-Rauf, *A Muslim's Reflections on Democratic Capitalism*, Washington, 1984; M.N. Siddiqi, *The Economic Enterprise in Islam*, Lahore, 1972; and

S.N. Haider Naqvi, *Ethics and Economics – An Islamic Synthesis*, Leicester, 1981.

9. See S.H. Nasr, *Islamic Science – An Illustrated Study*, London, 1976; and Nasr, *Science and Civilization in Islam*, Cambridge.
10. See T. Burckhardt, *op. cit.*
11. No human collectivity at this late stage of human history could be perfect or even nearly so according to the Islamic conception of history itself. Therefore there were certainly shortcomings in traditional Islamic society in realizing and guaranteeing the ethical conditions of work in both a qualitative and quantitative manner. What is amazing, however, is the degree to which Islam did succeed in bestowing an ethical dimension on all kinds of work and in extending the ethical to include even the quantitative aspect of the work in question.
12. On these movements and their significance socially and economically as well as religiously see B. Lewis, 'The Islamic Guilds', *Economic History Review*, vol. 8, 1937, pp. 20–37; Y. Ibish, 'Brotherhoods of the Bazaars', *UNESCO Courier*, vol. 30, no. XII, 1977, pp. 12–17; and *ibid*, 'Economic Institutions', R.B. Sarjeant (ed.), *The Islamic City*, Paris, 1980, pp. 114–125.
13. This fact is of course as true for Hinduism, Christianity or any other religion as it is for Islam. The works of A.E.R. Gill in England, who sought to revive the crafts and bestow a religious and ethical character upon work again, is an example of the principle in question. See Gill, *A Holy Tradition of Working*, Ipswich 1983; also the numerous works of A.K. Coomaraswamy, by whom Gill was deeply influenced; for example, R. Lipsey (ed.), *Coomaraswamy, 1: Selected Papers – Traditional Art and Symbolism*, Princeton, 1977, pp. 13ff.
14. One must recall that in Arabic *ḥusn* means at once 'goodness' and 'beauty' and *qubh* 'evil' and 'ugliness'.
15. On the traditional doctrine of art in which ethical and aesthetic elements are interrelated and in which art and work are inseparable see, in addition to the works of Coomaraswamy and T. Burckhardt, F. Schuon's illuminating expositions such as *Esoterism As Principle and As Way*, pp. 177ff; see also Nasr, *Knowledge and the Sacred*, chapter 8.
16. *Ṣaḥīḥ Muslim*, vol. IV, p. 1541.

Chapter Three

The Male and the Female in the Islamic Perspective

'O Mankind! Lo! We have created you male and female. The noblest among you, in the sight of Allah, is the best in conduct.'
– (Quran; XLVI; 13)

No tradition can pass over in silence the central question of the relationship between man and woman in religious as well as in social life. Islam is no exception to this rule. On the contrary, traditional Islam, basing itself on the explicit teachings of the Quran and the guiding principles of the life of the Prophet, has developed the doctrine of the relationship between the male and the female and formulated the norms according to which the two sexes should live and cooperate in the social order. At a time when innovations of every sort have destroyed for most contemporary people, including many Muslims, the perennial teachings of Islam concerning the male and female relationship, from its metaphysical and spiritual to its most outward aspects, it is particularly necessary to reinstate the traditional Islamic point of view, beginning with the metaphysical principles which govern human nature and the complementary relationship between the male and the female on the highest level.

To speak of creation or manifestation is to speak of the manifold, or multiplicity, whose first stage is that primordial polarization between the two contending and complementary principles that are seen throughout cosmic manifestation and which in human life appear as the male and female sexes. In relation to the Divine Unity, all multiplicity is a veil, and from the perspective of the Divine Substance everything else is an accident embracing all the reverberations of the One in the mirror of the many which we call the world; or in fact the many worlds that at once hide and manifest the One. But from the point of view of the created order, the polarization or duality expressed by the differentiation of the microcosm into man and woman is far from being an accident. It is a most profound feature of what constitutes human nature. That is why in the Quranic verse quoted above, as well as in certain other verses, God refers to His creating mankind in pairs, in two different forms, as both man and woman. God is Himself the creator of both man and woman, and whatever ensues from the distinction between the two sexes must be related to His Wisdom and Providence. The distinction between the sexes is not a later accident or accretion but is essential to the meaning of the human state, without this distinction in any way destroying the significance of the androgynic reality (identified with the Universal or Perfect man – *al-insān al-kāmil*) which both men and women carry within the depths of their being.[1]

Since God has created mankind in pairs, logically and metaphysically there must exist some element of difference which distinguishes one member of the pair from the other, for if two things were the same in every way they would be identical. There is, therefore, of necessity a difference between the two sexes. They are not the same, at least if one takes the totality of being of each sex into consideration, while they may be equal under certain aspects and features. From the Islamic point of view, their equality in fact first and foremost involves the entelechy of the human state as such, in which both men and women participate by virtue of belonging to the human race. Both man and woman were created for immortality and spiritual deliverance. Below that level, however, there are differences between the two sexes whose reality cannot be ignored in the name of any form of egalitarianism.

Furthermore, the difference between the two sexes cannot be only biological and physical because, in the traditional perspective, the corporeal level of existence has its principle in the subtle state, the subtle in the spiritual and the spiritual in the Divine Being Itself. The difference between the sexes cannot be reduced to anatomy and biological function. There are also differences of psychology and temperament, of spiritual types and even principles within the Divine Nature which are the sources *in divinis* of the duality represented on the microcosmic level as male and female. God is both Absolute and Infinite. Absoluteness – and Majesty, which is inseparable from it – are manifested most directly in the masculine state; Infinity and Beauty in the feminine state. The male body itself reflects majesty, power, absoluteness; and the female body reflects beauty, beatitude, and infinity. But these principles are also reflected in all the intermediate realms of existence which, in each type of microcosm, male and female, separate the corporeal state from the Divine Presence.

But since God is one and man, that is, the human being of whichever sex it might be, a theomorphic being who reflects God's Names and Qualities,[2] each human being also reflects the One and seeks to return to the One. Hence there is at once complementarity and rivalry between the sexes. There is union and polarization. The female is at once Mary, who symbolizes the Divine Mercy in the Abrahamic traditions and the beatitude which issues from this Mercy, and Eve, who entices, seduces and externalizes the soul of man, leading to its dissipation, although in Islam Eve is not the cause of man's loss of the Edenic state. The female is at once the source of concupiscence and the theater for the contemplation of the Divinity in Its uncreated aspect. Likewise, man is at once the symbol of the Lord and Creator and a being who, having lost sight of his ontological dependence upon the Lord, would seek, as a usurper, to play the role of Lord and Creator while he remains a mortal and perishable being. The veil of cosmic manifestation, the *ḥijāb* of Islamic metaphysics, makes the relation between the sexes an ambivalent one. But the profound metaphysical relationship between the two sexes is such that there is at once the inclination for union with a member of the opposite sex, which means ultimately the need to regain the consciousness of beatific union possessed by the androgynic ancestor of humanity in the paradisal state, and rivalry between the sexes, since each human being is in turn a total image of the primordial *insān*.

While some religions have emphasized the negative aspect of sexuality, Islam bases itself on its positive aspect as a means of perfection of the human state and, on the highest level, a symbol of union with God, sexual relations being of course governed by the injunction of the Divine Law. Addressing itself to man in his primordial nature (*al-fiṭrah*), to 'man as such',[3] Islam envisages the love of man and woman as being inseparable from the love of God, and leading to God on the highest level.[4] There exists in Islamic spirituality, as a result of this perspective, a hierarchy of love stretching from what is called 'metaphorical love' (*al-'ishq al-majāzī*) to 'real love' (*al-'ishq al-ḥaqīqī*), which is the love of God Himself.[5] The well-known but elliptical *ḥadīth* of the Prophet, that of the things of this world he loved above anything else women, perfume, and prayer alludes, spiritually speaking, to the positive aspect of sexuality in Islam, as well as to the relation of the spiritual nature of womanhood to prayer, which is the most direct means of access to God for human beings, and to the most subtle of sensual experiences having to do with the olfactory faculty.[6] Moreover, the Quran (XXIV; 26) specifically relates the symbolism of perfume to sexual union.

It is because of the positive role accorded to sexuality in the Islamic perspective that the theme of love, as realized gnosis, dominates its spirituality, that God appears as the Beloved and the female as a precious being symbolizing inwardness and the inner paradise which is hidden from man as a result of the loss of 'the eye of the heart' and the power to perceive beings *in divinis*.[7] The fall of man into the state of separation and forgetfulness has brought about an exteriorization and inversion in that contemplation of female beauty which can aid man to return to the Center once again, and which brings with it the beatitude in whose quest he spends his efforts, knowingly or unknowingly. This power has ceased to operate for most human beings, except in a potential manner. Yet its echo persists; even the physical joy of sexual union reflects something of its paradisal archetype and is itself proof of the sacred union which is the celestial prototype of all earthly union between the sexes, and which imparts upon the biological act, despite the ontological hiatus between archetype and earthly reflection as well as the element of inversion which is also present between the symbol and the symbolized, something of the experience of the Infinite and the Absolute.

Ibn 'Arabī goes to the point of describing the contemplation of

God in woman as the highest form of contemplation possible; he writes:

> When man contemplates God in woman, his contemplation rests on that which is passive; if he contemplates Him in himself, seeing that woman comes from man, he contemplates Him in that which is active; and when he contemplates Him alone, without the presence of any form whatsoever issued from Him, his contemplation corresponds to a state of passivity with regard to God, without intermediary. Consequently his contemplation of God in woman is the most perfect, for it is then God, in so far as He is at once active and passive, that he contemplates, whereas in the pure interior contemplation, he contemplates Him only in a passive way. So the Prophet – Benediction and Peace be upon him – was to love women because of the perfect contemplation of God in them. One would never be able to contemplate God directly in absence of all (sensible or spiritual) support, for God, in his Absolute Essence, is independent of all worlds. But, as the (Divine) Reality is inaccessible in respect (of the Essence), and there is contemplation (*shahādah*) only in a substance, the contemplation of God in women is the most intense and the most perfect; and the union which is the most intense (in the sensible order, which serves as support for this contemplation) is the conjugal act.[8]

Since religion concerns the final ends of man and his perfection, Islam has legislated and provided spiritual and ethical principles which, in conformity with its perspective, make use of this very important aspect of human nature, namely sexuality, to help perfect human beings and bring them felicity in both this world and the hereafter. This is especially true since Islam is a social order as well as a spiritual path, a *Sharī'ah* as well as a *Ṭarīqah*.[9] Also as already mentioned, Islam envisages the quest after God, which is the ultimate goal of human existence, upon the basis of social and personal equilibrium. Islamic spirituality is always based on the foundation of an equilibrium which is inseparable from the name of *al-islām*, 'peace': an equilibrium which is reflected in a blinding fashion in all authentic manifestations of Islam, especially its sacred art.[10]

To make this equilibrium and the spiritual life based upon it possible, Islam has envisaged a human order in which the sexes are seen in their complementary rather than contending aspects. On the social and family levels, it has legislated for a social order in which there should be a maximum amount of stability, the greatest possible degree of attachment of men and women to a family structure, and emphasis upon marriage as a religious duty. Marriage is not seen, however, as a sacrament, since from an 'alchemical' and also a metaphysical point of view – which is that of Islam – the sexual act is already a sacred act which must be kept within the bounds of the Sacred Law to govern human passions, but which does not need another sacrament in order to become sacralized. Islamic legislation and the social structure based upon it do not, of course, imply an order in which everyone could be satisfied in every way, for to speak of manifestation and multiplicity is to speak of separation from the unique source of goodness, and hence to be in the realm of imperfection. What the Islamic social order has always sought to achieve is the creation of the maximum amount of equilibrium possible, upon whose basis human beings can lead a life centered around and pointing to man's entelechy and end. Otherwise, there is no doubt that some people have been unhappy in a polygamous family situation, as others have been unhappy in a monogamous one – or even as totally 'free' persons living as atomized beings within an atomized society where each entity is, or at least appears to be, free to do and move about at will. The question for Islam has not been how to make everyone happy, because that is something which is not possible in this world. In fact, the world would not be the world (*al-dunyā* in the language of the Quran) if it were possible. The question has rather been how to create a state in which there would be the maximum amount of harmony and equilibrium, and which would be most conducive to man's living as God's vice-gerent (*khalīfatallāh*) on earth and with awareness of His Will during this fleeting journey called human life.

Since sexuality, far from being just a biological accident, possesses a profound metaphysical significance,[11] it has been possible for Islam to place its perspective on the positive rather than negative aspect of this powerful and profound force within human life.[12] Although both man and woman are *insān*, that is, both are the image of God and carry the androgynic reality within the depth of their beings, they cannot reach this interior and also superior reality through the attainment of a kind of least common denominator between the two sexes. Of course, both sexes contain something of both the male and female principles, the *yin* and *yang* of the Far Eastern traditions, within themselves; only in men, the male principle, and in women, the female principle, are dominant. To attain this state is to move in the other direction. Islamic spirituality tends in fact towards a clarification and complete differentiation of the two human types. Its social patterns and art of dress, among other things help to create masculine types who are very masculine and feminine types who are very feminine. If sexual union symbolizes the androgynic totality which both sexes seek consciously or even unconsciously, this union itself requires the distinction and separation of the two sexes, which can in fact participate in the sacred act precisely because of their very distinctness.

Moreover, each sex symbolizes in a positive manner a Divine aspect. Therefore, not only is sexual deviation and perversion a further step away from spiritual perfection, and a great obstacle to it, but also the loss of masculinity and femininity, and movement both psychologically and emotionally toward a neuter common type and ground implies, from the Islamic perspective, an irreparable loss and further fall from the perfection of the primordial *insān*, who was both male and female. The 'neuter' person is in fact a parody of the primordial human being, who was both Adam and Eve. Islamic teachings have emphasized this point very clearly. There are in fact *ḥadīths* of the Prophet which allude to men dressing and acting like women and vice-versa as being signs of the world coming to an end. In Islam, both the male and the female are seen as two creatures of God, each manifesting certain aspects of His Names and Qualities, and in their complementary union achieving the equilibrium and perfection that God has ordained for them and made the goal of human existence.

The tenets of Islam based upon sexual purity, separation of the sexes in many aspects of external life, the hiding of the beauty of women from strangers, division of social and family duties and the like all derive from the principles stated above. Their specific applications have depended on the different cultural and social milieus in which Islam has grown and have been very diverse. For example, the manner in which a Malay woman hides her female beauty is very different from the way of a Syrian, a Pakistani or a Senegalese; and even within a single country, what is called the veil (*ḥijāb*) has never been the same among nomads, villagers and city dwellers. Nor has the complementary role of the two sexes in all walks of life prevented Muslim women from participating in nearly all aspects of life, from ruling countries to owning major businesses in bazaars or even running butcher shops. Nor has the Islamic world been without eminent female religious and intellectual figures such as Fāṭimah, the daughter of the Prophet, who was a perfect saint; 'Ā'ishah, the wife of the Prophet through whom so much of Sunni *ḥadīth* has been transmitted; Zaynab, the granddaughter of the Prophet, who gave one of the most eloquent discourses in Islamic history before Yazīd after the death of her brother Imām Ḥusayn in Karbala'; Rābi'ah, one of the most celebrated of Muslim saints; or Sayyidah Nafīsah, who was a renowned authority on Islamic Law. The existence of these and many other personalities, from antiquity right down to our own day, demonstrates the undeniable fact that learning as well as the fields of commerce, agriculture, etc. were open to those women who chose to or were allowed to pursue them. But the principle of complementarity, as opposed to uniformity and competition, dominated.

This complementarity was rooted in equity rather than equality and sought to base itself on what served best the interests of society as a sacred body and men and women as immortal beings. Although spiritually it saw woman as symbolizing God as Infinity and the aspect of the Divinity above creation to the extent that Jalāl al-Dīn Rūmī refers to woman as 'uncreated', on the cosmic and human levels it recognized the role of the male as the immutable pole around which the family was constructed and in whose hand responsibility for the welfare of the women and children, as well as protection for God's Law and social order, were placed. In the Quran, man is given domination over woman but he is not given this responsibility as a two-legged animal. Rather, he has been entrusted with this task as the *imām* of God and His vice-gerent, whose soul is surrendered to Him. In a sense, man's soul must be the consort of the Spirit in order for him to be able to play his full role as husband for his wife and father for his children. The revolt of the female sex against the male did not precede but followed in the wake of the revolt of the male sex against Heaven.

But even the relative predominance given to the male function, which brings with it not privilege but rather responsibility, has not in any way compromised the view of Islam that both men and women were born for immortality, that the rites of religion are incumbent upon both of them and that its rewards are accessible to men and women alike. The *Sharī'ite* rites of Islam are meant for members of both sexes and the Quran explicitly states:–

> Lo! Men who surrender unto Allah, and women who surrender, and men who believe and women who believe, and men who obey and women who obey, and men who speak the truth and women who speak the truth, and men who persevere (in righteousness) and women who persevere, and men who are humble and women who are humble, and men who give alms and women who give alms, and men who fast and women who fast, and men who guard their modesty and women who guard (their modesty), and men who remember Allah much and women who remember – Allah hath prepared for them forgiveness and a vast reward.[13]

Even in instances where certain rites are reserved for men, such as the prayer for the dead, this does not imply a particular privilege for though God has not made women responsible for such rites, He still asks them to seek to reach those highest spiritual goals that are the *raison d'être* of such rites. As for the spiritual practices associated with Sufism, they have always been accessible to women and there have always been many women followers in various Sufi orders, some of whom have attained the level of sanctity and become spiritual guides. There is, in fact, a feminine dimension within Sufism which possesses a distinct perfume of its own.[14]

In conclusion we must remember again the Origin which, in its essence, is above the sexes and all other dualities but which yet, in its Majesty and Beauty, contains the roots of what on the plane of cosmic existence appears as the masculine and feminine principles, and on the human level as male and female. Individual human beings are born as men and women, not accidentally but according to their destiny. They can fulfil their function in life, reach the perfection which alone can bestow felicity and even transcend all traces of separative existence and return unto the One, only in accepting their destiny and transcending from above the form into which they have been born, not by rebelling against it. In the Holy Name of God, there is neither male nor female, but no-one can penetrate into the inner sanctum of that Name without having fully integrated into his or her own being the positive elements of the sex into which he or she has been born. The Universal Man is inwardly the androgynic being who possesses the perfection of both sexes, but he or she does not come to that perfection save by remaining faithful to the norms and conditions his or her sex implies. The revolt of the sexes against that equilibrium which results from their complementarity and union is both the result and a concomitant of the revolt of modern man against Heaven. Man cannot reach that peace and harmony which is the foretaste of the paradise human beings carry at the center of their being, except by bringing to full actualization and realization the possibilities innate in the human state, both male and female. To reject the distinct and distinguishing features of the two sexes and the Sacred Legislation based on this objective cosmic reality is to live below the human level; to be, in fact, only accidentally human. It is to sacrifice and compromise the eternal life of man and woman for an apparent earthly justice based on a uniformity which fails, ultimately even on the purely earthly level, since it does not take into consideration the reality of that which constitutes the human state in both its male and female aspects.

Notes

1. It is significant to note that the Quranic term for 'man' is *insān*, which refers to the human state as such and not to one of the sexes. The Arabic term is closer to the Latin *homo* or the German *mensch* than the English *man*.
2. On the meaning of man as a theomorphic being, a doctrine which does not at all imply any kind of anthropomorphism, see F. Schuon, *Understanding Islam*, pp. 13ff.
3. Schuon begins his well-known work, *Understanding Islam*, with the phrase, 'Islam is the meeting between God as such and man as such: that is to say, man envisaged, not as a fellow being needing a miracle to save him, but as man, a theomorphic being endowed with intelligence

capable of conceiving of the Absolute and with a will capable of choosing what leads to the Absolute.'

4. 'Loving each other, Adam and Eve loved God; they could neither love nor know outside God. After the fall, they loved each other outside God and for themselves, and they knew each other as separate phenomena and not as theophanies; this new kind of love was concupiscence and this new kind of knowing was profanity.' Schuon, *Islam and the Perennial Philosophy*, p. 191.
5. This theme is particularly developed among certain Sufis who have been aptly called the *fedeli d'amore* of Islam. See H. Corbin, *En Islam iranien*, Vol. III, Paris, 1972, (sub-titled *Les Fidèles d'amour*), especially pp. 9–146, concerning Rūzbahān Baqlī, the patron saint of Shiraz.
6. Ibn 'Arabī devotes many pages of the last chapters of his *Fuṣūṣ al-ḥikam* to an exposition of the metaphysical significance of this *ḥadīth* of the Prophet and why in fact women, perfume and prayer are mentioned in this order.
7. The beauty of woman is, for spiritual man, an unveiling of the beauty of the paradise that he carries at the center of his being and to which the Quran alludes when it speaks of the *houris* of paradise. Likewise, the goodness of man is for woman a confirmation and support of her inner goodness. According to an Arabic proverb, goodness is outward and beauty inward in man, while in woman beauty is outward and goodness inward. There is not only a complementarity between the sexes but also an inversion of relationships. From a certain point of view, man symbolizes outwardness and woman inwardness. She is the theophany of esotericism and, in certain modes of spirituality, Divine Wisdom (which, as *al-ḥikmah*, is feminine in Arabic) reveals itself to the gnostic as a beautiful woman.
8. See Muḥyī al-Dīn Ibn 'Arabī, *The Wisdom of the Prophets*, translated from the Arabic into French with notes by T. Burckhardt; translated from the French by A. Culme-Seymour, Gloucestershire, 1975, p. 120.
9. See S.H. Nasr, *Ideals and Realities of Islam*, chapters I, IV and V.
10. T. Burckhardt has dealt with this subject in many of his penetrating studies of Islamic art. See especially his *The Art of Islam*.
11. On the metaphysical principles pertaining to sexuality and its character as found in sources drawn mostly from the Western traditions see G. Evola, *Metafisica del sesso*, Rome, 1958.
12. Since sexuality is a double-edged sword, the other point of view, which is based on the monastic ideal, has also its metaphysical basis and had to manifest itself in certain religions such as Buddhism and Christianity. Even in Islam the positive attitude of monasticism as separation from the world is realized inwardly, since there is no institution of monasticism in Islam. And despite the emphasis of Islam upon marriage and the positive role accorded to sexuality in Islamic spirituality, there have been many saintly men and women who have practiced sexual abstinence. In fact, it would not be possible to experience the paradisal archetype of sexual union without the primary

phase of asceticism which allows the soul to experience phenomena as symbols rather than facts. That is also why the experience of the spiritual aspect of sexuality remains inaccessible outside the cadre of tradition and sacred laws which regulate all human relations, including sexuality.

13. Quran (XXXII; 35), Pickthall translation. On this point see Aisha Lemu, 'Women in Islam', in A. Gauhar (ed.), *The Challenge of Islam*, London, 1978, pp. 249–267. The Quran also asserts 'Whosoever doeth right, whether male or female, and is a believer, him verily We shall quicken with good life, and We shall pay them a recompense in proportion to the best of what they used to do.' (XVI; 97).

    On Islamic views concerning women and their rights and responsibilities from a religious as well as sociological and anthropological point of view see Muhammad Abdul-Rauf, *The Islamic View of Women and the Family*, New York, 1977; E.W. Fernea and B.Q. Bezirgan (ed.), *Middle Eastern Women Speak*, Austin, 1977; and D.H. Dwyer, *Images and Self-Images: Male and Female in Morocco*, New York, 1978. There is, needless to say, a vast literature on the subject but most of the works are written from the perspective of current prejudices in the West, as well as from the profane point of view as far as the nature of the human state itself is concerned. There is also very little which, by way of translation, would make accessible authentic writings by Muslim women on religious and spiritual themes.

14. A great master such as Ibn 'Arabī had female spiritual guides (*shaykhah* in Arabic) while he was in Andalusia. On the female element in Sufism see A.M. Schimmel, *Mystical Dimensions of Islam*, Chapel Hill, 1975, 'The Feminine Element in Sufism', pp. 426ff.; and L. Bakhtiar, *Sufi Art and Imagination*, London, 1976; see also J. Nurbakhsh, *Sufi Women*, New York, 1983.

Chapter Four

Traditional Shi'ism in Safavid Persia

The events of the last years have caused so much partisan debate concerning Twelve-Imam Shi'ism, its tradition and present significance, that few aspects of Islam are as much in need of disinterested and objective study today. Whereas a few years ago only a small number of works existed on Shi'ism in European languages, today there is a sizeable collection of books, monographs and articles on the subject, but still only a few which do not allow present-day events to color their evaluation and appreciation of traditional Shi'ism. With the intense interest in the subject caused by the political events of the past decade, there is great need to understand the nature of traditional Shi'ism as an integral aspect of the Islamic tradition itself. Moreover, a major manifestation of this traditional Shi'ism is to be found in Safavid Persia when, for the first time in history, Twelve-Imam Shi'ism became the official religion of a Muslim country. Despite the claims of certain 'Shi'ite revolutionaries', who have sought to dissociate Safavid Shi'ism from ''Alīd

Shi'ism', Shi'ism in Safavid Persia represents a major phase in the historical unfolding of traditional Shi'ism and is therefore of much significance for the understanding of this particular aspect of the Islamic tradition in its encounter with the modern world. No aspect of the religio-political history of 14th/20th century Iran can be fully understood without consideration of religion and especially Shi'ism in Safavid Persia.

The Safavid period marks a definite turning point in the history of Persia and the beginning of a new phase in the history of Islam in that country. Yet, despite its distinct character and the break it seems to display with respect to the centuries preceding it, there was definitely a long religious and intellectual history which prepared the ground for the sudden establishment of a Shi'ite order in Persia and the transformation of the country into a predominantly Shi'ite area.[1] There were several centuries of growth in Shi'ite theology and jurisprudence, the development of Sufi orders with Shi'ite tendencies and the establishment of Shi'ite political power – albeit of a transient character – all preceding the Safavid period.

As far as Shi'ite thought is concerned, the advent of the Mongols and the destruction of the major centers of Sunni political power in Western Asia enabled Shi'ism to flower in Persia more than ever before, culminating in the establishment of Shi'ism as state religion for a brief period under Sultan Muḥammad Khudābandah. But the most significant aspect of the post-Mongol period as far as Shi'ism is concerned was the appearance of intellectual figures of outstanding merit, such as Khwājah Naṣīr al-Dīn Ṭūsī and his student 'Allāmah Ḥillī, with whom Shi'ite theology became definitely established, the *Tajrīd* of Ṭūsī as commented upon by Ḥillī being the first systematic treatise of Shi'ite *kalām*. Other outstanding Shi'ite theologians followed, such as Ibn Makkī al-'Āmilī, known as al-Shahīd al-awwal, author of the well-known *al-Lum'at al-dimashqiyyah*, followed by Zayn al-Dīn al-'Āmilī, al-Shahīd al-thānī, whose commentary upon this work, *Sharḥ al-lum'ah*,[2] is famous to this day. The works of these and other figures were the props of Shi'ism at the outset of the Safavid period; in fact they are of such importance that the history of Shi'ism during the Safavid and subsequent periods would be incomprehensible without them.

Parallel to this development in the religious sciences, one can observe a remarkable spread of activity in post-Mongol Persia in the domain of religious philosophy and in that combination of

Peripatetic philosophy, Illuminationist doctrines and gnosis which came to be known as *al-ḥikmat al-ilāhiyyah* or theosophy and which gradually moved into the orbit of Shi'ism.[3] Such figures as Ibn Abī Jumhūr, Ibn Turkah, Rajab Bursī and especially Sayyid Ḥaydar Āmulī, who sought to harmonize and in fact identify the Sufism of Ibn 'Arabī with esoteric Shi'ite doctrines,[4] are the direct intellectual ancestors of the Safavid sages such as Mīr Dāmād and Mullā Ṣadrā.

As for Sufism, the period between the Mongols and the Safavids was witness, not only to a remarkable flowering of Sufism as exemplified by the appearance of such great poles of sanctity as Mawlānā Jalāl al-Dīn Rūmī, Najm al-Din Kubrā, Ṣadr al-Dīn Qunyawī and the like, but it was also the period during which Sufism became a bridge between Sunnism and Shi'ism, and in many instances prepared the ground for the spread of Shi'ism.[5] The role of the Kubrawiyyah,[6] the Nūrbakhshiyyah and the Ni'matallāhiyyah orders bears close study in the light of their relation to the later spread of Shi'ism in Persia through a dynasty of Sufi origin. This leads in turn to the Ṣafawī order itself, to the two and a half centuries which separate Shaykh Ṣafī al-Dīn of Ardabil from Shah Ismā'īl, to the transformation of a simple Sufi order organized around a saint and ascetic to a militant movement with extreme Shi'ite tendencies under Sultan Junayd and Ḥaydar, and finally to the establishment of the military basis which made the Safavid conquest of Persia possible.[7]

Finally, as far as political aspects of religion are concerned, the brief rule of Shi'ism under Muḥammad Khudābandah, as well as such Shi'ite dynasties as the Sarbadārān in Khurasan, the Musha'sha'ah in Iraq as well as the Safavid shaykhs themselves preceding Shah Ismā'īl, present historical antecedents of great importance.[8] They point to political and social transformations of a religious nature which are directly related to the whole question of religion in Safavid Persia.

In reality, the discussion of religion in its vastest sense as tradition (*al-dīn*) in the Safavid period includes every facet of life in Safavid society inasmuch as we are dealing with a traditional world in which all activity is related to a transcendent norm. Whether it be literature as reflected in the poetry of Ṣā'ib-i Tabrīzī and Muḥtashim-i Kāshānī, or architecture and city planning as seen in the central region of the city of Isfahan[9], or even sports as in the case of the *Zūr-khānah*, we are in fact dealing with something that is directly related to religion. Even the cosmic elements, the water that flowed in geometrically-shaped gardens and the earth from which the mud walls of structures were made, possess a religious significance if seen from the point of view of the men who lived and breathed in the traditional Islamic world, whether it was Abbasid, Seljuq or Safavid. Here, however, it is only with religion and religious thought in the strict sense of the word that we shall deal, leaving the ramifications of religion in art and society out of consideration.

The most noteworthy feature of religion in Safavid Persia is, first of all, the rapid process by which Persia became Shi'ite. Although the ground for this transformation had been prepared by subtle religious changes during the Īlkhānid period, when Shah Ismā'īl was crowned, probably the majority of Persians were still Sunnis. Certainly the city of Tabriz, where the crowning took place, was about two-thirds Sunni, although the Shi'ite element was at that time strongest among the Turkish-speaking segments of the population. It was the policy, ardently followed by the Safavids, to establish Shi'ism as the state religion that led to the rapid change.

To make the process of transforming Iran into a Shi'ite land possible, many outstanding Shi'ite scholars were invited to Persia from both Bahrayn and the Jabal 'Amil in present-day Lebanon, both of which had been for some time seats of Shi'ite learning. In fact, so many scholars from these two regions came to Persia that two works, the *Lu'lu'at al-baḥrayn* and *Amal al-'āmil*, are entirely devoted to their biographies. These scholars ranged from simple *mullās* who fulfilled small religious functions, to men like Shaykh Bahā' al-dīn al-'Āmilī and Sayyid Ni'matallāh al-Jazā'irī, both of whom came to Persia at a very young age but soon developed into leading religious authorities.

Few modern scholars have examined the effect of the presence of all of these Arabic-speaking scholars on the role of Arabic in Persian intellectual circles at this time. Many present-day traditional authorities[10] in Persia, however, believe that, because of the great power and prestige of these men, some of whom, like Sulṭān al-'Ulamā', hardly knew Persian, there came into being a new emphasis upon Arabic among the religious authorities, and it even became fashionable to use Arabic in situations where in earlier times Persian had been commonly used. Certainly the dearth of Persian prose writings in the religious field at this time in comparison with either the Seljuq and Mongol or the Qajar periods bears this out.[11] More Persian religious works were written in the Indian sub-continent during this period than in Persia itself. The immigration of this class of Arabic-speaking scholars, who became rapidly Persianized and absorbed within the matrix of Persian society, had, therefore, an effect upon both the religious life of the country and the type of religious language employed.

The result of the spread of Shi'ism, which, as already mentioned, did not completely replace Sunnism but became the most dominant form of Islam in Persia[12], implied the establishment of such typically Shi'ite institutions as the religious sermons depicting mostly the tragedy of Karbala' or *rawḍah-khānī*, held especially during Muḥarram, the *ta'ziyah* or passion play, the religious feast or *sufrah*, religious processions, visits to tombs of holy men or *imām-zādahs*, in addition to the daily prayers, the pilgrimage and the fasting, all of which still comprise the main day-to-day religious activity of Persians.[13] As far as the ritual and practical aspects of religion in the Safavid period are concerned, the situation was nearly the same as that which could be observed up until recent years.

The role and function of other aspects of religion in Safavid Persia after the early period of transformation can perhaps be best understood by studying such things as classes of religious scholars, the various religious functions in society, the types of religious thought of the period, and finally the position of Sufism and of the guilds, which played a paramount role in the religious life of the Persians at this time. As far as the classes of religious scholars are concerned, it is important to note that during the Safavid period, as in most other periods of Islamic history, and even more so because of the particular politico-religious structure of Shi'ism, there were two classes of religious scholars or *'ulamā'*: one, the class supported and appointed by the Safavid kings and their representatives, and the other, that which remained completely aloof from central political power and gained its authority from the support of the populace.[14]

As far as the first group is concerned, its members were chosen from the class of *'ulamā'* and were then appointed to a hierarchy of functions which, in a sense, paralleled the administrative structure of the Safavid state. There was, first of all, a learned person of high repute called the *mullā bāshī* whom many Safavid kings chose as a close companion to counsel them on religious matters and read prayers for them on different occasions.[15] Then there was the position of the *ṣadr*, the highest religious office of the land, whose incumbent was chosen directly by the king and who rivalled the grand *mufti* of the Ottomans. The *ṣadr* was responsible for all the official religious duties of the country, especially the supervision of the endowments (*awqāf*), which he administered with the help of such officials as *mustawfīs, mutaṣaddis* and *wazīrs* of *awqāf*. Sometimes the function of the *ṣadr* was in fact divided into two parts: one, that of *ṣadr-i mamālik*, which concerned the supervision of the general endowments, and the other, that of *ṣadr-i khāṣṣah*, which was related to the royal endowments. The *ṣadr* also appointed judges (*qāḍīs*) and the chief official religious dignitaries (*shaykh al-islām*) of the bigger cities with the consent of the king.[16]

As for the class of '*ulamā*', who stood aloof from the central political power, at their head were the *mujtahids*, literally those who could practice *ijtihād* (that is, give fresh opinions on questions of Sacred Law): men who were and still are highly revered by society because of their knowledge and piety, and because it is they whom the Shi'ites consider as the representatives of the Hidden Imām.[17] From among them was chosen the person who was emulated according to Shi'ite doctrine (*marja'-i taqlīd*)[18] and who at times gained a power rivaling that of the king himself. The *mujtahids*, while usually supporting the Safavid monarchy, also often acted as protection for the people against the tyranny of some local government officials and fulfilled a major function of both a religious and social nature. The aloofness of these scholars from centers of political power must not, however, be seen as opposition by them to the political system itself.

Besides the *mujtahids*, there were other religious scholars of lower rank whose authority relied upon the people and who provided their daily needs. Foremost among these were the leaders of prayers (*imāms*) of various mosques. Because of the stringent ethical conditions set in Shi'ism for those who lead the daily prayers, these men, behind whom people accepted to pray and who also catered to other religious needs of the populace, were never appointed by any government authorities. Rather, they were freely chosen by the members of the religious community itself. Of course, occasionally such functions were fulfilled by men who also held state-appointed offices, and sometimes this reached the highest level when a leading *mujtahid* also became an official religious dignitary, but this was an exception which nevertheless did not destroy the basic separation between the two types of religious authority just mentioned.

From the point of view of religious thought, however, both classes of *'ulamā'* mentioned belonged to the single category of specialists in jurisprudence and other Islamic legal sciences. They were *faqīhs* first and foremost. But there developed in the Safavid period, upon the basis of earlier examples, another type of religious scholar who, rather than being a specialist in law and jurisprudence, was a master of Islamic metaphysics and theosophy. The *ḥakīm-i ilāhī*, or theosopher, who came to the fore during this period, was the successor to earlier Muslim philosophers from al-Fārābī and Ibn Sīnā, through Suhrawardī and Naṣīr al-Dīn Ṭūsī to Ibn Turkah and Sayyid Ḥaydar Āmulī, who were the immediate predecessors of the Safavid sages. During this period the attempt begun by Suhrawardī and later Ibn Turkah to harmonize rational philosophy, intellectual intuition and revealed religion[19] reached its apogee, and *ḥikmat-i ilāhī* during the Safavid period became more than ever before a most important if not the central expression of religious thought.[20] Therefore the *ḥakīm-i ilāhī* also became a much more central figure in the religious life of the community than before.

The founder of this remarkable period of Islamic philosophy, which has come to be known as the School of Isfahan, is Mīr Dāmād, himself the son-in-law of one of the most influential of the early Safavid *'ulamā'*, Muḥaqqiq-i Karakī.[21] Mīr Dāmād was also an authority in the 'transmitted sciences' (*al-'ulūm al-naqliyyah*), including jurisprudence, but he was before everything else a *ḥakīm* who opened up new horizons for Islamic philosophy and who was responsible for the rapid spread of *ḥikmat-i ilāhī* through his numerous writings and by the training of many students. Among his disciples, Ṣadr al-Dīn Shīrāzī, the greatest metaphysician of the age and perhaps the foremost *ḥakīm* in Islamic history in the domain of metaphysics, stands out particularly.[22] Ṣadr al-Dīn also studied with Shaykh Bahā' al-Dīn al-'Āmilī in the field of the 'transmitted sciences' and possibly with another of the outstanding *ḥakīms* of the Safavid period, Mīr Abu'l-Qāsim Findiriskī. But as far as *ḥikmat-i ilāhī* is concerned, Mullā Ṣadrā built most of all upon the foundations laid by Mīr Dāmād. He followed the attempt of Mīr Dāmād to synthesize the teachings of Ibn Sīnā and Suhrawardī within Shi'ite esotericism but went further by making a grand synthesis of all the major intellectual perspectives of nearly a thousand years of Islamic intellectual life that went before him. The teachings of the Quran, of the Holy Prophet and the Imams, of the Peripatetic philosophers, of the Illuminationist theosophers and of the Sufis were like so many colors of the rainbow which became unified and harmonized in the transcendent theosophy (*al-ḥikmat al-muta'āliyah*) of Mullā Ṣadrā. No other figure of the Safavid period characterizes as well as Mullā Ṣadrā the special genius of this age for intellectual synthesis and the expression of unity in multiplicity, which is also so evident in the extremely rich art of the age.

Mullā Ṣadrā himself was an inexhaustible source for the doctrines of *ḥikmat-i ilāhī* and responsible for the spread of its teachings; he continues to dominate traditional religious thought in Persia to this day. He was at once a prolific writer[23] and a peerless teacher, his foremost students, Mullā Muḥsin Fayḍ Kāshānī and 'Abd al-Razzāq Lāhījī, being themselves among the most outstanding intellectual figures of Persia. Moreover, these masters themselves taught a generation of important *ḥakīms*, like Qādī Sa'īd Qummī, and the tradition continued despite much difficulty down to the very end of the Safavid period; it was then revived by Mullā 'Alī Nūrī and Mullā Ismā'īl Khājū'ī in the 13th/19th century.[24]

It is characteristic of the religious life of Safavid Persia that a dynasty that began as a Sufi order moved so much in the direction of exotericism that Mullā Muḥammad Bāqir Majlisī, the most powerful *'alim* of the later Safavid period and the author of the monumental encyclopedia, *Biḥār al-anwār*, repudiated the Sufism of his father, Mullā Muḥammad Taqī, and forced the last great *ḥakīm* of the Safavid period in Isfahan, the saintly Mullā Ṣādiq Ardistānī, into exile. It is an irony that both Sufism and *ḥikmat-i ilāhī*, which also possesses an esoteric character, were finally forced into a kind of marginal existence at the end of the reign of a dynasty of Sufi origin.

As far as Sufism itself is concerned, because of the very fact that the Safavid dynasty was originally a Sufi order, its coming into political power eventually made the life of Sufism in Shi'ite Persia difficult for several decades. At the beginning of the Safavid period, many Sufi orders were fully active in Persia. The Nūrbakhshī order, founded by Shaykh Muḥammad Nūrbakhsh, was at its height. In fact, the student of the founder of the order, Shaykh Muḥammad Lāhījī, who is the author of that ocean of gnosis in the Persian language, the *Sharḥ-i gulshan-i rāz*, was a contemporary of Shah Ismā'īl. The order wielded much influence during the first few decades of Safavid rule but then gradually disappeared from the scene.

The Dhahabī order, which is still strong in Persia today, was also active at that time. Some of the great Sufis of this age, such as Pīr-i Pālāndūz (Muḥammad Karān-dihī), Shaykh Ḥātam Harāwandī and Shaykh Muḥammad 'Alī Sabziwārī Khurāsānī, the author of the well-known *al-Tuḥfat al-'abbāsiyyah*[25], are considered by later Dhahabīs as poles of their order. But although the Dhahabīs continued their life into the Zand period, they too became less visible toward the end of the Safavid era.

Other orders mentioned by various sources, both Persian and European, as being active during the Safavid period include the Qāḍirīs, Baktāshīs, Khāksārs, Mawlawīs and Ni'matallāhīs.[26] The case of the Khāksār and the Ni'matallāhī orders, which are still very much alive today, in contrast to the Baktāshīs and Mawlawīs, which no longer have any following in Persia, is of particular interest. The Khāksārs somehow fell out of favor at the time of Shah 'Abbās and some of their leaders retired to cities far away in the south of the country. As for the Ni'matallāhīs, their leaders, such as Niẓām al-Dīn 'Abd al-Bāqī and Ghiyāth al-Dīn Mīr Mīrān, were closely associated with the court and held positions of great eminence at the beginning of the Safavid period, and the order itself had a wide following. But soon they too fell out of favor and were persecuted so severely that their outward organization in Persia disappeared completely. They retired to the Deccan in India and their very history in Persia was interrupted. It was in fact from the Deccan that the order was re-established in Persia during the early Qajar period.[27]

The reason for this rather violent opposition to Sufism and even *ḥikmat-i ilāhī* in the late Safavid period lies partially in the fact that the Ṣafawī order, which had become a ruling dynasty, tended because of this fact to lose its spiritual discipline as a Sufi order and to become diluted through the intrusion of worldly elements into its very structure. This fact in turn caused the resentment of other Sufi orders, which were eventually suppressed by the Safavids, as well as of the exoteric religious authorities. In the second case, it was not possible to suppress the exoteric authorities, for the very power of the Safavids lay in the support of Shi'ism. Hence the Safavid kings, if not all the members of the order, tended to become ever more detached from their Sufi background and to support exoteric authorities in their opposition to Sufism. As a result, if before the rise of the Safavids a figure such as Sayyid Haydar Āmulī could say that 'True Sufism is Shi'ism and true Shi'ism is Sufism,' at the end of the Safavid period the opposition between Shi'ism and the organized Sufi orders became so great that, even in later periods of Persian history, Sufism could return to the centers of Shi'ite learning only under the name of *'irfān* or under the guise of *ḥikmat-i ilāhī*. The situation that prevails in such centers as Najaf and Qum to this day is inherited from the complete polarity and opposition between the most powerful Shi'ite *'ulamā'* and organized Sufism at the end of the Safavid period.[28]

Finally, a word must be said about the guilds and forms of craft initiation that were widespread in the Safavid period and which bridged the gap between the most inward principles of the tradition and various aspects of everyday life, from selling merchandise in the bazaar to constructing mosques. The tradition of 'chivalry' (*futuwwat* or *jawānmardī*) as related to various social and artistic activities was already strong in the pre-Safavid period and continued on into the period itself.[29] Those remarkable architects who designed the various mosques, palaces and caravanserais of this era, the rug weavers who have created some of the most remarkable color harmonies of any school of art, and the masters of plaster and tile design were mostly members of guilds with a spiritual discipline related to various Sufi orders, especially the Khāksār. In fact, what has remained of the techniques of the traditional arts is to this day of an oral nature preserved within the still-existing guilds and transmitted by the way of a master-disciple relationship, still to be observed in some Persian cities and towns, which is a remnant of the fully active guilds of the Safavid period. What remains of the art of this period, even those forms which are not strictly speaking religious according to Western categories, is related in the profoundest way to the religious life of the Safavids. No account of religion in Safavid Persia would be complete without taking the role of the guilds and the deep religious nature of their activity into account.

Religion in the Safavid period is not only the key to the understanding of the Safavid period itself; it also represents a new chapter in Islamic history and a new crystallization of the possibilities inherent within the Islamic tradition. The study of the very complex and rich pattern of religious life in Safavid Persia – a study which has still to a large extent to be accomplished – is necessary for an understanding of the life of not only Persia but of other parts of the Islamic world at a time when the central region of this world became divided into three major empires: the Mughal, the Safavid and the Ottoman. Moreover, this study is basic for an understanding of the subsequent religious history of Persia itself to this day, for the basic religious institutions, practices and forms of thought established during the Safavid period comprised the foundation of the religious and intellectual life of Persia down to the present day and represent its link with the classical tradition of Islam dominant in Persia before its particular crystallization in the Safavid period in the form of a religious order dominated by Twelve-Imam Shi'ism.

Notes

1. Of course, if one remembers that much of present-day Afghanistan, Pakistan, Baluchistan, Caucasia and Central Asia was part of Persia at that time, it becomes clear that all of Persia did not become Shi'ite and that the solidly Shi'ite part came mostly within what comprises Persia today.
2. See M. Mazzaoui, 'Shi'ism in the Medieval Safavid and Qajar Periods: A Study in *Ithnā 'asharī* Continuity', in *Iran: Continuity and Variety*, New York, 1971, pp. 39ff.
3. See S.H. Nasr, 'Spiritual Movements, Philosophy and Theology in the Safavid Period', first part, *Cambridge History of Iran*, vol. VI, Cambridge, 1985.
4. See H. Corbin's prolegomena to Sayyid Ḥaydar Āmulī, *Jāmi' al-asrār wa manba' al-anwār*, ed. by H. Corbin and O. Yahya, Tehran-Paris, 1969; also P. Antes, *Zur theologie der Schi'a, Ein Untersuchung der Ǧami' al-asrār wa manba' al-anwār von Sayyid Ḥaydar Āmolī*, Freiburg, 1971.
5. See S.H. Nasr, 'Shi'ism and Sufism', *Sufi Essays*, London, 1972; also K. al-Shaybī, *al-Ṣilah bayn al-taṣawwuf wa'l-tashayyu'*, 2 vols., Baghdad, 1963–64; also H. Corbin, *En Islam iranien*, vol. IV, Paris, 1972, livre IV.
6. See M. Molé, 'Les Kubrawiya entre Sunnisme et Schiisme aux

huitième et neuvième siècles de l'Hegire', *Revue des Études Islamiques*, XXIX (1961), pp. 61–142. There are certain scholars who deny the Shi'ite character of the Kubrawiyyah order or its role in the spread of Shi'ism in pre-Safavid Iran. See the introduction by H. Algar to Rāzī, *The Path of God's Bondsmen*, New York, 1982, especially pp. 6–7, where he argues for the Sunni character of the Kubrawiyyah order.

Even if the view of these scholars be accepted, however, one cannot deny the role of the spread of this order in creating a more congenial background for the later acceptance of Shi'ism with the order's emphasis upon the *ahl al-bayt* and especially 'Alī.

7. On the background of the Safavid movement see E. Gassen, *Die Frühen Safaviden nach Qāẓī Aḥmad Qumī*, Freiburg, 1968, pp. 86–96. On the exploits of Shaykh Ḥaydar, the rise of the Qizil-bāsh and the religious wars leading to the establishment of Safavid rule, see V. Minorsky, *Persia in A.D. 1478–1490*, London, 1957, pp. 61ff. On the Safavids themselves see also R. Savory, *Iran under the Safavids*, Cambridge, 1980.
8. See M. Mazzaoui, *The Origins of the Safavids, Shi'ism, Ṣūfism and the Gulāt*, Wiesbaden, 1972, chapter III.
9. On the spiritual significance of the art and architecture of this period see N. Ardalan and L. Bakhtiyar, *The Sense of Unity, The Sufi Tradition in Persian Architecture*, Chicago, 1973, including the introduction by S.H. Nasr.
10. This, for example, is the view of Sayyid Muḥammad Kāẓim 'Aṣṣār, one of the leading *mujtahids* and *ḥakīms* of Persia during the present century.
11. Arabic has, of course, always been the primary language of the Islamic sciences in Persia as in the Arab world itself. But a relatively large number of works have also been composed in Persian in the fields of Quranic commentary, philosophy and the like from the fourth Islamic century onward. It is this type of writing which decreased in quantity during the Safavid period relative to the periods both before and after. There is, for example, no major Quranic commentary in Persian at this time of the dimensions of *Kashf al-asrār* of Mībudī, and Mullā Ṣadrā wrote only one philosophical work in Persian compared with the many Persian writings of Suhrawardī and Naṣīr al-Dīn Ṭūsī.
12. Debates between Sunni and Shi'ite authorities became in fact much more pronounced than before as a result of the political identification of the first with the Ottomans and the second with the Safavids. See E. Eberhard, *Osmanische Polemik gegen die Safawiden im 16. Jahrhundert nach arabischen Handschriften*, Freiburg, 1970.
13. For the meaning of various Shi'ite practices, see Nasr, 'Islam in Persia, Yesterday and Today', *Islam and the Plight of Modern Man*, London, 1975, pp. 101–121. As for Shi'ism in general see 'A.S.M. Ṭabāṭabā'ī, *Shi'ite Islam*, trans. S.H. Nasr, Albany (N.Y.), 1975.
14. Concerning the *'ulamā'* of this period, chapter VIII of E.G. Browne, *A Literary History of Persia*, vol. IV, Cambridge, 1959 on *mujtahids*

and *mullās* is still valuable. As for first hand sources of biographies of the *'ulamā'* of this period, such works as *Rawḍat al-jannāt*, *Majālis al-mu'minīn*, *Kashf al-ḥujub wa'l asrār*, *Nujūm al-samā'* and *Mustadrak al-wasā'il* may be mentioned.

As a result of current interest in Shi'ite political thought, many works have appeared during the past few years concerning the *'ulamā'*, their relation to the government and the question of the legitimacy of their political authority. There is, however, much difference of opinion concerning these politically crucial questions, not only among traditional and 'revolutionary' Shi'ites, but also among Western scholars. See for example, J. Eliash, 'Some Misconceptions Regarding the Juridical Status of the Iranian *'ulamā''* *International Journal of Middle East Studies*, vol. 10, 1979, pp. 9–25; H. Enayat, *Modern Islamic Political Thought*, London, 1982; and S.A. Arjomand, *The Shadow of God and the Hidden Imām*, Chicago, 1984, N. Calder in his 'Accommodation and Revolution in Imami Shi'i Jurisprudence: Khumayni and the Classical Tradition', *Middle East Studies*, vol. 18, no. 1, 1983, pp. 3–20, typifies the kind of scholarship that reads the present-day situation backwards into the classical period as far as the question of legitimacy is concerned and fails to distinguish between the traditional doctrines and the present 'revivalist' or 'fundamentalist' interpretations.

15. See *Tadhkirat al-mulūk*, part 1, ed. by M. Dabīr-siyāqī, Tehran, 1332 (A.H. solar), pp. 1–4.
16. Concerning this hierarchy of functions, see the perceptive description of the 17th-century traveller to Persia E. Kaempfer, *Amoenitatem exoticarum, politico-physico medicarum fasciculi V, quibus continentur variae relationes, observationes & descptiones rerum Persicarum & ulterioris Asiae . . .*, Lemgovia, 1712, pp. 98ff. There is also a fine Persian translation based on Hinz by K. Jahāndārī, *Dar darbār-i shāhanshāh-i Īrān*, Tehran, 1350 (A.H. solar).
17. On the class of *mujtahids* and their importance in Shi'ite society see H. Algar, *Religion and State in Iran 1785–1906*, Berkeley and Los Angeles, 1969; and A.K. Lambton, 'A Reconsideration of the Position of the *Marja' al-Taqlīd* and the Religious Institution', *Studia Islamica*, vol. XX (1964), pp. 115–135.
18. On the meaning of *marja'-i taqlīd*, see 'Allāmah Ṭabāṭabā'ī et al., *Marja'iyyat wa rūḥāniyyat*, Tehran, 1341 (A.H. solar).
19. On Suhrawardī see H. Corbin, *En Islam iranien*, vol. II, Paris, 1971: S.H. Nasr, *Three Muslim Sages*, Albany, 1976, chapter II. As for Ibn Turkah see Corbin, *op. cit.*, vol. III, Paris, 1972, pp. 233ff.
20. On the relation between *ḥikmat-i ilāhī* and Islamic theology, see S.H. Nasr, *'al-Hikmat al-ilāhiyyah* and *Kalām*', *Studia Islamica*, vol. XXXIV (1971), pp. 139–149.
21. See S.H. Nasr, 'The School of Isfahan', M.M. Sharif, *A History of Muslim Philosophy*, vol. II, Wiesbaden, 1966, pp. 904–932; and Corbin, *En Islam iranien*, vol. IV, Paris, 1972, livre V.
22. At last Mullā Ṣadrā is beginning to gain the recognition he deserves in

the West. Concerning this remarkable figure see H. Corbin's introduction to his own edition of Mullā Ṣadrā's *Kitāb al-mashā'ir (Le livre des pénétrations métaphysiques)*, Tehran: 1964; Corbin, *En Islam iranien*, vol. IV, chapter II; S.H. Nasr, 'Ṣadr al-Dīn Shīrāzi', in Sharif (ed.), *A History of Muslim Philosophy*, vol. II, pp. 932–961; Nasr, *Ṣadr al-Dīn Shīrāzī and His Transcendent Theosophy*, Tehran-London, 1978.

23. For a bibliography of Mullā Ṣadrā see biblio., chapter 2 of *Ṣadr al-Dīn Shīrāzī*.
24. The immense richness of the intellectual life of the Safavid period as far as *ḥikmat-i ilāhī* is concerned is beginning to reveal itself through current research, especially the anthology of the writings of the philosophers of this and later periods in Persia prepared by S.J. Ashtiyani and H. Corbin, of whose seven projected volumes four have already appeared. See S.J. Ashtiyani and H. Corbin, *Anthologie des philosophes iraniens*, Tehran-Paris, 1972–1978. Although as a result of the death of Corbin this major project was never completed, the volumes which have already appeared reveal the remarkably rich intellectual activity of the Safavid period. See also H. Corbin, *La philosophie iranienne Islamique aux XVIIe XVIIIe siècles*, Paris, 1983.
25. See the introduction to *al-Tuḥfat al-'abbāsiyyah*, Shiraz, 1336 (A.H. solar).
26. It is remarkable that despite the very extensive activity of Sufism during the Safavid period, there are very few written sources to go by and one must rely mostly on oral traditions that have survived within the existing Sufi orders.
27. On the history of the Ni'matallāhī order see J. Nurbakhsh, *Masters of the Path*, New York, 1980; and N. Pourjavady and P. Wilson, *Kings of Love*, Tehran, 1978.
28. It is of great interest that Mullā Ṣadrā wrote his *Sih aṣl*, ed. by S.H. Nasr, Tehran, 1340 (A.H. solar), to refute exoteric authorities who did not understand esotericism and the *Kasr al-aṣnām al-jāhiliyyah*, ed. by M.T. Daneshpazhuh, Tehran, 1340 (A.H. solar), to refute those who 'pretended to be Sufis.' There existed definitely a decayed form of Sufism or pseudo-Sufism often cut off from the *Sharī'ah* at that time which incited the rather violent and excessive reaction of exoteric authorities at the end of the Safavid period.
29. See M. Sarraf, *Traités des compagnons-chevaliers*, introduction analytique par H. Corbin, Tehran-Paris, 1973; also *Tuḥfat al-ikhwān*, ed. by M. Dāmādī, Tehran, 1351 (A.H. solar).

Part Two
Traditional Islam and Modernism

Chapter Five

Islam in the Present-Day Islamic World – An Overview

To discuss Islam in the present-day Islamic world means already to distinguish between Islam as a religious and spiritual reality and the manifestation of this reality in a particular social order or historic context. Such a distinction, although not even accepted by many modern interpreters and students of religion, lies at the heart of the traditional perspective, which always distinguishes between levels of reality and also between the archetype in relation to its spatio-temporal manifestations. From that point of view, it is therefore not only possible to make such a distinction but even necessary to do so in order not to confuse everything that is called Islamic by this or that group with traditional Islam as it has manifested itself over the centuries in accordance with the essential reality of Islam, and which has also displayed various modes of development but always within the possibilities inherent in that reality and according to its principles. It is especially imperative to speak of Islam as traditionally understood, *and* the present-day Islamic world, precisely because of the bewildering confusion that reigns in this domain, combined with intense interest in the subject in the Western world as a result of factors to which we have already referred.[1]

As far as Islam is concerned, its meaning is clear from the traditional point of view. Islam is a divinely revealed religion whose roots are contained in the Noble Quran, and the traditions of the Blessed Prophet – both written and oral – and whose branches embrace fourteen hundred years of a sacred and religious history which, in its orthodoxy, has embraced both Sunnism and Shi'ism as well as the esoteric dimension of the tradition contained in Sufism. It has produced not only the schools of law (*Sharī'ah*) but also theology, philosophy, a whole array of arts and sciences, and a distinct educational system not to speak of political, economic, social and family structures and the ethical and moral norms to which those structures are related.

This tree, which has its roots in the revelation, has also produced a sacred and traditional art, both auditory and visual, ranging from the various methods of chanting the Noble Quran to calligraphy and architecture and finally various forms of Islamic literature. While Islam remains a trans-historical reality, it has also had this long historical deployment which has linked and continues to link every generation of Muslims through time to the Origin. This direct access to the spiritual world is made possible by the rites and the *barakah* issuing from the Quranic revelation, which link each Muslim to the Origin through a hierarchic 'space' which is present and accessible here and now. Islam is at once that inexhaustible trans-historical reality and the whole of the Islamic tradition as reflected in Islamic history and including as already mentioned not only the roots but also the trunk, branches and fruits which have issued from the roots of the 'tree of Islam'.

As for the Islamic world, that term needs some elucidation. In traditional Islamic language the world is divided into *dār al-islām*, the 'abode of Islam' or where Islam rules as a majority religion, that is, where the Islamic Sacred Law or *Sharī'ah* governs human life; *dār al-ṣulḥ* the 'abode of peace' where Muslims live as the minority but where they are at peace and can practice their religion freely; and finally *dār al-ḥarb*, the 'abode of conflict or war', where Muslims are not only in a minority but where they are in a state of conflict with and struggle against the external social and political environment in order to be able to practice their religion. Had there not been the intrusion of secularism into the Islamic world since the 19th century, one could have simply defined the 'Islamic world' as *dār al-islām*. But today the situation is made complicated by the fact that, in many parts of *dār al-islām* itself, non-Islamic forces have gained a footing, sometimes under the name of a foreign ideology or a Western form of nationalism and sometimes even under the name of Islam itself, which, as already noted, has during the last few years been used more and more in a cunning and sometimes insidious fashion to hide the real nature of the forces at work. Moreover, Muslims in both *dār al-ṣulḥ* (such as India and parts of Africa), where they are in fact not always able to live in peace, and even *dār al-ḥarb* (such as Muslims in Europe and America, many of whom can live peacefully) have come to play an important role in *dār al-islām* and modern means of communication have linked Muslims in the three 'worlds' in a new fashion. It is, therefore, not so easy to define exactly what is meant by the Islamic world. For the sake of this discussion, however, let us define it as that part of the world in which there is either an Islamic majority or a substantial Muslim population, even if the degree of attachment of the Muslims in all these regions to Islam is not exactly the same.

This question of the kind and degree of attachment of Muslims to Islam is itself a crucial question in the discussion of the role of Islam in the Islamic world today. Before modern times, the degree of penetration of Islam within a particular region or ethnic group was mostly a question of the length of the process of Islamization. For example, in parts of Indonesia or Black Africa, where Islam had penetrated for only a century, the process of Islamization had not been as complete as where this process had commenced, let us say, four centuries earlier. But in parts of the Islamic world in which Islam had had time to sink its roots and establish its institutions, the attachment of Muslims to Islamic practices was of such intensity that one could not easily say whether, let us say, the Egyptians or Syrians or Persians or Punjabis were more strongly attached to Islam, although some communities accentuated more the formal, legal aspects and others inner attachment and faith, according to the emphasis of the different schools of law and theology which they followed. Wherever the orthodox schools of Islam, whether Sunni or Shi'ite, were firmly rooted, the complete practice of Islamic precepts and attachment to the teachings of Islam were taken for granted. Differences existed only in such questions as pietistic attitudes, emphasis upon secondary forms of worship, such as pilgrimage to local shrines or certain supererogatory prayers, theological speculations, expressions of sacred art, etc., which often demonstrated as much local variation as differences between various Islamic communities and ethnic groups and which at the same time reflected the positive elements of the ethnic genius of the people in question, elements which Islam did not destroy but allowed to flower within the context of the Islamic universe.

In modern times, however, forces such as Western-style nationalism, tribalism, and linguistic affinities, as well as the different ways in which various parts of the Islamic world have experienced the modern world and such forces as colonialism, secular nationalism, racialism and Western lay humanism have caused a significant variation in the manner and degree of attachment of many Muslims to Islam. There are Muslims who never miss their daily prayers and live as much as they can by the *Sharī'ah*, who consider their manner of following Islam to be the only manner. But in contrast to the days of old, there are also others who do not follow all the injunctions of the *Sharī'ah* and do not even pray regularly, yet consider themselves as being definitely Muslim. And there are even others who do not do anything specifically Islamic except follow a kind of 'humanistic' ethics which is vaguely Islamic and who yet call themselves Muslims and would protest if called anything else. And again there is another group which performs the Islamic rites meticulously and yet breaks many of the moral injunctions of the *Sharī'ah*, including, for example, honesty in business, while claiming to be devout.

From another point of view, there is the majority for whom Islam is essentially an all-embracing ethical and social code: a way of life embodied in the *Sharī'ah* and for those who wish to follow the spiritual life in the *Ṭarīqah*. and there are those for whom it is felt more than anything else as a culture and now, as a result of Western influence and reaction against it, an ideology and political force with which to combat other ideologies. There are authentic as well as antitraditional and modernistic interpretations, and there are, as a result, many kinds of degrees of attachment to Islam, especially in those parts of the Islamic world which have been long exposed to various types of modernistic influences. Those who speak of a 'monolithic' Islam or a uniform wave of 'fundamentalism' sweeping over the Islamic world, or who try to scare the West by depicting Islam as a violent enemy unified to oppose the rest of the world – these are all too unaware of the differences and nuances which exist in the perception of Islam and attachment to it by contemporary Muslims. If Islamic history has taught anything in this domain, it is that, even in traditional times, no part of *dār al-islām* could speak for the whole and that the reaction of the whole of the Islamic world to such major events and forces as the introduction of Graeco-Hellenistic learning into the Islamic world, the Crusades or the Mongol invasion was never uniform. How much more is this true today when the degree of exposure of a college student in any cosmopolitan center of the Middle East to non-Islamic elements is totally different from the exposure of a villager from the same country to these elements, not to speak of radical differences in the degree and manner of modernization and secularization in, let us say, the Yemen and Turkey.

Another point of central importance in the study of Islam in the Islamic world today is the all-embracing nature of Islam itself. This still holds good despite the recent process of secularization which has influenced the degree and manner of attachment of many Muslims to Islam, especially in the big cities, which are centers of decision-making. For most Muslims, all of their other relations and concerns are intertwined with their understanding of their religion as a reality inseparable from these other relationships. For example, a traditional Muslim has bonds to his family, city, nation, business, friends, etc., which he does not juxtapose to religion but sees in the context of that totality which for him is, in one way or another, Islam. He does not see Islam only as an ideal, although it is of course an ideal, especially as far as the ethical norms exemplified by the Blessed Prophet and the great figures of the religion are concerned. But for the ordinary Muslim it is, more than anything else, a reality with which he lives day and night. Therefore, in many cases he makes use of religious sentiments to solve family problems or further his economic or social goals or for the exercise of power, if he feels that such sentiments will aid in reaching his aims. There are, of course, many Muslims who practice their religion only out of the fear and love of God. But it would be a dangerous idealization of Islamic society and forgetful of human frailty to think that every person who is ostentatious in his attachment to Islam has nothing but the satisfaction of God in mind and that he would continue such ostentatious acts were the rest of his life, work, family, etc., disrupted or destroyed. For many people, all of these forces, bonds and relationships are intertwined in a manner that can cause unexpected social and political upheavals in the name of religion but, at the same time, rapid changes of direction and aim without the religious elements appearing to be sacrificed or compromised.

Precisely because Islam is still a powerful force pervading the lives of its believers, the misuse of it to further various personal and group interests is always a possibility. It has, in fact, been and is being made use of, not only by some Muslims themselves, but also by many forces originating outside the Islamic world. Obviously this kind of recourse to religious sentiments and practice is very different from the following of religion for the sake of God alone, a difference which can have devastating effects upon the whole world if there is a manipulation of Islam for non-Islamic ends.

With these general traits of the Islamic world in mind, it is now necessary to turn to the more particular types of reactions which have arisen within that world as a result of its encounter with the modern West: reactions which must be elucidated and fully understood if we are to grasp the nature of Islam in the Islamic world today. During the first twelve centuries of its historic existence, Islam lived with full awareness of the truth and realization of God's promise to Muslims that they would be victorious if they followed His religion. Such verses as 'There is no victor but God' (*Lā ghāliba illa'Llāh*, which adorns the walls of the Alhambra, also adorned the soul and mind of Muslims. They were victorious in the world, the Crusades and the short conquest of the Islamic world by the Mongols notwithstanding, since the Crusaders were defeated and the grandson of Hulagü, Uljaytü, became a Muslim and in fact a patron of Islamic learning and the arts. The authenticity of the Quranic message was born out by the experience of history.

Then came the conquest of various parts of the Islamic world by the British, the French, the Dutch and the Russians, not to speak of the more peripheral conquests of the Portuguese and the Spanish. Although Muslims were at first somewhat indifferent to the long-range significance of these events, the conquest of Egypt by Napoleon caused a shock which made Muslim leaders aware of the dimension and meaning of the Western conquest of Islam. In the early 19th century, the Muslim intelligentsia realized that clearly something had gone wrong which, as mentioned by W.C. Smith among other Western scholars of Islam, was of the dimension of a cosmic crisis.[2] How was it that the Islamic world was being defeated by non-Islamic forces everywhere and in such an irreversible fashion? Logically one of three attitudes could be taken:

1. Something had gone wrong with the world, as God Himself had mentioned in His Book concerning the end of the world and the Blessed Prophet had described in his traditions. In such a case, the eclipse of Islam was itself a proof of the validity of the Islamic message which, however, also foretold the imminent appearance of the Mahdi and the final eschatological events leading to the end of the world.

2. Muslims had ceased to follow Islam properly and should return to the practice of their religion in its pure form and with full vigor so as to defeat the non-Islamic forces and escape the punishment they were receiving from the hands of God for their negligence of their religion. Such a reaction resulted mostly in the Wahhābī and neo-Wahhābī movements associated with the Deoband school in India, the followers of Muḥammad ʿAbduh and the Salafiyyah in Egypt and Syria, the Muḥammadiyyah movement in Indonesia, etc., but was also connected with the much less studied inner revivals within Sufi orders or the establishment of new ones, such as the Darqāwiyyah and Tījāniyyah in Morocco and West Africa, the Sanūsiyyah in Libya, the Yashruṭiyyah in the Arab Near East, the Niʿmatallāhiyyah in Persia, the Chishtiyyah and Qādiriyyah in India and many others.

3. The Islamic message had to be changed, modified, adapted or reformed to suit modern conditions and to be able so to adapt itself to the modern world as to be able to overcome Western domination. Out of this attitude grew all the different types of modernism influenced by the French Revolution and the rationalism of such men as Descartes and Voltaire, in some quarters, Locke and Hume and later Spencer and Bergson, in others. So-called Arab liberalism, as well as modernistic movements in Turkey, Persia and the Indian subcontinent, were also results of this third possible reaction to the subjugation of the Islamic world by the West.

In some cases these elements mixed with each other, Mahdiism, puritanical or 'fundamentalist' tendencies and modern reformist elements combining together in the thoughts and teachings of a single figure or school. Sometimes even Sufi figures had a Mahdiist aspect, as the study of the life of such figures as ʿAbd al-Qādir in

Algeria, Usman dan Fadio in Nigeria and al-Ḥajj 'Umar of Futa Toro in East Africa reveals. In such cases, Sufism itself undertook the task of reviving the Islamic community as a whole, a task which has not received nearly as much attention from Western scholarship as the fruit of the efforts of the neo-Wahhābī and modernistic reformers.[3]

These reactions continued to animate certain segments of Islamic society for the next century down to the Second World War, although the wave of Mahdiism gradually died down after giving birth to such diverse phenomena as the Aḥmadiyyah movement in India and Pakistan, the Bābī-Bahā'ī movement in Persia and the Mahdiist state in the Sudan.

After the Second World War, certain events took place which revived or altered the movements which had grown out of the original reaction of Islam to its domination by the West. First of all, nearly the whole of the Islamic world became politically 'independent', but as national states along the model of European states. This apparent freedom brought with it the expectation of greater cultural and social independence, especially as the less Westernized elements of Islamic society began to gain political and economic power. Secondly, the vast array of wealth pouring into much of the Islamic world brought with it the acceleration of the processes of industrialization and modernization, and at the same time heightened the tensions already present between Islam and the ethos of modern western civilization – tensions which had not been solved either intellectually or socially and which had been mostly glossed over by well-known earlier figures, usually known as 'reformers', as well as by the *'ulamā'*, or religious scholars, who had hardly concerned themselves with them.

These events within the Islamic world were complemented by transformations within the Western world itself which were also to have profound consequences for movements within the Islamic world. From the moment the West conquered the Islamic world until the Second World War, the Islamic world saw in the West another model or philosophy for human existence which, although rejected by many in that world, was accepted wholeheartedly by many leaders within these movements.

Few, however, doubted the success of this model, at least from the point of view of man's life on earth, whatever the consequences might have been for man's immortal soul. Before the Second World

War, few Muslims were seriously affected by Spengler's *Decline of the West*, which in fact had been translated into Arabic and Persian, and fewer still had read the gloomy descriptions of Western civilization given by such literary figures as T.S. Eliot (although this poet has exercised a great influence on certain Arab poets during the past few decades). And practically no-one, save a small circle in Cairo and Karachi, had read the 'prophetic' works of R. Guénon, such as *The Crisis of the Modern World* and *The Reign of Quantity and the Signs of the Times*, predicting the collapse of the modern world, although Guénon had moved permanently to Cairo in 1931.[4] It was only after the Second World War that the Islamic intelligentsia in general became aware that within the Western world itself there were profound criticisms of that civilization and that the Western model which so many Muslims had tried to emulate was itself breaking down.

This movement in the West was combined with an attempt on the part of many to seek their roots once again, to rediscover tradition and to regain access to the sacred. So, while much of what remained of the Western tradition was floundering and giving place to despair and nihilism, there was also a reassertion of traditional teachings, a rediscovery of myth and symbols, a positive appreciation of non-Western religions and even a reappraisal of the medieval Western heritage, which ceased to appear as dark as its purblind Renaissance and 18th-century critics had made it out to be.[5] All these developments were bound to, and in fact did, affect the few but influential intellectual and religious leaders, critics, writers, scholars, and other leaders within the Islamic world.

Finally, a change began to appear in the attitude of non-Islamic powers, both Western and communist, toward the forces within the Islamic world. After the Second World War, for some time Islam as a religion was belittled as a force to be reckoned with by the outside world, but various nationalistic forces, which in most cases were in fact combined with religious elements in one way or another, were manipulated in every conceivable way to aid the causes and aims of the powers in question to the largest extent possible. The history of the various forms of Arab nationalism during the past decades is a good example of the way these forces were at work. Then, as the situation changed, the same policy of manipulation began to be pursued in the case of religious forces themselves through indirect aid or by hindrance of a particular religious school or organization or the sudden aggrandisement of a particular force or movement and the belittling of others which might not be of immediate political or economic benefit to the interested powers. This external manipulation, although relying on existing movements, tendencies, forces and personalities in the Islamic world, has played and continues to play an important role in the manner in which these forces and processes develop and change and also the way the personalities in question are able or not able to exercise influence and leadership. This manipulation is not the only factor but is certainly one to be reckoned with if one wishes to understand the present state of Islam and specifically Islamic forces at work within the Islamic world.

With the earlier reactions of the Islamic world to the West in mind and with full consideration of the new forces and changes brought upon the scene since the Second World War, it is now possible to describe the present state of forces, movements and tendencies within Islam as they affect and mold the contemporary Islamic world.

There are, first of all, a number of forces, differing in many basic features among themselves, which are more or less heir to or related to the type of the earlier Wahhābī reactions against the Western world, and others which are of a counter-traditional nature. Yet, both are usually termed 'fundamentalist', although this term has particular Christian and, in fact, Protestant connotations, which do not apply exactly to the Islamic situation. Despite the basic difference between these two types of forces, however, they share in common a disdain for the West, a distrust of foreign elements, a strong activist tendency and usually opposition or indifference to all the inward aspects of Islam and the civilization and culture which it created, aspects such as Sufism, Islamic philosophy, Islamic art,[6] etc. They are all outwardly oriented in the sense that they wish to reconstruct Islamic society through the re-establishment of external legal and social norms rather than by means of the revival of Islam through inner purification or by removing the philosophical and intellectual impediments which have been obstacles on the path of many contemporary Muslims. These movements, therefore, have rarely dealt in detail with the intellectual challenges posed by Western science and philosophy, although this trait is not by any means the same among all of them, some being of a more intellectual nature than others.

Politically also there has not been a uniformity of program among them. Some have sought to revive the caliphate; others have supported other traditional forms of government, such as the sultanate or amirate; and yet others have opted for a Western type of democracy in an Islamic context. The counter-traditional movements, however, possess a violent and revolutionary political nature and in some of these the most fanatical and volcanic elements of Western republicanism and Marxist revolutionary theory and practice have been set in what the followers of these groups consider to be an Islamic context. There is only one political aim in which these so-called 'fundamentalist' forces are united, and that is the unification of the Islamic world, or what is called Panislamism. In this sense, they are all heirs to the campaign of Jamāl al-Dīn Astarābādī, known as al-Afghānī, who in the 19th century called for the reunification of the Islamic world. But although Panislamism has continued as an ideal espoused by nearly all Islamic leaders and intellectual figures during the past century and remains encrusted in the traditional Islamic vision of the perfect state to be established by the Mahdi before the end of time, the manner of its execution as part of a practical political program has hardly been agreed upon by the diverse groups who speak of it. Some preach the re-establishment of a single caliphate or central political authority, as during the time of the four 'rightly-guided caliphs' (*khulafā' rāshidūn*). Others speak of a commonwealth of Muslim nations and yet others, while using Panislamism as a slogan to arouse the religious sentiments of the people, remain deliberately vague as to how it would be carried out in practice. The manipulation of these so-called 'fundamentalist' Islamic forces by external powers, to achieve ends as diverse as creating a wall of defense against communism and ensuring that what is commonly termed economic development does not go beyond a certain stage, is particularly dangerous because of the ambivalent and vague aspect of the political dimension of these forces. The effect that such manipulations are having and will have upon the Islamic community is bound to be very different from what so-called experts who provide the programs for such manipulation have envisaged.

Of the 'fundamentalist' forces, the oldest are without doubt those which inherited the earlier Wahhābī movement and have carried that movement into our own day. These forces are centered mostly in Saudi Arabia, which follows officially the Wahhābī interpretation of Islam, and from the beginning they were associated with a group of Islamic scholars in the Hejaz and especially Madinah. They also include neo-Wahhābīs in Egypt, Syria, Jordan and other countries of the Arab Near East, many of whom were influenced by the Salafiyyah movement, whose base was in Egypt and Syria until the Second World War and which withdrew later into the Hejaz. Its influence is felt directly in many Muslim seats of learning such as al-Azhar, but it is less of a distinct political force of an activist nature than it was in the 19th century.

In the subcontinent of India, this type of 'fundamentalist' movement has had many expressions, of which perhaps the most significant today is the Jamā'at-i islāmī (literally, 'Society of Islam') of Pakistan, founded by Mawlānā Abu'l-'Alā' Mawdūdī. This organization is closely knit and of a semi-secret nature, its purpose being the revival of the Islamic way of life. It has direct political and social goals and is of an activist nature, although it is milder than the violent revolutionary movements and is more interested in promoting the consideration of the more intellectual dimensions of the confrontation between Islam and modernism. There are organizations of a similar nature among Muslims of India itself as well as in Indonesia, which have close links to the Pakistani 'society'.

An organization with a somewhat longer history but of more limited political power at the present moment is the famous Muslim Brotherhood (al-Ikhwān al-Muslimīn), founded in Egypt before the Second World War but later extended to other Muslim countries, especially those in the Persian Gulf region, where many of its members settled after the execution in Egypt of its leader, Sayyid Quṭb, during the rule of Jamāl 'Abd al-Nāṣir. This organization, which has also been involved in political plots of various kinds and even accused of political assassinations, has also produced a religious literature which has had some influence among sections of the young in the Arab world and even elsewhere. Adherents to its cause are also found in the Arab countries of North Africa, although in much smaller numbers, and an organization called the Fadā'iyān-i islām (literally, 'those who sacrifice themselves for Islam') was founded in Iran in the 1940s on the model of the Ikhwān and claiming to follow the same programs, including the elimination of certain political figures.

In Turkey, the appearance of a remarkable politico-religious figure, Sayyid Sa'īd Nūrsī, during the time of Ataturk and the outward secularization of Turkey, made possible the founding of a secret organization whose aim was the protection of Islam from secularism. The members of this organization grew rapidly in number and represent today a very significant voice in Turkey. They are usually given more to Islamic education and the rejuvenation of the Islamic faith based on the Quranic commentary of their founder than to political activism or direct violence, although they do have their own specific programs for the founding of an Islamic state. There are, however, Islamic movements in Turkey which have used violence, especially when faced with Marxists, and who espouse the cause of the re-establishment of the caliphate abolished by Ataturk.

The nature of 'fundamentalism' in Iran is more complicated, both because of the presence of certain elements which are the veritable parody of traditional Islam and also because Iran is mostly Shi'ite and traditionally Shi'ism always disdained political power. Until just a short time ago, the majority of Shi'ite scholars followed the traditional interpretation of Shi'ism, leaving it to the Mahdi to actually take the reins of power into his own hands. Moreover, protest over modernism as a threat to Islamic values, the intrusion of the so-called 'Islamic Marxism' into the arena of Islamic action, the direct participation of non-Islamic powers, both communist and Western-oriented, in the guise of Islam in events which have been carried out in the name of Islam, together with many other complications, have created a remarkably complex mixture in which genuine Islamic sentiments have become combined with all kinds of extraneous forces. Only the passage of time will allow the sifting of these elements and a correct judgement upon the nature of all the forces at play to be made.

The types of 'fundamentalism' thus far described, can also be found in other Muslim countries, such as Sudan and Nigeria, or among the Afghans before and even after the Soviet invasion. The only part of the Islamic world where such forces have made no headway at all, in contrast to the hope and expections of certain elements in the West who have sought to manipulate these forces, is among the Muslims of the Soviet Union and China. As far as the former are concerned, the cause for the continued presence of Islam and its vitality is in fact to be sought, not at all in some kind of externalized, 'fundamentalist' revival, but in the Sufi orders which have kept the flame of faith burning within the hearts of men despite adverse external circumstances.

'Fundamentalist' movements have also been related in many ways to the several international Islamic conferences, leagues and the like which have their centers in such places as Saudi Arabia, Pakistan and even in Europe, and whose goal is the unity of the Islamic world. Although the political perspectives of these organizations are not the same, they share the goal of achieving some form of unity and bringing the Islamic peoples closer together. These therefore often attract people who are also attracted to one form or another of the neo-Wahhābī, puritanical or 'fundamentalist' movements, although there is no necessary link between the two and one can in fact remain a completely traditional Muslim and yet strive for the unity of the Islamic peoples, as is in fact the case in many instances. But there is also no doubt that many of the leaders and administrators of these international Islamic organizations are also the leaders of various kinds of 'fundamentalist' movements. This nexus seems in fact to be found most often in the Indo-Pakistani world and in Southeast Asia.

The second reaction referred to earlier in this chapter, namely the espousal of one form or another of modernism, has also led to the creation of powerful forces within the Islamic world today, forces whose nature and degree of Islamicity has, however, been open to debate. Since the Second World War, the very advent of political independence to many Islamic countries once again brought to the fore the question of the relationship between nationalism and Islam. From this debate have grown several forms of what might be called 'Islamic nationalism'; that is, a way of thinking which, accepting both Islam and a particular nationhood, seeks to wed the two together. Pakistan offers the most outstanding example of such a wedding between the idea of a nation or state in the modern sense and Islam. Because Pakistan was created for the sake of Islam, obviously its nationalism could not be anti-Islamic, as had been the case with certain earlier forms of strong nationalism, like that of Turkey. In fact, many Pakistanis, in giving a positive connotation to their wedding of Islam and nationalistic sentiments, consider this type of coupling of sentiments as positive both from an Islamic point of view and from that of the geo-political realities of their century. The same attitude can be found among most Bengladeshis, Malays, Senegalese, etc. In fact, in many Islamic countries, such as Persia, where a sense of nationhood, or at least separate existence as a distinct entity, preceded the intrusion of the modern European concept of nationalism, Islamic and national sentiments developed a *modus vivendi* which allowed Islam to flourish in its authentic, traditional form within the state without being abused for ends beyond itself.

As for Arab nationalism, since it is already based, not on an actual political entity such as Egypt, Syria or Iraq, but upon the unification of various present-day states into a larger unit, it is of a unique nature and has created a phenomenon which is different from other types of nationalism within the Islamic world. But what is interesting from the point of view of this study is that earlier Arab nationalism was essentially a secular movement led often by Christian rather than Muslim Arabs. It has left behind at least one important political expression, which is the Ba'th party. Later Arab nationalism, whether in the form of Nasserism or Qadhafi's version or any other brand, has become more and more mixed with Islamic elements. For most Arabs today, it is impossible to separate their 'Arabism' (*'urūbah*) from Islam, and in fact among the masses, when they use *'urūbah*, the connotation in their minds is almost completely Islamic. Arab nationalism has in a sense nationalized Islam, with all the dangers that such an act implies for the universal teachings of Islam, which are opposed to all forms of parochialism, especially the fanatical and narrow form of nationalism that grew out of the French Revolution, in contrast to the natural love of a man for his nation and country to which the Prophet of Islam was referring when he said, 'The love of one's nation comes from faith [in religion].' Nevertheless, this process has caused most Arab nationalistic sentiments and forces to possess also strong Islamic elements, although the secular type of Arab nationalism is of course still also very much present, especially in the eastern Arab countries.

Another type of movement that has grown out of the modernizing quarters within the Islamic world and which has been in vogue among many young Muslims during the past two decades is so-called 'Islamic Socialism' and lately 'Islamic Marxism'. Many of those who follow these movements have been influenced of course by the Soviet and socialist worlds in their apparent espousal of pro-Arabic and pro-Islamic causes in such matters as the Arab-Israeli question, while overlooking their disregard for the plight of

Muslims within the socialist world itself, not to speak of those in Afghanistan. Many people who accept the slogan of 'Islamic Socialism' understood by 'socialism', 'social justice', and in their desire to promulgate justice in their own societies adopt an 'Islamic Socialist' stance. In certain states, this ideological position is directly supported by the state and is made use of by existing political forces more or less sympathetic to the Soviet world. Although the theoretical constructs upon which this movement is based have come mostly out of leftist circles in France and the movement itself is strongest among Islamic countries which were culturally French originally, such as Algeria and more recently Iran (as far as a circle educated in France is concerned), it can also be found in the Arab Near East, where 'Islamic Socialism' has come to replace the Arab Socialism of two decades ago (which still survives in Syria and Iraq). There are also defendants of this amalgamation of Islam and socialism in Pakistan, India and Southeast Asia.

As for 'Islamic Marxism', this thesis is of a much more recent origin, associated with certain extremist groups in the Middle East which consider themselves as Muslims but which use an almost completely Marxist political ideology and also Marxist means of achieving their goals. In fact, the so-called 'Islamic Marxists' interpret Islam itself as a political revolutionary force in the sense that revolution has been understood in the context of the Marxist and post-Marxist schools in European thought. This movement has naturally received much attention as well as support from the so-called intellectually Marxist circles in France and other European countries and the figures whose works have been used by the 'Islamic Socialist' and 'Marxist' groups have been in close contact with leftist circles in the West. Today, this type of modernism within the Islamic world is an important force to contend with, not because of the number of its adherents or the degree of its popularity among the mass of the people, but because of its being used as a means of allowing totally un-Islamic, and in fact anti-Islamic, forces to gain access to power within certain of the Islamic countries.

The cataclysmic events of recent years have also brought back to life the movement of Mahdiism, which had been dormant for over a century since the wave caused by the first encounter between Islam and the modern world. The fact that much of the Islamic world is under the cultural and economic domination of non-Islamic forces, that the very attempt to free oneself from this domination through industrialization and related processes brings with it a greater destruction of Islamic values, that the world as a whole seems to be confronted with so many apparently insoluble problems, such as the ecological crisis, and that forces of destruction have become such that all peoples are threatened with extinction at all times, have helped to bring back a sense of the imminent appearance of the Mahdi: the one who will destroy inequity and re-establish the rule of God on earth. The fact that the Blessed Prophet had promised that at the beginning of every century a renewer (*mujaddid*) would come to revive Islam from within has only strengthened this feeling of expectation for the Mahdi. Already in the fall of 1979, the holiest site in Islam, namely the House of God in Makkah, was captured in the name of the Mahdi, although the forces at work were far from being those of simply pious Muslims helping to bring about the parousia. During the Iranian Revolution also, many simple people believed that the coming of the Mahdi was imminent. Without doubt, as the forces of destruction in the world increase, as the natural system strains ever more under the burden of a technology which is alien to the natural rhythms of the life of the cosmos, and as movements which speak in the name of Islam itself fail to create the ideal Islamic order which they always promise, this sense of expectation of the Mahdi and movements associated with it will increase among traditional and devout Muslims. This force is certainly a reality among present-day Muslims and is bound to continue as a powerful one in the future.

Finally, there is a fourth kind of force or presence in contemporary Islam which must be mentioned, especially since it has received practically no attention so far in Western analyses of the Islamic world. This force is the revival of the Islamic tradition from within by those who have encountered the modern world fully and who, with complete awareness of the nature of that world and all the problems of a philosophical, scientific and social nature which it poses, have returned to the heart of the Islamic tradition to find answers and to revive the Islamic world as a spiritual reality amidst the chaos and turmoil created throughout the world by what is called modernism. The number of this group has of necessity been small. Their theater of action has been not mass meetings or political gatherings, but the hearts and minds of individuals gathered in small circles. For this group, Islam is traditional Islam with its roots sunk in heaven and its branches spread through a vast world stretching in space from the Atlantic to the Pacific and encompassing a time-span of some fourteen centuries. They reject nothing of the Islamic tradition, whether it be its art or its science or its philosophy, not to speak of Sufism, which they consider as the heart of the whole body of Islam, whose limbs, governed by the *Sharī'ah*, are animated by the blood flowing from this heart. To this group, it is Islamic metaphysics which provides answers to problems posed by such modern ideologies and 'isms' as rationalism, humanism, materialism, evolutionism, psychologism and the like. For them the revival of the Islamic world must come with a revival within the Muslims themselves. Their idea of reform is not the modern one which always begins with the outward: which wishes always to reform the world but never man himself. They emphasize inner reform of Islamic society as a whole. Their attitude to the world, including the modern world, is not that of passive acceptance. They criticize the modern world in the light of immutable principles and view it as a canvas, alluring from afar but shown to be of an illusory nature when examined from close quarters. They stand at the center of Islamic orthodoxy and consider all violent movements which incorporate the worst elements of Western civilization in order to combat that civilization to be a disservice to Islam and below the dignity of God's last revelation.

This group believes in inner revival (*tajdīd*), which is a traditional Islamic concept, and not external reform (*iṣlāḥ*), which is a modern idea grafted upon the body of Islam. The model for this group is an al-Ghazzālī, an 'Abd al-Qādir al-Jīlānī or a Shaykh Aḥmad Sirhindī, and not some 19th-century or 20th-century leftist revolutionary who would simply be given a Muslim name. This group acts without acting, in the sense that its function is more that of knowledge and presence than of action. But it is from this group that there has flowed and continues to flow some of the most profound and religiously significant Islamic responses to the modern world. And it is this group that in the long run will leave the deepest effect upon the Islamic community, as has ever been the case in the past.[7]

The four types of groups or movements within the Islamic world today, namely the 'fundamentalist', 'modernist', 'Mahdiist' and 'traditionalist', are not of course always exclusive of each other, although certain positions, such as that of the traditionalist, exclude others, such as that of the modernist. For example, in the various groups usually gathered together under the category of 'fundamentalist', there are some who are attached to Sufism and close to the traditionalist perspective, others who share certain affinities with the modernists and yet others who are strongly attracted by the Madhiist type of sentiment. And of course there are the counter-traditional elements which talk of Islam but in fact represent the very antithesis of traditional Islam. Finally, there are Mahdiists, who really belong to the traditional world, while others have allied themselves with the 'fundamentalists' of the counter-traditional type. If all the diverse forces present in the contemporary Islamic world have been divided into these four categories, it has been to facilitate discussion and also to point to four fundamental types or attitudes which are discernible in the Islamic world today. Moreover, these four categories are in reality not at all opposed to the division between traditional, anti-traditional and counter-traditional made earlier and can be analyzed just as well in those terms. Of course it is essential to remember that, in many parts of the Islamic world, the majority of Muslims continue their lives in the traditional manner and are not involved in any of the theological, religious or political reactions to the modern world already mentioned. The vast number of Muslims, whose belonging to the Islamic tradition is still defined in terms of the traditional Islamic categories rather than of reactions to modern ideologies and thought patterns, must always be kept in mind.

Islam is still very much alive in the Islamic world today; but there are also so-called 'Islamic forces' within that world which are often manipulated and altered in such a manner that, although they remain forces, it is doubtful whether they are still Islamic. Not everything that happens to occur in the Islamic world is Islamic, nor does every birth in that part of the world herald an Islamic renaissance. After all, according to authentic Islamic traditions, the anti-Christ is also to be born in the Islamic world. Close attention must be paid to the Islamic character of all that is chosen to be called Islamic in a world in which the use and misuse of practically anything can take place as long as it serves the aims of the powers that be. In any full discussion of Islam today, one must ask in every instance what is meant by 'Islamic'. Islam is not a vague idea. It is a religion with its Sacred Book, the traditions of its Blessed Prophet, sacred law, theology, philosophy, mystical paths and a specific manner of looking at the world of nature and of creating art. There are certainly such things as Islamic orthodoxy and orthopraxy, and therefore their opposites exist as well. There are traditional, anti-traditional and counter-traditional forces, and such basic differences cannot be glossed over by the simple use of the term 'Islamic'.

Today we are witness to a vast religious community which is still alive and whose teachings on all levels, from the most esoteric to those concerned with daily laws, are kept intact. But we are also witness to the destruction of certain elements of this religious world, not only through modernistic forces alien to its genius but also through modernistic forces which, in order not to appear alien, put on the guise of Islamicity so as to enter within the citadel of Islam. It will serve neither the interests of the Islamic world, nor of Christianity, nor even of the secularized West to remain oblivious of fundamental differences between the forces at play here. Mass media dominated by a new version of triumphalism in the Islamic world itself and opportunism combined with ignorance in the West should not be allowed to blind people to the difference between Islamic forces seeking genuine political and social expression and totally anti-Islamic or at best non-Islamic political forces using the guise of Islam to further their own ends. Nor is it wise to neglect the more hidden forms of inner revival and rejuvenation which have always been and will always be at the heart of every authentic religious regeneration.

It is the hope of every Muslim concerned with the future of Islam that the energy and vitality of Islam will react in a constructive manner along with other religions similarly faced with the withering effects of modern secularism and that this vitality will not be channelled into volcanic eruptions and violent reactions that will, in the long run, leave both the Islamic world and the world at large impoverished spiritually, whatever they might do in the short term to serve the immediate aims of present-day powers. Let us hope that Islamic movements and groups will channel and guide their activities in a manner which is worthy before the sight of God and not according to what might appear politically or economically opportune. Islamic history stands as witness to the fact that only those acts that have been performed in the light of eternity and according to the Will of the One, the surrender to whose Will is the *raison d'être* of Islam itself, have had an enduring effect upon the heart and soul of Muslims and upon the Islamic world at large.

Notes

1. We have also dealt with certain aspects of this subject in our *Islam and the Plight of Modern Man*, chapter 7.
2. See W.C. Smith, *Islam in Modern History*, Princeton, 1957.
3. Some attention has been paid to the Sanūsiyyah in Western languages but much more needs to be done in this field in general. On the Sanūsiyyah see N. Ziadeh, *Sanusiya: a Study of a Revivalist Movement in Islam*, London 1958. As for a general treatment of various movements within the Islamic world, there exists a vast literature which, until a few years ago, possessed a general over-emphasis upon the modernists but more recently upon the 'fundamentalists'. For a recent general survey covering the whole of the Islamic world rather than just the Middle East see J. Voll, *Islam: Continuity and Change in the Modern World*, Boulder (Colorado), 1982.
4. Again there were notable exceptions. For example, 'Abd al-Ḥalīm Maḥmūd, who was later to become rector of al-Azhar University, was aware of the works of Guénon and other Western critics of the West.
5. See our *Knowledge and the Sacred*, chapter 3.
6. See the Prologue to this book.
7. This group represents on the highest intellectual level the vast number of Muslims who remain traditional and who are neither modernist nor 'fundamentalist'. This circle is the voice of traditional Islam and those traditional Muslims who remain more or less intellectually silent but who live the traditional life of faith and share with this intellectual élite (*khawāṣṣ*), in the time-honored meaning of the term, the same traditional world-view.

Chapter Six

Reflections on Islam and Modern Thought

Few subjects arouse more passion and debate among Muslims today than the encounter between Islam and modern thought. The subject is of course vast and embraces fields ranging from politics to sacred art, subjects whose debate often causes volcanic eruptions of emotions and passions and vituperation, which are hardly conducive to an objective analysis of causes and a clear vision of the problems involved. The whole discussion is also paralysed by a psychological sense of inferiority and a feeling of enfeeblement before the modern world, a feeling which prevents most modernized Muslims from making a critical appraisal of the situation and of stating the truth irrespective of whether it is fashionable and acceptable to current opinion or not. Let us then begin by defining what we mean by 'modern thought'.

It is amazing how many hues of meaning have been given to the term 'modern', ranging from 'contemporary' to simply 'innovative', 'creative', or in tune with the march of time. The question of principles, and in fact the truth itself, is hardly ever taken into consideration when modernism is discussed. One hardly ever asks whether this or that idea, form or institution conforms to some aspect of the truth. The only question is whether it is modern or not. The lack of clarity, precision and sharpness of both mental and artistic contours, which characterizes the modern world itself, seems to plague the contemporary Muslim's understanding of modernism, whether he wishes to adopt its tenets or even to react against it. The influence of modernism seems in fact to have dimmed that lucidity and blurred that crystalline transparency which distinguish traditional Islam in both its intellectual and artistic manifestations.[1]

When we use the term 'modern', we mean neither 'contemporary' nor 'up-to-date'; nor does it signify for us something that is successful in the conquest and domination of the natural world. Rather, for us 'modern' means that which is cut off from the Transcendent, from the immutable principles which in reality govern all things and which are made known to man through revelation in its most universal sense. Modernism is thus contrasted with tradition (*al-dīn*); the former, as already mentioned, implies all that is merely human and now ever more increasingly subhuman, and all that is divorced and cut off from the Divine source.[2] Obviously, tradition has always accompanied and in fact characterized human existence, whereas modernism is a very recent phenomenon. As long as man has lived on earth, he has buried his dead and believed in the afterlife and the world of the Spirit. During the 'hundreds of thousands' of years of human life on earth, he has been traditional in outlook and has not 'evolved' as far as his relation with God and nature, seen as the creation and theophany of God, are concerned.[3] Compared to this long history, during which man has continuously celebrated the Divine and performed his function as God's vice-gerent (*khalīfah*) on earth, the period of the domination of modernism stretching from the Renaissance in Western Europe in the 15th century to the present day appears as no more than the blinking of an eye.[4] Yet, it is during this fleeting moment that we live; hence the apparent dominance of the power of modernism before which so many Muslims retreat in helplessness, or which they join with that superficial sense of happiness that often accompanies the seductions of the world.

A word must also be said about the term 'thought', as it appears in the expression 'modern thought'. The term 'thought' as used in this context is itself modern rather than traditional. The Arabic term *fikr*, or the Persian *andīshah*, which are used as its equivalents, hardly appear with the same meaning in traditional texts. In fact, what would correspond to the traditional understanding of the term would be more the French *pensée* as used by a Pascal: a term which would be rendered better as 'meditation' rather than 'thought'. Both *fikr* and *andīshah* are related to meditation and contemplation rather than to the purely human, and therefore non-divine, mental activity which the term 'thought' usually evokes.[5] If then we nevertheless use the term 'thought', it is because we are addressing an audience nurtured on all that this term implies and are using a medium and language in which it is not possible, without being somewhat contrite, to employ another term with the same range of meaning, embracing many forms of mental activity but devoid of the limitation, in the vertical sense, that the term 'thought' possesses in contemporary parlance.

All these forms of mental activity, which together comprise modern thought and which range from science to philosophy, psychology and even certain aspects of religion itself, possess certain common characteristics and traits which must be recognized and studied before the Islamic answer to modern thought can be provided. Perhaps the first basic trait of modern thought to be noted is its anthropomorphic nature. How can a form of thought which negates any principle higher than man be anything but anthropomorphic? It might, of course, be objected that modern science is certainly not anthropomorphic, but rather that it is the pre-modern sciences which must be considered as man-centred. Despite appearances, however, this assertion is mere illusion if one examines closely the epistemological factor involved. It is true that modern science depicts a universe in which man as spirit, mind and even psyche has no place and the Universe thus appears as 'inhuman' and not related to the human state. But it must not be forgotten that, although modern man has created a science which excludes the reality of man from the general picture of the Universe[6], the criteria and instruments of knowledge which determine this science are merely and purely human. It is human reason and the human senses which determine modern science. The knowledge of even the farthest galaxies is held in the human mind. This scientific world from which man has been abstracted is, therefore, nevertheless based on anthropomorphic foundations as far as the subjective pole of knowledge, the subject who knows and determines what science is, is concerned.

By contrast, the traditional sciences are profoundly non-anthropomorphic in the sense that, for them, the locus and container of knowledge is not the human mind but ultimately the Divine Intellect. True science is not based on purely human reason but on the Intellect which belongs to the supra-human level of reality yet illuminates the human mind.[7] If medieval cosmologies placed man at the centre of things, it is not because they were humanistic in the Renaissance sense of the term, according to which terrestrial and fallen man was the measure of all things, but it was in order to enable man to gain a vision of the cosmos as a hierarchy of states, the lowest of which was occupied by man and was a crypt through which he must travel and which he must transcend. Certainly one cannot begin a journey from anywhere except where one is located.[8]

If the characteristic of anthropomorphism is thus to be found in modern science, it is to be seen in an even more obvious fashion in other forms and aspects of modern thought, whether it be psychology, anthropology or philosophy. Modern thought, of which philosophy is in a sense the father and progenitor, became profoundly anthropomorphic the moment man was made the criterion of reality. When Descartes uttered, 'I think, therefore I am' (*cogito ergo sum*), he placed his individual awareness of his own limited self as the criterion of existence, for certainly the 'I' in Descartes' assertion was not the Divine 'I' who, through Ḥallāj, exclaimed, 'I am the Truth' (*ana'l-Ḥaqq*): the Divine 'I' which alone, according to traditional doctrines, has the right to say 'I'.[9] Until Descartes, it was Pure Being, the Being of God, which determined human existence and the various levels of reality. But with Cartesian rationalism, individual human existence became the criterion of reality and also the truth. In the mainstream of Western thought, and excluding certain peripheral developments, ontology gave way to epistemology, epistemology to logic and finally, by way of reaction, logic became confronted with those antirational 'philosophies' so prevalent today.[10]

What happened in the post-medieval period in the West was that higher levels of reality became eliminated in both the subjective and the objective domains. There was nothing higher in man than his reason and nothing higher in the objective world than what that reason could comprehend with the help of the normal human senses. This was of course bound to happen if one remembers the well-known principle of adequation (the *adequatio* of St. Thomas Aquinas) according to which to know anything there must be an instrument of knowledge adequate and conforming to the nature of that which is to be known. And since modern man refused to accept a principle higher than himself, obviously all that issued from his mind and thought could not but be anthropomorphic.

A second trait of modernism closely related to anthropomorphism is the lack of principles which characterizes the modern world. Human nature is too unstable, changing and turbulent to be able to serve as the principle for something. That is why a mode of thinking which is not able to transcend the human level and which remains anthropomorphic cannot but be devoid of principles. In the realm of the active life, namely the domain of morality (although morality cannot be reduced simply to the realm of action) and, from another point of view, politics and economics, everyone senses this lack of principles. But one might object as far as the sciences are concerned. Here again, however, it must be asserted that, neither empiricism, nor the validification through induction, nor reliance upon the data of the senses as confirmed by reason, can serve as principles in the metaphysical sense. They are all valid on their own level, as is the science created by them. But they are divorced from immutable principles, as is modern science, which has discovered many things on a certain level of reality but, because of this divorce from higher principles, has brought about disequilibrium through its very discoveries and inventions. Only mathematics among the modern sciences may be said to possess certain principles in the metaphysical sense; the reason is that mathematics remains, despite everything, a Platonic science and its laws, discovered by the human mind, continue to reflect metaphysical principles, as reason itself cannot but display the fact that it *is* a reflection of the Intellect. The discoveries of the other sciences, to the extent that they conform to some aspect of the nature of reality, of course possess a symbolic and metaphysical significance; but that does not mean that these sciences are attached to metaphysical principles and integrated into a higher form of knowledge. Such an integration could take place but, as a matter of fact, it has not. Modern science, therefore, and its generalizations, like the other fruits of that way of thinking and acting which we have associated with modernism, suffer from the lack of principles which characterize the modern world, a lack which is felt to an even greater degree as the history of the modern world unfolds.

It might be asked what other means of knowledge were available to other civilizations before the modern period. The answer is quite clear, at least for those Muslims who know the intellectual life of Islam: revelation and intellectual intuition or vision (*dhawq*, *kashf* or *shuhūd*).[11] The Muslim intellectual saw revelation as the primary source of knowledge, not only as the means to learn the laws of morality concerned with the active life. He was also aware of the possibility of man purifying himself until the 'eye of the heart' (*'ayn al-qalb*), residing at the centre of his being, would open and enable him to gain direct vision of the supernal realities. Finally, he accepted the power of reason to know, but this reason was always attached to and derived sustenance from revelation on the one hand, and intellectual intuition on the other. The few in the Islamic world who would cut this cord of reliance and declare the independence of reason from both revelation and intuition were never accepted into the mainstream of Islamic thought. They remained marginal figures while, in a reverse fashion in the post-medieval West, those who sought to sustain and uphold the reliance of reason upon revelation and the Intellect remained on the margin, while the mainstream of modern Western thought rejected both revelation and intellectual intuition as means of knowledge. In modern times even philosophers of religion and theologians rarely defend the Bible as a source of sapiential knowledge which could determine and integrate *scientia* in the manner espoused by a St. Bonaventure. The few who look upon the Bible for intellectual guidance are usually limited by such shallow literal interpretations of the Holy Book that, in their feuds with the modern sciences, the devotees of the rationalistic camp almost inevitably come out the victors.[12]

When one ponders over these and other salient features of modernism, one comes to the conclusion that, in order to understand modernism and its manifestations, it is essential to comprehend the conception of man which underlines it. One must seek to discover how modern man conceives of himself and his destiny, how he views the *anthropos vis-à-vis* God and the world. Moreover, it is essential to understand what constitutes the souls and minds of men and women whose thoughts and ideas have molded and continue to mold the modern world. For surely, if such men as Ghazzālī and Rūmī, or for that matter an Erigena or Eckhart, were the occupants of chairs of philosophy in leading universities in the West, another kind of philosophy would issue forth in that world. A man thinks according to what he is; or as Aristotle said, knowledge depends upon the mode of the knower. A study of the modern concept of man as being 'free' of Heaven, complete master of his own destiny, earth-bound but also master of the earth, oblivious to all eschatological realities which he has replaced with some future state of perfection in profane historical time, indifferent if not totally opposed to the world of the Spirit and its demands, and lacking a sense of the sacred, will reveal how futile have been and are the efforts of those modernistic Muslim 'reformers' who have sought to harmonize Islam and modernism in the sense that we have defined it. If we turn even a cursory glance at the Islamic conception of man, at *homo islamicus*, we shall discover the impossibility of harmonizing this conception with the modern concept of man.[13]

Homo islamicus is at once the slave of God (*al-'abd*) and His vice-gerent on earth (*khalīfatallāh fi'l-arḍ*).[14] He is not an animal which happens to speak and think but a being who possesses a soul and spirit created by God. *Homo islamicus* contains within himself the plant and animal natures, as he is the crown of creation (*ashraf al-makhlūqāt*); but he has not evolved from the lower forms of life. Man has always been man. The Islamic conception of man envisages that man is a being who lives on earth and has earthly needs; but he is not earthly and his needs are not limited to the terrestrial. He rules over the earth, but not in his own right; rather he is God's vice-gerent before all creatures. He therefore also bears responsibility for the created order before God and is the channel of grace for God's creatures. *Homo islamicus* possesses the power of reason, of *ratio* which divides and analyses, but his mental faculties are not limited to reason. He possesses the possibility of inward knowledge: the knowledge of his own inner being, which is in fact the key to the knowledge of God according to the famous prophetic *ḥadīth*, 'He who knows himself knoweth his Lord' (*man 'arafa nafsahᵘ faqad 'arafa rabbahᵘ*). He is aware of the fact that his consciousness does not have an external, material cause but that it comes from God and is too profound to be affected by the accident of death.[15] *Homo islamicus* thus remains aware of the eschatological realities, of the fact that, although he lives on this earth, he is here as a traveller far away from his original abode. He is aware that his guide for this journey is the message which issues from his home of origin, from *the* Origin, and this message is none other than the revelation to which he remains bound, not only in its aspect of law as embodied in the *Sharīʿah*, but also in its aspect of truth and knowledge (*Ḥaqīqah*). He is also aware that man's faculties are not bound and limited to the senses and reason but that, to the extent that he is able to regain the fullness of his being and bring to actuality all the possibilities that God has placed within him, man's mind and reason can become illuminated by the light of the spiritual world and he is able to gain direct knowledge of that spiritual and intelligible world to which the Noble Quran refers as the Invisible (*ʿālam-al-ghayb*).[16]

Obviously such a conception of man differs profoundly from that of modern man, who sees himself as a purely earthly creature, master of nature, but responsible to no one but himself; and no amount of wishy-washy apologies can harmonize the two. The Islamic conception of man removes the possibility of a Promethean revolt against Heaven and brings God into the minutest aspect of human life.[17] Its effect is therefore the creation of a civilization, an art, a philosophy or a whole manner of thinking and seeing things which are completely theocentric and which stand opposed to the anthropomorphism that is such a salient feature of modernism. Nothing can be more shocking to authentic Muslim sensibilities than the Titanic and Promethean 'religious' art of the late Renaissance and the Baroque, which stand directly opposed to the completely nonanthropomorphic art of Islam. In Islam man thinks and makes in his function of *homo sapiens* and *homo faber* as the *ʿabd* of God, and not as a creature who has rebelled against Him. His function remains, not the glorification of himself, but of his Lord, and his greatest aim is to become 'nothing', to undergo the experience of *fanāʿ* which would enable him to become the mirror in which God contemplates the reflections of His own Names and Qualities and the channel through which the theophanies of His Names and Qualities are reflected in the world.

Of course, what characterizes the Islamic conception of man has profound similarities with the conception of man in other traditions, including Christianity, and we would be the last to deny this point. But modernism is *not* Christianity or any other tradition and it is the confrontation of Islam with modern thought that we have in mind here, not its comparison with Christianity. Otherwise what could be closer to the Islamic teaching that man is created to seek perfection and final spiritual beatitude through intellectual and spiritual growth, that man is man only when he seeks perfection (*ṭālib al-kamāl*) and attempts to go beyond himself, than the scholastic saying *Homo non proprie humanus sed superhumanus est*, which means that to be properly human man must be more than human.

The characteristics of modern thought discussed earlier, namely its anthropomorphic and, by extension, secular nature, the lack of principles in its various branches and the reductionism which is related to it and which is more evident in the realm of the sciences, are obviously in total opposition to the tenets of traditional Islamic thought, just as the modern conception of man from which these thought patterns issue is opposed to the traditional Islamic conception of man. This opposition is clear enough not to need further elucidation here.[18] There is one characteristic of modern thought, however, which needs to be discussed in greater detail as a result of its pervasive nature in the modern world and its lethal effect upon the religious thought and life of those Muslims who have been affected by it, namely, the theory of evolution.[19]

In the West, no modern theory or idea has been as detrimental to religion as the theory of evolution, which instead of being considered as a hypothesis in biology, zoology, or paleontology, is paraded around as if it were a proven scientific fact. Furthermore, it has become a fashion of modern thought, embracing fields as far apart as astrophysics and the history of art. Nor has the effect of this manner of thinking been any less negative on Muslims influenced by it than it has been on Christians. Usually modernized Muslims have tried to come to terms with evolution through all kinds of unbelievable interpretations of the Noble Quran, forgetting that there is no possible way to harmonize the conception of man (Ādam) as he to whom God taught all the 'names' and whom He placed on earth as His *khalīfah*, and the evolutionist conception which sees man as having 'ascended' from the ape. It is strange that except for a number of traditionalist and also 'fundamentalist' Muslim thinkers who have rejected the theory of evolution mostly on purely religious grounds without providing intellectual and rational arguments for their rejection of the theory, few Muslims have bothered to see its logical absurdity and to consider all the scientific evidence brought against it by such men as L. Bounoure and D. Dewar[20], despite the ecstatic claims of its general acceptance by various standard dictionaries and encyclopedias. In fact, as has been stated so justly by E.F. Schumacher, 'evolutionism is not science; it is science fiction, even a kind of hoax'.[21] Some Western critics of evolution have gone so far as to claim that its proponents suffer from psychological disequilibrium[22], while recently a whole array of arguments drawn from information theory have been brought against it.[23]

It is not our aim in this study to analyse and refute in detail the theory of evolution, although such a refutation by Muslim thinkers is essential from the scientific as well as the metaphysical, philosophical, logical and religious points of view, as has already been carried out in the Occident. What is important to note here is that the evolutionary point of view, which refuses to see permanence anywhere, for which the greater somehow 'evolves' from the 'lesser' and which is totally blind to the higher states of being and the archetypal realities which determine the forms of this world, is but a result of that loss of principles alluded to above. Evolutionism is but a desperate attempt to fill the vacuum created by modern man's 'cutting off' of the Hands of God from His creation and negating any principle above the merely human, which then falls of necessity to the level of the subhuman. Once the Transcendent Principle is forgotten, the world becomes a circle without a centre and this experience of the loss of the centre remains an existential reality for anyone who accepts the theses of modernism, whether he be a Christian or a Muslim.

Closely allied to the idea of evolution is that of progress and utopianism, which have both philosophically and politically shaken the Western world to its roots during the past two centuries and are now affecting the Islamic world profoundly. The ideal of unilateral progress has fortunately ceased to be taken seriously by many noted thinkers in the West today and is gradually being rejected in the Islamic world as an 'idol of the mind' before which the earlier generation of modernized Muslims prostrated without any hesitation.[24] But the utopianism which is closely related to the idea of progress bears further scrutiny and study as a result of the devastating effect it has had and continues to have on a large segment of the modernized Muslim 'intelligentsia'.

'Utopianism' is defined by the *Oxford English Dictionary* as 'Impossible ideal schemes for the amelioration or perfection of social conditions'. Although the origin of this term goes back to the well-known treatise of Sir Thomas More, entitled *Utopia* and written in 1516 in Latin, the term 'utopianism' as employed today has certain implications antedating the 16th century, although the term itself derives from More's famous work. The Christian doctrine of the incarnation, combined with a sense of idealism which characterizes Christianity, were of course present before modern times. Utopianism grafted itself upon the caricature of these characteristics and, whether in the form of the humanitarian socialism of such figures as St. Simon, Charles Fourier or Robert Owen, or the political socialism of Marx and Engels, led to a conception of history that is a real parody of the Augustinian *City of God*. The utopianism of the last centuries, which is one of the important features of modernism, combined with various forms of Messianism, led and still leads to deep social and political upheavals whose goals and methods cannot but remain completely alien to the ethos and aims of traditional Islam.[25] Utopianism seeks to establish a perfect social order through purely human means. It disregards the presence of evil in the world in the theological sense and aims at doing good without God, as if it were possible to create an order based on goodness but removed from the source of all goodness.

Islam has also had its descriptions of the perfect state of society in works such as those of Fārābī describing the 'virtuous society' or *al-madīnat al-fāḍilah*, or the texts of Shaykh Shihāb al-Dīn Suhrawardī, which refer to the land of perfection called in Persian *nā kujā-ābād*, literally 'the land of nowhere': *u-topia*. But then it was always remembered that this land of perfection *is nowhere*; that is, beyond the earthly abode and therefore identified with the eighth clime above the seven geographic ones of this world. The realism present in the Islamic perspective, combined with the strong emphasis of the Noble Quran upon the gradual loss of perfection of the Islamic community as it moves away from the origin of revelation, until quite recently prevented the kind of utopianism present in modern European philosophy from growing upon the soil of Islamic thought. Moreover, the Muslim remained always aware that, if there were to be a perfect state, it could only come into being through Divine help. Hence, although the idea of the cyclic renewal of Islam through a 'renewer' (*mujaddid*) has always been alive, as has the wave of Mahdiism which sees in the Mahdi the force sent by God to return Islam to its perfection, Islam has never faced within itself that type of secular utopianism which underlies so many of the socio-political aspects of modern thought. It is therefore essential to be aware of the profound distinction between modern utopianism and Islamic teachings concerning the *mujaddid*, or renewer of Islamic society, or even the Mahdi himself. It is also basic to distinguish between the traditional figure of the *mujaddid* and the modern reformer, who usually, as a result of his feeble reaction to modern thought, can hardly be said to have brought about the renewal of Islam. One must also be aware of the real nature of that revivalism, based on utopianism but using Islamic images, that one finds in certain types of Islamic 'fundamentalism'.

There is, finally, one more characteristic of modern thought which it is essential to mention and which is related to all that has been stated above. This characteristic is the loss of the sense of the sacred. Modern man can practically be defined as that type of man who has lost this sense, and his thought is conspicuous in its lack of awareness of the sacred. Nor could it be otherwise, seeing that modern humanism is inseparable from secularism. But nothing could be further from the Islamic perspective, in which there does not even exist such a concept as the profane or secular[26]; for in Islam, as already mentioned, the One penetrates into the very depths of the world of multiplicity and excludes no domain from the tradition. This is to be seen not only in the intellectual aspects of Islam[27], but also in an arresting fashion in Islamic art. The Islamic tradition can never accept a thought pattern which is devoid of the perfume of the sacred and which replaces the Divine Order by one of purely human origin and inspiration. The confrontation of Islam with modern thought cannot take place on a serious level if the primacy of the sacred in the perspective of Islam and its lack in modern thought is not take into consideration. Islam cannot even carry out a dialogue with the secular by placing it in a position of legitimacy. It can only take the secular for what it is, namely the negation and denial of the sacred, which may ultimately be said to be that which alone *is*, while the profane or secular only *appears* to be.

In conclusion, it is necessary to mention that the reductionism which is one of the characteristics of modern thought has itself affected Islam in its confrontation with modernism. One of the effects of modernism upon Islam has been to reduce Islam in the minds of many to only one of its dimensions, namely the *Sharīʿah*, and to divest it of those intellectual weapons which alone can ward off the assaults of modern thought upon its citadel. The *Sharīʿah* is of course basic to the Islamic tradition. But the intellectual challenges posed by modernism in the form of evolutionism, rationalism, existentialism, agnosticism and the like can only be answered intellectually and not juridically. Nor can they be answered by ignoring or disregarding those issues and expecting some kind of magical wedding between the *Sharīʿah* and modern science and technology to take place. The successful encounter of Islam with modern thought will not take place simply through the expression of anger and the display of self-righteousness. It can only come about when modern thought is fully understood in both its roots and ramifications, and the whole of the Islamic tradition brought to bear upon the solution of the enormous problems which modernism poses for Islam. At the center of this undertaking lies the revival of that wisdom, that *ḥikmah* or *ḥaqīqah*, which lies at the heart of the Islamic revelation and which will remain valid as long as men remain men and bear witness to Him according to their theomorphic nature and in the state of servitude before the Lord (*ʿubūdiyyah*), the state which is the *raison d'être* of human existence.

Notes

1. Islam is based on intelligence, and intelligence is light as expressed in the *ḥadīth*, *innaʾl-ʿaql*^{a} *nūr*^{un} ('Verily intelligence is light'). The characteristic expression of Islam is the courtyard of an Alhambra, whose forms are so many crystallizations of light and whose spaces are defined by the rays of that light which in this world symbolizes the Divine Intellect.
2. If we are forced to re-define such terms as 'tradition' and 'modernism' in this and other works, it is because, despite the considerable amount

of writing devoted to the subject by the outstanding traditional writers such as Guénon, Schuon, A.K. Coomaraswamy, T. Burckhardt, M. Lings and others, there are still many readers, especially Muslim ones, for whom the distinction between tradition and modernism is not clear. They still identify tradition with customs and modernism with all that is contemporary.

Many Western students of Islam also identify 'modern' with 'advanced', 'developed' and the like, as if the march of time itself guarantees betterment. For example, C. Leiden, a political scientist and student of contemporary Islam, writes, 'Equally important is how the term *modernisation* can itself provide insight into these questions. This is not the first time in history that societies have undergone confrontation with other "advanced" societies and have learned to accommodate to them. Every such confrontation was, in a sense, a clash or contact with modernisation.' J.A. Bill and C. Leiden, *The Middle East – Politics and Power*, Boston, 1974, pp. 48–49. The author goes on to cite as examples the confrontation of the Romans with the Greeks and the Arabs with the Byzantines and Persians. However, despite the decadent nature of late Greek culture, neither the Greeks nor certainly the theocratic Byzantines and Persians were modern in our definition of the word, according to which this *is* in fact the first time that traditional societies confront modernism.

3. Despite the totally anti-traditional character of the perspective which dominates modern anthropology, even certain anthropologists have come to the conclusion that, from a metaphysical and spiritual point of view, man has not evolved one *iota* since the Stone Age. If in the early decades of this century this view was championed by a few scholars, such as A. Jeremias and W. Schmidt, in recent years it has received more powerful support based on extensive evidence reflected in the studies of such men as J. Servier and, from the point of view of religious anthropology, M. Eliade.
4. It must be remembered that even during this relatively short period of five centuries, the Muslim world has remained for the most part traditional and did not feel the full impact of modernism until a century ago. See S.H. Nasr, *Islam and the Plight of Modern Man*.
5. In the famous Persian poem –

   Invoke until thy invocation gives rise to mediation (*fikr*)
   And gives birth to a hundred thousand virgin 'thoughts' (*andīshah*)

   – the relation of mental activity in a traditional context to spiritual practice and contemplation is clearly stated.
6. There have been recent attempts to escape from the reductionism of classical physics and to introduce both life and even the psyche as independent elements in the Universe. But the general view of modern science remains the reductionist one which would reduce spirit to mind, mind to the external aspects of the psyche, the external aspects of the psyche to organic behaviour and organisms to molecular structures. The man who knows and who has the certitude of his own

consciousness is thus reduced to chemical and physical elements which in reality are concepts of his own mind imposed upon the natural domain. See A. Koestler and J.R. Smythies (eds.), *Beyond Reductionism*, London 1959, especially the article of V.E. Frankl, 'Reductionism and Nihilism' where he writes, 'the present danger does not really lie in the loss of universality on the part of the scientist, but rather in his pretence and claim of totality . . . The true nihilism of today is reductionism . . . Contemporary nihilism no longer brandishes the word "nothingness"; today nihilism is camouflaged as *nothing-butness*. Human phenomena are thus turned into more epiphenomena.' See also the remarkable work of E.F. Schumacher, *A Guide for the Perplexed*, New York, 1977, especially chapter 1, where this question is discussed.

7. See F. Brunner, *Science et réalité*, Paris, 1956, where the author displays clearly the non-anthropomorphic nature of the traditional sciences based on their reliance upon the Divine Intellect rather than upon mere reason.
8. Concerning the study of the cosmos as a crypt as far as Islam is concerned see S.H. Nasr, *An Introduction to Islamic Cosmological Doctrines*, London, 1978, chapter 15.
9. See S.H. Nasr, 'Self-awareness and Ultimate Selfhood', *Religious Studies*, vol. 13, no. 3, Sept. 1977, pp. 319–325.
10. The classical study of E. Gilson, *The Unity of Philosophical Experience*, is still valuable in tracing this development in Western thought.
11. It was especially Ṣadr al-Dīn Shīrāzī who elucidated, perhaps more than any other Muslim philosopher, the relation between the three paths of reason, intuition and revelation open to man in his quest for the attainment of knowledge. See S.H. Nasr, *Ṣadr al-Dīn Shīrāzī and his Transcendent Theosophy*, London, 1978.
12. We have dealt with this issue extensively in our *Knowledge and the Sacred*, chapter 4.
13. There are of course many men and women living in the modern world who would not accept this description of modern man as far as it concerns themselves. But such people, whose number in fact grows every day in the West, are really contemporary rather than modern. The characteristics which we have mentioned pertain to modernism as such and not to a particular contemporary individual who may in fact stand opposed to them.
14. On the Islamic conception of man see S.H. Nasr, 'Who is Man? The perennial answer of Islam', in J. Needleman (ed.), *The Sword of Gnosis*, Penguin Books Inc. 1974, pp. 203–17, and *Knowledge and the Sacred*, chapter 5.
15. Consciousness has no origin in time. No matter how we try to go back in the examination of our consciousness, we cannot obviously reach a temporal beginning. At the heart of this consciousness in fact resides the Infinite Consciousness of God, who is at once the absolutely transcendent Reality and the infinite Self residing at the center of our being. In general, Sufism has emphasized more the objective and

Hinduism the subjective pole of the One Reality, which is at once pure Object and pure Subject, but the conception of the Divinity as pure Subject has also been always present in Islam, as the reference in the Noble Quran to God as the Inward (*al-bāṭin*), the prophetic *ḥadīth* already cited and such classical Sufi treatises as the *Conference of the Birds* (*Manṭiq al-ṭayr*) reveal. See F. Schuon, *Spiritual Perspectives and Human Facts*, trans. D.M. Matheson, London, 1953, pp. 95ff.

16. It is of interest to note that one of the outstanding treatises of Islamic philosophy dealing with metaphysics and eschatology is a work by Ṣadr al-Dīn Shīrāzī entitled *Mafātiḥ al-ghayb*, literally *Keys to the Invisible World*.

17. 'In Islam, as we have seen, the Divine ray pierces directly through all degrees of existence, like an axis or central pivot, which links them harmoniously and bestows upon each degree what is suited to it; and we have also seen how the straight ray curves on its return and becomes a circle that brings everything back to its point of departure . . .' L. Schaya, 'Contemplation and Action in Judaism and Islam', in Y. Ibish and I. Marculescu (eds.), *Contemplation and Action in World Religions*, Seattle and London, 1978, p. 173.

18. Of course, the ramification of this opposition and the details as they pertain to each field are such that they could be discussed indefinitely. But here we have the principles rather than their applications in mind. We have discussed some of these issues in detail in our *Islam and the Plight of Modern Man*.

19. '. . . in the modern world more cases of loss of religious faith are to be traced to the theory of evolution as their immediate cause than to anything else . . . for the more logically minded, there is no option but to choose between the two, that is, between the doctrine of the fall of man and the 'doctrine' of the rise of man, and to reject altogether the one not chosen . . .' M. Lings, review of D. Dewar, *The Transformist Illusion*; in *Studies in Comparative Religion*, vol. 4, no. 1, 1970, p. 59.

One might also explain the rapid spread of the theory of evolution as a pseudo-religion in the West by saying that, to some extent at least, it came to fill a vacuum already created by a weakening of faith. But as far as Islam is concerned, its effect has been to corrode and weaken an already existing faith, as it was for those Christians who still possessed strong religious faith when the theory of evolution spread in the late 19th century, as it continues to do in fact up to the present day.

20. See L. Bounoure, *Determinisme et finalité, double loi de la vie*, Paris, 1957; *ibid.*, *Recherche d'une doctrine de la vie. Vrai savants et faux prophètes*, Paris, 1964; and D. Dewar, *The Transformist Illusion*, Newfreesboro (Tenn.), 1957. We have also dealt with this question in our *Man and Nature*, London, 1977.

21. Schumacher, *Guide for the Perplexed*, p. 114: 'It is far better to believe that the earth is a disc supported by a tortoise and flanked by four elephants than to believe, in the name of "evolutionism", in the coming of some "superhuman" monster.'

F. Schuon, *Spiritual Perspectives and Human Facts*, p. 112: 'A literal interpretation of cosmological symbols is, if not positively useful, at any rate harmless, whereas the scientific error – such as evolutionism – is neither literally nor symbolically true; the repercussions of its falsity are beyond calculation.'

22. 'If we present, for the sake of argument, the theory of evolution in a most scientific formulation, we have to say something like this: "At a certain moment of time the temperature of the Earth was such that it became more favourable for the aggregation of carbon atoms and oxygen with the nitrogen-hydrogen combination, and that from random occurrences of large clusters molecules occurred which were most favorably structured for the coming about of life, and from that point it went on through vast stretches of time, until through processes of natural selection a being finally occurred which is capable of choosing love over hate and justice over injustice, of writing poetry like that of Dante, composing music like that of Mozart, and making drawings like those of Leonardo." Of course, such a view of cosmogenesis is crazy. And I do not at all mean crazy in the sense of slangy invective but rather in the technical meaning of psychotic. Indeed such a view has much in common with certain aspects of schizophrenic thinking.' K. Stern, *The Flight from Woman*, New York, 1965, p. 290. The author is a well-known psychiatrist who has reached this conclusion not from traditional foundations but from the premises of various contemporary schools of thought.
23. See especially the works of A.E. Wilder Smith, such as *Man's Origin, Man's Destiny*, Wheaton (I11.), 1968, and his *Herkunft und Zukunft des Menschen*, Basel, 1966. We have assembled many references to anti-evolutionary Western literature in *Knowledge and the Sacred*, pp. 249–50.
24. We have discussed the idea of progress and its refutation in our *Islam and the Plight of Modern Man*, and in our 'Progress and Evolution: A Reappraisal from the Traditional Perspective', *Parabola*, vol. VI, no. 2, Spring 1981, pp. 44–51. See also M. Jameelah, *Islam and Modernism*, Lahore, 1968. For an eloquent refutation of the notion of progress see M. Lings, *Ancient Beliefs and Modern Superstitions*, London, 1967; also Lord Northbourne, *Looking Back on Progress*, London, 1968.
25. On the deeper roots of utopianism in the West see J. Servier, *Histoire de l'utopie*, Paris, 1967.
26. This is proven by the lack of such a term in classical Arabic or Persian.
27. We have dealt with the sacred quality of all aspects of Islamic learning, even science, in our *Science and Civilization in Islam*, Cambridge (U.S.A.), 1968; also *Islamic Science – An Illustrated Study*, London, 1976.

Chapter Seven

Value and Development in the Contemporary Islamic World

Since the the late 19th century, when Western ideas became prevalent among a notable section of the ruling classes of the Islamic world, the ideas of 'progress' and later 'development' became widely accepted and for some time was considered as the normal consequence of the flow of historic time. Rarely were these notions analyzed objectively and in the light of both the 'values' they imply and of the Islamic ideas and norms which they threaten. In the earlier days of contact with the West, philosophical definitions of progress did encounter an intellectual rebuttal from the traditional intelligentsia, but once the general notion of development became prevalent in the present century, there was for some time even less questioning than before concerning the implication of development for the value system existing within the Islamic world.

It was only during the past two or three decades, thanks to the crisis of modern civilization and some of the bitter fruits of what has been taken for granted as the natural course of development, that some of the more perceptive people in the Islamic world began to question the nature and meaning of development as understood in the modern West and its implications for the Islamic system of 'values'. During the past few years one has begun to hear such questions as 'what is development?' – and 'development towards what goal?' In fact the most significant development during the past few years in the Islamic world is the questioning of development itself as it had been understood in the West and by Westernized Muslims for some years.

In this short discourse, at least some of the more important issues which development poses for Islamic values can be delved into. One of the most basic of these values concerns the nature of time and the historical process itself. The idea of continuous development and progress grew in the West from a utopianism which is itself a parody of the traditional doctrine of time ending with the intervention of God in history to re-establish the primordial harmony of the Edenic state. As already mentioned in the previous chapter, it is significant to note how difficult it actually is to translate the modern idea of utopia into Arabic and Persian. How different is in fact the meaning of that 'ideal city' or *nā kujā ābād* of Suhrawardī in the eighth clime beyond our ordinary experience of space and 'utopia' as currently understood, despite the fact that the term used by Suhrawardī means literally *u-topia*. The Islamic conception of time is based essentially upon the cyclic rejuvenation of human history through the appearance of various prophets and ending finally in the eschatological events identified with the appearance of the Mahdi. This re-establishes harmony and peace in the world through direct Divine intervention and not through the secular changes brought about by means of mere human agency. The first challenge of the modern Western theory of development to the Islamic world concerns the very nature and meaning of history as the final end of human action in historical time. Between traditional Islamic eschatological doctrines and Western philosophical utopianism, there is a chasm which cannot be bridged in any way: a chasm which has also created a profound tension within the mind and soul of those Muslims who are caught between traditional Islamic culture and Western ideas.

Development implies activity directed towards a particular goal.

In Islam all human activity must be carried out in accordance with God's Will as embodied in the Divine Law (*Sharī'ah*) and, as far as the making of things is concerned, in accordance with the norms and principles of Islamic art, which are also derived from the Islamic revelation. Human action must be pleasing and acceptable in God's eyes. Obviously that aspect of development in its modern sense which deals with human welfare, with such problems as providing food and housing, can be easily justified and in fact supported from the religious point of view. But such is not the case with the goal of development as indefinite growth associated with man considered merely as an earthly creature, an economic animal. Islam, as other religions, sees the end of man in the perfection of his spiritual possibilities and defines man as the creature born for transcendence, for going beyond himself. Obviously a development which concentrates solely upon the material and the worldly cannot but destroy the Islamic conception of the meaning of human life and activity. It is true that in Islam the gaining of a livelihood and the provision of material needs are stressed and are in fact basic to the *Sharī'ah*, but even these worldly activities (*al-dunyā*) are judged praiseworthy only in relation to man's final end or the other world (*al-ākhirah*). The Quran states in clear terms in an already cited verse, 'Verily the *ākhirah* is better for you than this world.' (XVI; 30) The modern idea of development, therefore, which has been until recently essentially materialistic and purely economic, disrupts the Islamic balance between the spiritual and material aspects of human life and the need to live and be active with some degree of detachment and with full awareness of man's last ends.

Islamic society is one in which the individual is related to an organic social manifold within which he finds meaning and support. Islamic society is based neither upon individualism, in which society is pulverized into atomic units, nor upon the ant heap, in which the individual loses his inner freedom and is faced with the danger of the stultification of his creative powers through regimentation and uniformity. Modern development, especially since it has implied until now indiscriminate and blind industrialization, has also tended to destroy the very basis of the organic structure of traditional societies, where the individual is related to a greater whole through the extended family, local bonds, guilds and – on a more inward plane – through Sufi orders. The value system of such a society is obviously challenged by any force which would break or disrupt such relationships. Development in the Islamic world has certainly strained these relationships, although it has not as yet been able to break them.

Development, as it has been conceived and as it has taken place in the Islamic world during past decades, affects the relationships between man and society, man and nature, and finally man and God. It tends to create an anthropomorphic philosophy based on terrestrial man and his earthly well-being, a philosophy which stands opposed to the theomorphic conception of Islam. The man affected by this view tends to regard society, not as the *ummah* or religious community governed by God's law, but as an aggregate of atomized units bent on producing and consuming at an ever greater speed. He tends to see nature, not as God's handiwork to be contemplated and lived with in harmony, but as an 'it': an object to be plundered and exploited as rapidly as possible. Finally, he sees God, not as the all-powerful presence Who dominates every moment of human life and before whom man is responsible for his every deed and action, but at best a Being watching His creation from a great distance.

Of course, these are tendencies which are prevalent but have not destroyed the Islamic system of values. In fact, these values are strong enough to have caused a reaction in many spheres against the stresses caused by the notions of development that have been dominant until recently. Furthermore, attempts are now being made in the Islamic world to re-define the process of development itself in the light of Islamic values at a moment when many perspicacious observers of the human condition in the West itself are re-examining the modern notions of development based on secular humanism, utopianism or historical determinism. Whatever the future may hold as far as the 'development' of the Islamic world is concerned, there is no doubt that, from the Islamic point of view, development cannot but mean the realization by man of all that he can become and all that he actually is here and now, even if he remains unaware of his God-given possibilities.

Part Three
Tradition and Modernism – Tensions in Various Cultural Domains

Chapter Eight

Islamic Education, Philosophy and Science – A Survey in the Light of Present-Day Challenges

If in the previous section our aim was to examine the tension between traditional and modern Islam, both generally and in various particular fields of thought and action, in this section our goal is rather to turn to more specific subjects. It is in fact to present the traditional teachings of Islam as they encounter various forces within the modern world in such fields as education, science, philosophy and architecture. By doing so, it is possible to gain great understanding of the nature of the actual forces at play and the tensions which exist in specific disciplines and issues between traditional Islam and the modern world. To bring out these tensions, however, it is necessary first to present some of the traditional teachings themselves as they apply in each specific domain, teachings with which not everyone concerned with the confrontation of traditional Islam and the modern world is fully acquainted.

As far as Islamic education and science are concerned, they both cover such a vast expanse of intellectual space and historical time that it is hardly possible to do justice to them in this appraisal, except by pointing out some of the chief principles and salient features which have always characterized them as authentic manifestations of traditional Islam and notable aspects of Islamic civilization. If some of the achievements of Muslims in these domains are mentioned, it is with the purpose of providing necessary examples to elucidate those principles and features, not in order to enumerate the achievements of Muslims in these fields in an exhaustive manner. Needless to say, even a cataloguing of what Muslims have accomplished in these fields would require volumes.[1]

Both the education and the science which developed in Islamic civilization over the centuries are essentially Islamic in character, whatever may have been their historical origin. The living organism which is Islamic civilization digested various types of knowledge from many different sources, ranging from China to Alexandria and Athens; but whatever survived within this organism was digested and made to grow within the living body of Islam. Whatever may have been the origin of the 'material' for education and the sciences, the form was always Islamic, and both Islamic education and the Islamic sciences are related in the most intimate manner to the principles of the Islamic revelation and the spirit of the Quran. The Quran contains, according to the traditional Islamic perspective, the roots of all knowledge but not of course its details, as is contended by certain apologists who would make the Sacred Book a textbook of science in the modern sense of the word. The Quran is *al-qur'ān* which, besides 'recitation', is also understood by some commentators to mean 'the gathering', namely the treasury in which are gathered all the pearls of wisdom. The Sacred Book is also called *al-furqān*, 'discernment', for it is the supreme instrument of knowledge whereby truth is distinguished from falsehood. It is the *umm al-kitāb*, 'the mother of all books', for all authentic knowledge contained in 'all books' is ultimately born from its bosom. It is *al-hudā*, 'the guidance', for in it is contained not only moral guidance but also educational guidance: the *hidāyah* or guidance which educates the whole being of man in the most profound and also complete sense.[2] No wonder then that the Quran, the Word of God, has always been the *alpha* and *omega* of all Islamic education and science, being at once their source and goal, their inspiration and guide.

Enwrapped in the perpetual presence of the Quran, the life of the Muslim was witness to a continuous process of education based on the form and spirit of the Quranic revelation as contained in the Sacred Book and reflected in the very substance and being of the Prophet. From the *shahādah* uttered into the ear of the newly-born child until the moment of death, the words of the Book and the sayings of the Prophet molded the mind and soul of the Muslim, providing for him the primary content as well as the ambience of his education and the principles and goal of the sciences. The quest for knowledge and its veritable celebration[3] were dominated from beginning to end by its sacred quality and nature. In Islam, knowledge was never divorced from the sacred[4] and both the whole educational system and the sciences that it made possible breathed in a universe of sacred presence. Whatever was known possessed a profoundly religious character, not only because the object of every type of knowledge is created by God, but most of all because the intelligence by which man *knows* is itself a Divine gift: a supernaturally natural faculty of the human microcosm, even the categories of logic being the reflections of the Divine Intellect upon the plane of the human mind.[5]

Being related to holiness, hence wholeness, Islamic education had to be concerned with the whole being of the men and women whom it sought to educate. Its goal was not only the training of the mind but that of the whole being of the person. That is why it implied not only instruction or transmission of knowledge (*ta'līm*), but also training of the whole being of the student (*tarbiyah*).[6] The teacher was not only a *mu'allim*, a 'transmitter of knowledge', but also a *murabbī*, a 'trainer of souls and personalities'. This was true to such an extent that the term *mu'allim* itself came to gain the meaning of *murabbī* as well; that is, it came to be imbued with ethical connotations which in the modern world have become nearly totally divorced from the question of teaching and the transmission of knowledge, especially at higher levels of education. The Islamic educational system never divorced the training of the mind from that of the soul and the whole being of the person. It never considered the transmission of knowledge or its possession to be legitimate without the possession of appropriate moral and spiritual qualities. In fact, the possession of knowledge without these qualities was considered dangerous, so that the Persian poet, Sanā'ī, could call a person who possessed knowledge without moral and spiritual virtue a thief and assert:–

> *If a thief comes with a lamp, he will be able to*
> *steal more precious goods.*[7]

Although Islamic education encompassed the whole life of the traditional Muslim, there are distinct phases and periods to be detected in this organic whole. There was, first of all, the primary period of early family education in which the father and mother both played the role of teacher and educator in religious matters as well as in matters relating to language, culture, social customs, etc.[8] After this period, which was usually longer than the pre-kindergarden phase in the West today, the growing child went on to one of the Quranic schools, which corresponded more or less to elementary and early high school, then to the *madrasah*, which can be said to correspond to secondary school and undergraduate college, and finally the *jāmi'ah*, or place of highest formal education. In many parts of the Islamic world, the *madrasah* incorporated the *jāmi'ah* and provided what would at once correspond to secondary, as well as to college and university education.

The earliest Quranic school did not only acquaint the child with the religious foundation of his or her life, society and civilization, but also served as an introduction to the mastery of language. Although, of course, the situation for Arab children differed from non-Arab Muslims, there is no doubt that in both cases literacy was impregnated with religious meaning and the very process of reading and writing was seen as a religious activity. The word 'pen' (*al-qalam*) itself, as well as signifying the writing implement with the help of which the child wrote his or her first words, also signified the instrument of revelation by which God has even sworn in the Quran. Likewise, 'book' as such was first of all *the* Book, namely the Quran, with all that the term *kitāb* implied in the Islamic context. The habit of illiterate traditional Muslims of respecting any piece of printed material when printing first came to the Islamic world was based on this attitude of identifying the written with the sacred.

Outside the Arab world children were taught their own language, but since both the alphabet[9] and much of the basic vocabulary dealing with both religious and moral ideas were drawn from Quranic Arabic, the two types of training did not oppose but rather complemented each other. Many children were also taught at home rather than at a school located physically in a mosque. This was particularly true of girls, although in many places girls did also attend formal schools outside the home and even studied in *madrasahs*.[10] Also many children received an oral education of a high quality based upon the Quran and traditional literature, so that literacy was not at all synonymous with formal education. The remarkable literary knowledge of certain 'illiterate' Muslims even today testifies to the strength of the less formal, oral education which has usually started at an early age.[11]

As far as the *madrasah* is concerned, it became a formal educational institution early in Islamic history and developed into a fully fledged college and university system by the 4th/10th century. The radiance of such institutions and their significance was so great that soon they began to become a noticeable element throughout practically the whole of the Islamic world and in fact played a fundamental role in the foundation of the European centers of higher education, a role that is only now becoming fully recognized.[12] The *madrasahs* ranged from fairly modest schools with one or two hundred students, to major universities, such as the Qarawiyyin in Fez in Morocco which is over 1100 years old, the al-Azhar,[13] founded over a millennium ago in Cairo and still the greatest seat of Sunni learning, or the Shi'ite *madrasah* of Najaf,[14] established some nine hundred years ago. It even developed into a university system with several campuses and sites, as in the case of the Niẓāmiyyah established in Baghdad as well as in Khurasan by the Seljug *wazīr*, Khwājah Niẓām al-Mulk. Almost always the *madrasahs*, which were also endowed and where students received free room and board as well as compensation for other expenses, were constructed with great care in a beautiful setting. To this day in most Islamic cities, after the mosques, the *madrasahs*, which in fact were always related geographically to mosques, are the most notable architectural masterpieces to be found and some of them, like the Qarawiyyin, the Mustanṣariyyah of Baghdad and the Chahār Bāgh of Isfahan, are among the greatest achievements of Islamic art. Since in Islam knowledge was never divorced from the sacred and Islam saw in the sacred, especially in its noumenous aspect, the aura of Divine Beauty, Islamic education was always imparted in an ambience of beauty.[15] Great care was taken to create an atmosphere in which the sacred quality of knowledge and the religious nature of all educational pursuits in the traditional context were confirmed rather than denied.

The main activity of the *madrasahs* was instruction in the religious sciences, especially Divine Law (*al-Sharī'ah*), its principles (*al-uṣūl*), jurisprudence (*al-fiqh*), etc. The study of the Law was itself based on the careful study of the Quran and its commentaries (*tafsīr* and *ta'wīl*), of the traditions of the Prophet (*Ḥadīth*), and of the sacred history of Islam, which is related to both the Quran and *Ḥadīth*. These studies in turn required complete mastery of Arabic and all the literary disciplines connected with it. They also led to the study of theology (*kalām*) in its manifold schools, which developed from the first Islamic century and which reached a period of intense activity in the Baghdad of the 3rd/9th and 4th/10th centuries. These disciplines together were referred to as the transmitted (*naqlī*) sciences and they dominated the educational activity of most *madrasahs*.

There were, however, a series of other disciplines, including logic, mathematics, the natural sciences and philosophy, which, according to Muslim thinkers, could be arrived at by human intelligence and were not transmitted in the same way as the religious, linguistic and historical sciences. Hence they were called the 'intellectual sciences' (*'aqlī*) in contrast to and as complement of the *naqlī* sciences. This division of the sciences became reflected in the curriculum of the *madrasahs*[16], many of which taught at least some of the *'aqlī* as well as the *naqlī* sciences until a few centuries ago. In certain parts of the Arab world, the *'aqlī* sciences ceased to be taught after the 8th/14th century, while in Persia and such Turkish centers as Istanbul, as well as in the Indian subcontinent, they were taught until much later. Philosophy continues to be taught seriously in Persia to the present day. But there is no doubt that, when the modern Western educational system was brought to the Islamic world in the 19th century, there was practically no *madrasah* which had preserved its former vitality in the different fields of knowledge, especially in mathematics, and the natural and medical sciences.[17]

Moreover, even during the height of activity in the Islamic sciences, there is little doubt that in the domain of the *'aqlī* sciences, except for logic and philosophy, the natural and mathematical sciences were taught to a large extent outside of the *madrasahs*. This seems at least to be the conclusion when one reflects upon the curricula that have survived from the earlier period. One can therefore state with some assurance that, as far as the *'aqlī* sciences are concerned, the activity of the *madrasah* in traditional Islamic society was complemented and augmented by two other types of body: scientific institutions and private circles. Islam developed such scientific institutions as teaching and research hospitals and observatories in both of which instruction for a professional cadre was extensively carried out. In the hospital of Baghdad, which dates from the 3rd/9th century, where the famous Persian physician Muḥammad din Zakariyyā' al-Rāzī (the Latin Rhazes) taught and treated patients, there are records of how medical students were trained both theoretically and practically, how they had to undergo a period of internship and how they were finally examined and given the professional status of a physician.[18] Likewise, in the major observatories which were established in Islamic countries and which must be accounted as the first scientific institutions, instruction in mathematics and astronomy as well as in related disciplines like logic and philosophy was given, as in the first of these major observatories in Maraghah under Khwājah Naṣīr al-Dīn Ṭūsī.[19]

As for private circles, which exist to this day in Persia and are referred to as 'outside instruction or lessons' (*dars-i khārij*), they had always existed as a means of teaching less common disciplines to groups of chosen students, both in order to avoid the anathema of those religious scholars who might object to such subjects being taught and to have a more intimate ambience for the transmission of certain of the *'aqlī* sciences. This type of instruction has been especially important in the teaching of Islamic philosophy and must be considered in any serious study of the traditional Islamic educational system.

Another institution whose impact upon Islamic education has been immense is the Sufi center, called *zāwiyah* in the Arab world and *khānaqāh* in the Persian, Indian and Turkish worlds, the term *tekye* also being used for certain types of Sufi centers in the Ottoman empire. In such centers, whose function is to provide a place for the transmission of the highest form of knowledge, namely Divine

Knowledge (*al-ma'rifah* or *'irfān*) or what could be called *scientia sacra*[20], there has always been educational activity of a most intense nature. Sufism has always been concerned first and foremost with the training of the human soul to enable it to become a worthy receptacle of Divine Presence.[21] It has therefore been concerned with education as *tarbiyah* on the highest level. But Sufism is also concerned with a knowledge which is imparted to the disciple by the master, or more exactly which is caused to be born from within the depth of being of the disciple with the help of the master. This knowledge, although in essence metaphysical, also possesses cosmological and psychological dimensions. Moreover, since Sufism has usually expressed its teachings in the form of literature and music of the highest order, the Sufi centers have been also places for artistic education. Finally, it must be remembered that in certain periods of Islamic history, such as after the Mongol invasion when the formal educational system was destroyed, Sufi centers also took the task of formal education upon themselves and in some areas of the Islamic world for long periods of time they were the sole educational institutions which were still functioning. Altogether, Sufi centers must be considered as among the most basic institutions of Islamic education, in addition to being the place of assembly of the friends of God where the ecstasy of Divine Union is experienced and celebrated.

No discussion of Islamic education would be complete without mention of the practical education connected with the arts and crafts.[22] Within the guilds (*aṣnāf*, *futuwwāt*), as well as through individual instruction in homes or ateliers of master craftsmen, not only were the techniques for the production of objects of art ranging from carpets to tile work transmitted to the student, but a science was also taught which had both a microcosmic and macrocosmic significance. It concerned the soul of the student who, while making an object of traditional art, was also molding his own soul. The student also received instruction concerning the nature of the object at hand and in the symbolism involved in the making of the object in question. Islamic art is a science as Islamic science is an art.[23] Not all those who learned to weave carpets or make tiles were consciously aware of the profound metaphysical and cosmological significance of the symbolism of patterns, forms and colors with which they were dealing. Nevertheless, something of the science involved was transmitted from the beginning, the knowledge becoming more explicitly elucidated as the student advanced in the mastery of his craft and came to gain a more immediate awareness of the nature of the materials with which he was working and the principles by which his art was ennobling the material he was molding. There is no doubt that a vast oral tradition was transmitted over the centuries which enabled architects to construct domes of incredible beauty and durability or to create gardens with perfect harmonic ratios. A science of a high order was somehow preserved and transmitted as long as the traditional arts survived and in fact to the extent that they survive today. This process could not be called anything else but educational and this type of teaching, which concerned technological and scientific knowledge as well as an artistic one, cannot but be considered as a major component of the traditional Islamic educational system.

As far as the *'aqlī* sciences which the Islamic world fostered through this educational system are concerned, their development constitutes both an important chapter in the history of science in general and a dazzling achievement of Islamic civilization of which it was an integral part. The rapid geographical expansion of Islam from the vast plains of Western China to the snow-covered mountain peaks of southern France made it heir to most of the sciences of antiquity. Already within the first century of its existence, when it was building the very foundations of classical Islamic civilization, Islam was confronted with the learning of the Graeco-Alexandrian world as it had been cultivated, not only in the school of Athens, but especially in Alexandria and its offshoots in Pergamon, Antioch, Edessa and other cities of the Near East.[24] Islam became heir to the sciences of the Persians and, to a large extent, to those of the Indians through the university center of Jundishapur where the disciplines of both these sciences, including astronomy and medicine, had been taught extensively before the rise of Islam. The center in fact continued to flourish until the foundation of Baghdad by the Abbasids, when it was finally transferred to the new capital.[25] Islam also inherited some of the Babylonian and the more esoteric elements of the Hellenic and Hellenistic sciences through the Sabaeans of Harran.[26] It even had contact with China and traces of Chinese alchemy had already begun to appear in Islamic sources by the 2nd/8th century. As the last religion of mankind, Islam also became heir to nearly all the sciences of the ancient world. Thus

Islam constructed a number of sciences which, while being profoundly Islamic,[27] at the same time integrated in an unprecedented manner the scientific heritage of many different civilizations which had gone before.

The mere physical presence of these centers of learning could not, however, have been sufficient to generate a major movement within the Islamic world intent upon transmitting these sciences to the Muslims and translating their sources into Arabic. The Muslims had no military, economic or political compulsion to study Aristotle or Indian medicine. They already possessed perhaps the most powerful empire on earth. Nor could turning to these sciences have been merely utilitarian. Their interest in them was in fact most of all intellectual and spiritual, and directly related to the nature of Islam as a revelation based upon knowledge. As a way of knowing, Islam could not remain indifferent to other ways of knowing, to philosophies and sciences which also claimed to explain the nature of things. Moreover, since Islam accepted the religions that went before it as having come from the same source as itself, this principle being particularly emphasized in the case of Judaism and Christianity but also accepted for Zoroastrianism and even to some extent for the Sabaean eclecticism of the Harranians, and later Hinduism and Buddhism, the Muslims could not but engage in theological and philosophical debates with followers of these religions, all of whom had already developed their own theologies and philosophies. Muslims, therefore, had to confront the challenge of modes of knowing related to both the sciences of antiquity and to the philosophies and theologies of religious communities which lived in their midst.

The answer of the Muslims to this challenge was a concerted effort to translate philosophical and scientific works from Greek, Syriac, Sanskrit and Pahlavi into Arabic. Once they had determined to carry out this task, they had at their disposal a whole group of excellent translators belonging to various minority religious communities, especially Christians, some of whom, like Ḥunayn Ibn Isḥāq, as well as being accomplished scholars were also Arab themselves and therefore knew Arabic perfectly well. Schools and centers of translation were established, often supported by public funds, as was the case of the *Bayt al-ḥikmah* or House of Wisdom in Baghdad. As a result, in a period of less than two centuries ranging from the end of the 1st/7th to the 3rd/9th century, an immense corpus of learning was translated into Arabic, making the Arabic language the most important scientific language in the world for several centuries and a major depository for the sciences of antiquity to this day. There are many Greek works, especially of the Hellenistic period, which can be found only in Arabic, the originals having been lost.[28] Altogether, the transmission of the sciences of antiquity to Islam is a cultural event which, from the point of view of quantity and quality as well as of its later impact upon the world at large, must be considered as one of truly global significance.[29]

At the pinnacle of the Islamic intellectual sciences stands philosophy or 'divine wisdom' (*al-falsafah*, or *al-ḥikmat al-ilāhiyyah*). Islam has created one of the richest philosophical traditions, one which possesses great spiritual significance for Islam itself and which has survived as a continuous tradition to this day.[30] Heir to Pythagoreanism, Platonism, Aristotelianism, Neopythagoreanism, Hermeticism and Neoplatonism, and aware of many branches of Stoicism and the later schools of Hellenistic thought, Islam created a powerful and original philosophy within the intellectual universe of Abrahamic monotheism and the Quranic revelation, while incorporating those elements of Greek philosophy which conformed to the Islamic unitarian perspective. The origin of what is characteristically medieval philosophy, whether Jewish or Christian, is to be found in Islamic philosophy.

Being traditional philosophy based upon the supra-individual intellect rather than upon individualistic opinion, Islamic philosophy developed schools and perspectives which were followed over the centuries, rather than being changed and overthrown by one philosopher after another. Already in the 3rd/9th century, Peripatetic (*mashshā'ī*) philosophy, which itself represented a synthesis of Plato, Aristotle and Plotinus in the context of the Islamic world-view, was begun by al-Kindī, further developed by al-Fārābī, pursued in the 4th/10th century by al-'Āmirī and Abū Ya'qūb al-Sijistānī and reached its peak with Ibn Sīnā, the Latin Avicenna, who became the prototype of the philosopher-scientist for all later Islamic history.[31] Criticized by such theologians as al-Ghazzālī, al-Shahrastānī and Fakhr al-Dīn al-Rāzī, this school was temporarily eclipsed in the eastern lands of Islam but enjoyed a period of intense activity in Spain with Ibn Bājjah, Ibn Ṭufayl and Ibn Rushd or Averroes, the foremost expositor of this school in the Islamic West (al-Maghrib). As for the East, the school of Ibn Sīnā was resuscitated by Naṣīr al-Dīn al-Ṭūsī in the 7th/13th century and continued henceforth as an important intellectual tradition during the centuries which followed.[32]

Parallel with the genesis of Peripatetic philosophy, there developed an Ismā'īlī philosophy, which was closer to the Hermetic tradition than the Peripatetic but which itself developed into a distinct philosophy of great variety and richness. Growing out of the enigmatic *Umm al-kitāb*, this philosophy produced in the figures of such men as Abū Ḥātim al-Rāzī, Abū Sulaymān al-Sijistānī, Ḥamīd al-Dīn al-Kirmānī, Nāṣir-i Khusraw, many of whom wrote in Persian as well as in Arabic, a philosophy which vied with the better-known Peripatetic school. The *Rasā'il* of the Ikhwān al-Ṣafā', a collection which appeared in Iraq in the 4th/10th century and which possesses a strong Pythagorean tendency, is also related to this important school. Ismā'īlī philosophy continued even after the eclipse of the Fāṭimids, producing works of significance in Persia and Yemen and finally India, where Ismā'īlism, this important branch of Shī'ite Islam, found its final intellectual home.[33]

In the 6th/12th century, while Avicennan philosophy was being criticized by the theologians, a new intellectual perspective was being established by Shaykh al-ishrāq Shihāb al-Dīn Suhrawardī, who, because he was not directly translated into Latin, is not well known in the West. Suhrawardī, who claimed to be the resurrector of the perennial philosophy which had existed in both ancient Greece and Persia, established the School of Illumination (*al-ishrāq*), for which knowledge is derived from light and indeed the very substance of the Universe is ultimately degrees of light and shadow.[34] This school, elucidated and explained by Muḥammad Shams al-Dīn Shahrazūrī and Quṭb al-Dīn Shīrāzī in the 7th/13th century, has also had many exponents and followers during later centuries, especially in Persia but also among the Muslims of the Indian subcontinent.

During later centuries, while in most of the Arab world philosophy as a distinct discipline became integrated into either Sufism in its intellectual aspect or philosophical theology (*kalām*), in Persia and the adjacent areas including not only India but also Iraq and Turkey, various schools of philosophy continued to flourish. At the same time, the different intellectual disciplines, such as Peripatetic philosophy, the School of Illumination, theology and Sufi metaphysics were drawing closer together. The ground was thus prepared for the already-mentioned revival of Islamic philosophy in the Safavid period in Persia with Mīr Dāmād, the founder of the 'School of Isfahan', and especially Ṣadr al-Dīn Shīrāzī, his student, who is perhaps the greatest of the later Islamic metaphysicians.[35] Even through the gradual decay of the teaching of the 'intellectual sciences' in the *madrasahs*, this later school associated with the name of Ṣadr al-Dīn Shīrāzī, as well as those of Ibn Sīnā, Suhrawardī, Ibn 'Arabī and their commentators, continued to be taught and to produce noteworthy figures, some of whom have survived to the present day.[36]

The Islamic philosophical tradition, although of great diversity and richness, is characterized by certain features which are of special significance both for its understanding and for an appraisal of its import for the world at large. This philosophy breathes in a religious universe in which a revealed book and prophecy dominate the horizon. It is, therefore, 'prophetic philosophy', whatever might be the subject with which it is concerned. Moreover, it is a philosophy which, in conformity with the Islamic perspective, is based upon the intellect as a supernaturally natural faculty within man which is a sacrament and which, if used correctly, leads to the same truths as revealed through prophecy. It is therefore concerned most of all with the One who dominates the whole message of Islam.[37] This philosophy is also concerned with the basic issues of the harmony between reason and revelation and of providing, within the context of a religious universe dominated by monotheism, a metaphysics centered around the supreme doctrine of the One. It is also concerned with providing keys for the understanding of the manifold in relation to the One. It is therefore rich, not only in religious and ethical philosophy, but also in philosophies of nature and mathematics as well as of art. In fact, as far as the Islamic sciences are concerned, they were cultivated in the bosom of Islamic philosophy and almost always by men who were not only scientists but also philosophers.

Islamic philosophical texts provide, not only a study of metaphysics and logic, but a philosophy of nature. This provides the key for the understanding of both physical nature and the soul. Although the Peripatetics treat the soul as a part of natural philosophy, as seen in Ibn Sīnā's *Kitāb al-shifā'* and the Illuminationists as part of metaphysics (*ilāhiyyāt* rather than natural philosophy *ṭabī'iyyāt*), there is no doubt that both schools, as well as those of the Ismā'īlīs and of Ṣadr al-Dīn Shīrāzī and his followers, all provide a general matrix wherein individual sciences pertaining to both the world of nature without and the world of the soul within can be studied in the light of the principles which belong to metaphysics, as traditionally understood, and which relate the many to the One; that is to say, the points on the periphery of cosmic existence to the Divine Center.

A science which found special favor with the Muslims, and which accorded well with the unitarian, aniconic and 'abstract' character of Islamic thought, was mathematics, in which the accomplishments of the Islamic sciences were many.[38] The Muslims integrated Greek and Indian mathematics, and upon that basis continued the development of geometry, formulated algebra, developed plain and spherical trigonometry and number theory, expanding the definition of numbers to include irrationals. They received the Sanskrit numerals and developed them into the form that we now know as Arabic numerals, which revolutionized reckoning in medieval Europe. The name of the mathematician, al-Khwārazmī, whose work on arithmetic first introduced these numerals into the West, entered into European tongues as *algorism*, while the treatise on algebra by Khayyām, along with several other Arabic works on the subject, made this science, which still preserves its Arabic name, known to the West in a highly developed form. The trigonometric functions also still bear in their very names the traces of their Arabic origin. Furthermore the Muslims developed computation theory and even made computation machines, as seen in the work of Ghiyāth al-Dīn Jamshīd Kāshānī, who also discovered decimal fractions. Muslim mathematicians were, moreover, interested in problems which concerned the foundations of mathematics, as seen in their study of the theory of parallel lines and the hypotheses underlying Euclidian geometry.

In astronomy, Muslims began their activities early, encouraged by a practical concern to locate the direction of the *qiblah* and calculate the time for the daily prayers, as well as for more 'theoretical' and philosophical considerations. They first mastered the Indian and Iranian works of astronomy before becoming acquainted with Ptolemy, whose *Almagest* still bears, in the very name by which it is known in Western languages, the stamp of the influence of Islamic astronomy upon the West. The Muslim astronomers synthesized these schools upon the basis of which they established Islamic astronomy, whose distinct features can be seen already in the 3rd/9th century. By the time al-Bīrūnī wrote his *Mas'ūdic Canon* a century later, Islamic astronomy was the most complete and perfected astronomical science known anywhere in the world at that time.

The Muslims were interested in both observational and mathematical astronomy. They compiled numerous tables, called *zīj*, based on their observations, and discovered new stars, some of which still bear Arabic names. They founded the first fully-fledged observatory in Maraghah and made numerous instruments for observation, of which the astrolabe, that remarkable synthesis of science and art, is perhaps the one best known in the West. Parallel with observation of the heavens, they also refined mathematical astronomy, beginning a criticism of Ptolemaic astronomy in both Persia and Spain. While the anti-Ptolemaic astronomy of Spain was mostly philosophical, that of Persia, associated with Maraghah and the figures of Naṣīr al-Dīn Ṭūsī and Quṭb al-Dīn Shīrāzī, was combined with a mathematical study of the motion of two vectors (to use the modern terminology)[39] and led to new planetary models for Mercury and the Moon, which somehow reached the Poland of Copernicus and were most likely known by him.

In physics, the Muslim contribution is to be seen in three distinct domains: in the study of the nature of matter, of projectile motion and optics. For over a millennium, Muslim scientists, philosophers, theologians and even Sufis have studied and discussed the nature of matter, time, space and motion. They have developed numerous 'philosophies of nature', ranging from the atomism of the theologians and Muḥammad ibn Zakariyyā' al-Rāzī[40] to the physics of light of Suhrawardī and the School of Illumination. In the study of motion, such figures as Ibn Sīnā, al-Bīrūnī, Abu'l-Barakāt al-Baghdādī and Ibn Bājjah criticized prevalent Aristotelian concepts and developed ideas in mechanics and dynamics, which are of much importance for the history of physics in general and whose effect is to be seen, not only in the physics developed by Latin Scholastics, but even in the early work of Galileo.[41] As for optics, perhaps the greatest Islamic physicist, Ibn al-Haytham, placed this discipline upon a new foundation in his *Optics*, in which he used the experimental method in its contemporary sense to study the problem of vision, the *camera obscura*, reflection and refraction, etc., and made many basic discoveries in the field of the study of light. Upon the foundation of his work, some two centuries later Quṭb al-Dīn Shīrāzī and Kamāl al-Dīn Fārsī provided the first correct explanation of the phenomenon of the rainbow, which had preoccupied the men of science since antiquity.

The Muslims also showed interest in mechanical devices, which they treated as a branch of applied mathematics. In fact, most of the early masters of the subject, such as the Banū Mūsā and Ibn al-Haytham, were mathematicians. In such works, of which the most elaborate is the *Treatise on Automata* of al-Jazarī, many machines are described, some of which are quite complicated. It is important to realize, however, that while Muslims had developed many forms of technology of quite a refined nature but always closely related to the forces and rhythms of nature, they developed these complicated machines, which among the artifacts of Islamic civilizations most resemble products of modern technology, for amusement and play rather than for economic production.

As far as medicine and pharmacology are concerned, in these and related fields the achievements of Islamic science were no less startling than in mathematics and astronomy. Again making use of Greek as well as Iranian and Indian sources, the Muslim integrated the Hippocratic and Galenic traditions with Iranian and Indian elements to create a distinct school of medicine which survives as a living school to this day in certain parts of Asia. The early masters of this art, such as Rāzī, became as well known in Europe and Hindu India as in the Islamic world itself, while Ibn Sīnā, the author of the *Canon of Medicine*,[42] became known as the 'Prince of Physicians' in the West and in certain areas has given his name in its common Persian form of Bū 'Alī to Islamic medicine itself.[43] Islamic medicine combined a philosophical approach based on the cosmological principles which dominate the human body considered as microcosm, with the clinical and observational approaches. Muslim physicians emphasized preventive medicine, especially diet, and made an extensive study of the rapport between psychological and physical health. But they also developed surgery, as seen in the works of the Spanish master, Ibn Zuhr, and perfected many surgical instruments. Besides discovering the causes and distinguishing many diseases, such as measles, meningitis and whooping cough, Muslim physicians also dealt with physiology and anatomy, Ibn Nafīs having discovered the minor circulation of the blood long before Michael Servetus and William Harvey.

The cultivation of Islamic medicine has been inseparable from that of pharmacology which was usually studied by the same figures. Upon the basis of Dioscorides and the extensive pharmacological knowledge of the Iranians and Indians, Muslims developed pharmacopoeias which reflected extensive knowledge of both mineral and herbal drugs. As far as herbs were concerned, they were also studied from the more botanical point of view, especially in Spain, where the study of the plant world reached its peak with al-Ghāfiqī and Ibn al-Bayṭār. The study of plants, especially in relation to their medicinal properties, was one of the fields of Islamic science in which notable work continued in both Persia and Muslim India after the period of gradual decline of activity in the other Islamic sciences.

The study of botany by Muslims was also carried out in the context of their study of natural history and geography, which were deeply impregnated by the Quranic idea of studying the wonders of creation as signs (*āyāt*) of God and His wisdom. As a result of the possibilities of travel and the exchange of ideas throughout the Islamic world, to which the annual pilgrimage to Makkah contributed greatly, Muslim natural historians and geographers were able to assemble knowledge of a very wide range of flora and fauna, from those native to China to those of Western Europe. Al-Mas'ūdī, often called the 'Arab Pliny', composed works on natural history which were related to those of the Greeks but of a more comprehensive nature and deeply integrated into the religious world-view of Islam. As for geography, Muslims such as al-Idrīsī produced the first medieval maps and Muslims gained detailed geographical knowledge of such areas as the Indian Ocean. Paradoxically enough, it was Muslim geographers and sailors who led Europeans around the Cape of Good Hope to India, which in turn facilitated the destruction by Portuguese and later other European navigators of the trade routes that had been dominated by Muslims until the 16th century. This in turn prepared the ground for the colonization of much of the Islamic world in the centuries which followed.

No account of the Islamic sciences would be complete without reference to what the Muslims called 'the hidden sciences' (*al-'ulūm al-gharībah*) comprising such subjects as alchemy, physiognomy, geomancy and other disciplines which have been relegated to the category of pseudo-sciences as a result of the symbolic language which they employ and the cosmological principles upon which they are based having been forgotten. As far as Islamic alchemy is concerned, it reached its peak early in Islamic history with Jābir ibn Ḥayyān in the 2nd/8th century and continued as a long tradition embracing a range of meanings from spiritual psychology and cosmology to medicine and a symbolic science of materials. From the cadaver of spiritual alchemy was also born that science of material substances which is called chemistry today.[45] The word 'alchemy' itself, and the spread of alchemical ideas in the Occident, attest to the great influence and significance of the Islamic alchemical tradition in the West as well as within the Islamic world itself, while many of the instruments still used in the chemistry laboratory bear witness to the roots of modern chemistry in that aspect of medieval alchemy which had relinquished the internal task of transmuting the lead of the soul into the gold of the Spirit in favour of an external project for manufacturing physical gold.

From the point of view of the global history of science, the Islamic sciences stood for some seven centuries as the most developed among the sciences cultivated in the different civilizations. They influenced the sciences of Hindu India and China as well as those of the West. They were only eclipsed in the West with the advent of the Renaissance and the Scientific Revolution, which made use of the material of Islamic science but within a world-view diametrically opposed to that of Islam. The important question is not why Islam did not continue to devote its intellectual energies to the cultivation of an ever-changing science of nature divorced from higher orders of knowledge, as has happened in the West since the 17th century.[46] The basic fact to note is that Islam was able to create an educational system and a scientific tradition which produced knowledge of the world of nature and mathematics but within a world-view dominated by the Transcendent and imbued with the fragrance of the Divine Presence as contained in the Quranic revelation. In a world on the verge of destruction as a result of the application of a science which is both divorced from knowledge of a higher order and blind to the unity which pervades, not only nature, but all orders of reality leading to the One, Islamic science possesses a message that is of more than historical interest. This science is a reminder to contemporary man, whether he be Muslim or non-Muslim, that besides modern science, which is legitimate only if kept within the confines of its own limitations, there are other sciences of nature which unveil dimensions and aspects of nature and man's own being that have become hidden in the modern world but for which contemporary man yearns because of what by his essential nature he always truly is no matter where or when he happens to live.

The nature of this reality, which man is in his essence, is elucidated by traditional Islamic philosophy, for that is wedded at once to intellect and revelation and is related to God, the cosmos and human society. Islamic philosophy is one of the richest treasures of traditional wisdom that have survived to this day and it stands at the center of the battle which traditional Islam must wage on the intellectual front in the modern world. Likewise, the educational system, which over the centuries produced those philosophers and scientists as well as the jurists, the men of letters and the experts in other fields of knowledge, must remain as the basis upon which all attempts made in the field of education to accommodate conditions created by the encounter of Islam with the modern world should be carried out. The traditional educational institutions, as well as traditional Islamic philosophy and science, in addition to being glories of classical Islamic civilization, are of the utmost significance in the whole question of the encounter of traditional Islam with modernism.

It must be remembered that in them are embedded those perennial values and doctrinal truths which alone can aid contemporary Muslims in preserving their Islamicity in the face of the challenges posed by a world whose general world-view, both in terms of philosophy and of science, is based on forgetfulness of the One and the denial of the relevance of the Transcendent.

Notes

1. In the field of the Islamic sciences, despite thousands of articles and books in different languages, so many works remain to be studied and analyzed that practically every year there are major new discoveries. Although no exhaustive treatment of present-day knowledge of the Islamic sciences is available, as one would find for Western science or even Chinese science (thanks to the pioneering work of J. Needham

and his collaborators), there are several works which provide a panoramic view of the field. As far as general works on the Islamic sciences are concerned, see A. Mieli, *La Science arabe et son rôle dans l'évolution scientifique mondiale*, Leiden, 1966; M. Ullmann, *Die Natur-und Geheimwissenschaften im Islam*, Leiden, 1972; J. Vernet, *Der Islam im Europa*, Bussum, 1973; F.E. Peters, *Allah's Commonwealth*, New York, 1973; J.M. Millás Vallicrosa, *Nuevos estudios sobre historia de la ciencia española*, Barcelona, 1960; W. Hartner, *Oriens-Occidens*, Hildesheim, 1970; S.H. Nasr, *Science and Civilization in Islam*, and *ibid.*, *Islamic Science: An Illustrated Study*.

As for works in particular fields see E.G. Browne, *Arabian Medicine*, Cambridge, 1921; D.E.H. Campbell, *Arabian Medicine and Its Influence on the Middle Ages*, 2 vols., London, 1926; C. Elgood, *A Medical History of Persia and the Eastern Caliphate*, Cambridge, 1951; M. Clagett, *The Science of Mechanics in the Middle Ages*, Madison, 1964; E.S. Kennedy, *A Survey of Islamic Astronomical Tables*, Philadelphia, 1956; Nallino, C.A., *Raccoltá di scritti editi e inediti*, vol. 5, Rome, 1948; D. Pingree, *The Thousands of Abū Ma'shar*, London, 1968; A.M. Sayili, *The Observatory in Islam*, Ankara, 1960; H. Suter, *Die Mathematiker und Astronomen der Araber und ihrer Werke*, Ann Arbor, 1963; A.P. Yuschkewitsch, *Geschichte der Mathematik im Mittelalter*, Leipzig, 1964; A.S. Saidan, *The Arithmetic of Al-Uqlīdisī*, Boston, 1978, Daffa', A., *The Muslim Contribution to Mathematics*, London, 1977; P. Kraus, *Jābir ibn Ḥayyān*, 2 vols., Cairo, 1942–43; J. Ruska, *Tabula Smaragdina*, Heidelberg, 1926; and S.B. Omar, *Ibn al-Haytham's Optics*, Minneapolis, 1977.

Such general works on the history of science as G. Sarton, *An Introduction to the History of Science*, 3 vols. Baltimore, 1927–48; and Ch. Gillespie (ed.), *Dictionary of Scientific Biography*, as well as studies on Arabic and Persian manuscripts, especially F. Sezgin, *Geschichte der arabischen Schrifttums*, Leiden, 1970 on, likewise contain a wealth of information on the Islamic sciences. The pioneering work of Sarton still remains of great value for the general student of the subject and has in fact never been replaced by a more up to date work of the same scope.

As for education, there is even less available of a systematic nature which would consider the philosophy of education, its history, content of syllabi, etc. for the whole of the Islamic world. Among works which are available see, besides the already cited works, A.L. Tibawi, *Islamic Education: Its Traditions and Modernization into the Arab National Systems*, London, 1972; *ibid.*, *Arabic and Islamic Garland*, London, 1977; B. Dodge, *Muslim Education in Medieval Times*, Washington, 1962; al-Zarnūjī, *Ta'līm al-muta'allim*, trans. G.E. von Grunebaum and T.M. Abel, New York, 1974. See also the series on Muslim education edited by S.A. Ashraf and printed in London, of which several volumes have appeared since 1978.

For a more complete bibliography containing works in European languages on both science and education see S.H. Nasr, *An Annotated*

Bibliography of Islamic Science, Tehran, 1975–77, of which only two of seven projected volumes have been published so far.

2. The many names of the Quran, like those of the Prophet, contain in themselves a science which, if studied carefully, reveals the many facets of that reality to which the names related.
3. See F. Rosenthal, *Knowledge Triumphant, The Concept of Knowledge in Medieval Islam*, Leiden, 1970, where this veritable celebration of knowledge in Islam is recorded in detail.
4. See our *Knowledge and the Sacred*, where this theme has been treated extensively on a global scale and not limited to the case of the Islamic tradition.
5. See F. Schuon, *From the Divine to the Human*, trans. G. Polit and D. Lambert, Bloomington (Ind.), 1982; and also Schuon, *Logic and Transcendence*, trans. P. Townsend, New York, 1975.
6. To this day education in official circles in most of the Arab world is called *al-ta'līm wa'l-tarbiyah*, while in Persia, the Persian counterpart of this term, namely *Āmūzish wa parwarish*, has been used as the name for the ministry of education itself.
7. چو دزدی با چراغ آید گزیده‌تر برد کالا
8. The importance of this period in introducing the child to oral traditions existing within Islamic society was immense. Much of this oral tradition served later in life as a basis for the highest forms of metaphysical knowledge for those qualified to master such knowledge.
9. Before modern times this was true of most Islamic languages, the alphabets of which were drawn either from Arabic directly or from Persian, whose own alphabet is the same as that of Arabic, except for the addition of four letters.
10. There are several miniatures of student scenes in famous medieval Islamic universities showing female students and also references to women in the literature.
11. As mentioned by I. Illich in his many studies on education, including *De-Schooling Society*, New York, 1971, which contains many ideas similar to the traditional Islamic philosophy of education. In traditional society a book was not confined only to the reader but usually encompassed many people through the fact that, in most cases, while one person read aloud many listened. This practice is still to be seen in certain parts of the Islamic world, such as Persia, where many people who have never had a formal education know not only verses of the Quran but also poems from Firdawsī's *Shāh-nāmah* or Sa'dī's *Gulistān* as a result of listening to traditional story-tellers, who often actually recite stories and poems for them from the greatest literary masterpieces of the language.
12. It has of course always been known that such academic terms as 'chair' in English and *licence* in French are direct translations of Arabic terms (*al-kursī* and *ijāzah*, respectively), but in earlier works on the medieval European universities, such as the classical opus of H. Rashdall, *The Universities of Europe in the Middle Ages*, Oxford, 1895, this influence

has usually been played down. The full import of this influence is traced with great care and scholarship by G. Makdisi in his recent work, *The Rise of Colleges: Institutions of Learning in Islam and the West*, N.Y., 1981.

13. See the study of B. Dodge, *Al-Azhar; a Millennium of Muslim Learning*, Washington, 1961, which provides a detailed study of the history and significance of this venerable institution.
14. On this important but little studied *madrasah* see F. Jamali, 'The Theological Colleges of Najaf', *Muslim World*, vol. 50, 1960, pp. 15–22.
15. See T. Burckhardt, 'The Role of Fine Arts in Muslim Education', in Nasr (ed.), *Philosophy, Literature and Fine Arts*, Sevenoaks (Kent), 1982, pp. 41–48.
16. On this division see our *Science and Civilization in Islam*, pp. 59–64.
17. To this day, in fact, no *madrasah* in the Islamic world has been resuscitated successfully as far as encounters with modern forms and modes of knowledge are concerned, despite many different types of experiments carried out in Morocco, Tunisia, Egypt, India, etc. The traditional and modern educational systems have become contending and competing forces in most of the Islamic world.
18. See Abū Bakr al-Akhawaynī al-Bukhārī, *Hidāyat al-muta'allimīn*, ed. J. Matini, Meshed, 1965, which concerns medical education, whose origin can be traced to Rāzī and the hospital educational system of the 4th/10th century.
19. On the observatory as a scientific and educational institution see A. Sayili, *The Observatory in Islam*.
20. See our *Knowledge and the Sacred*, chapter 4.
21. On Sufi training of the soul see J. Nurbakhsh, *What the Sufis Say*, New York, 1980, part I.
22. The arts and the crafts are the same in Islam and no distinction of a fundamental nature can be made in the context of Islamic civilization between what are called the major and minor arts in the West.
23. This could in fact be said of all traditional art but is especially evident in Islamic art, with its mathematical clarity and harmony. See A.K. Coomaraswamy, *Christian and Oriental Philosophy of Art*, New York, 1956; and T. Burckhardt, *op. cit.*

    See also our *Knowledge and the Sacred*, Chapter 8, and our *Islamic Art and Spirituality*.
24. The reason for the spread of this learning eastward is itself a fascinating chapter of cultural history related to the separation of the eastern Christian churches from Constantinople. See the still valuable works of O. de Lacy O'Leary, *How Greek Science passed to the Arabs*, London, 1949; and M. Meyerhoff, *Von Alexandrien nach Baghdad*, Berlin, 1930.
25. On the significance of the school of Jundishapur built by the Sassanid king Shāpūr I on the model of the school of Antioch see, M. Mohammadi, 'The University of Jundishapur', *Regional Cultural Institute* (Tehran), vol. 2, 1969, pp. 152–166.

26. These Sabaeans are not to be confused with the present-day Sabaeans of Iraq and southern Iran. See J. Pedersen, 'The Sabians', in *A Volume of Oriental Studies presented to E.G. Browne*, ed. T.W. Arnold and R.A. Nicholson, Cambridge, 1922, pp. 383–391; and C. Buck, 'The Identity of the Ṣābi'ūn; An Historical Quest', *Muslim World*, vol. LXXIV, no. 3–4, July to October 1984, pp. 172–186, where the wide legal meaning of *Ṣābi'ūn* is emphasized. Buck writes, 'Exactly because it was imprecise, the word *Ṣābi'ūn* functioned as a term of great legal importance by contributing to an attitude of toleration towards minority religions under Muslim rule' (p. 186).
27. On the 'Islamic nature' of the Islamic sciences see our *Science and Civilization in Islam*, introduction; also our *An Introduction to Islamic Cosmological Doctrines*, prolegomena.
28. On Greek works in Arabic see M. Steinschneider, *Die arabischen Übersetzungen ans dem Griechischen*, Graz, 1960; F. Rosenthal, *The Classical Heritage in Islam*, trans. E. and J. Marmonstein, Berkeley, 1975; and A. Badawi, *La transmission de la philosophie grecque au monde arabe*, Paris 1968. See also F. Sezgin, *Geschichte*, where numerous references are made to Arabic translations of Greek texts.
29. It must be remembered that when the works of the Greek authorities, such as Aristotle, were being translated into Arabic, there was still a living oral tradition known to the translators who made use of the 'unwritten' text as well as the written one in their translations. Arabic translations of Greek texts, especially in philosophy, are therefore in a sense closer to the original than those made in modern European languages directly from the Greek but without a continuity of worldview and an oral tradition accompanying the written word. In any case, far from being less perfect renderings of the Greek originals, Arabic texts provide a precious document for the knowledge of antiquity independent of that type of interpretation in the modern world which is colored by Renaissance humanism and 17th-century irrationalism.
30. See S.H. Nasr, 'The Role and Meaning of Philosophy in Islam', *Studia Islamica*, vol. XXXVII, 1973, pp. 57–80.
31. On Ibn Sīnā and the philosopher-scientists in Islam see our *Three Muslim Sages*, chapter 1.
32. Most of the Western works on Islamic philosophy include only this school and even in this case limit their discussions to Ibn Rushd, as if Islamic philosophy had ceased to exist after him. The only history of Islamic philosophy which does justice to the much richer intellectual life of Islam are M.M. Sharif (ed.), *A History of Muslim Philosophy*, 2 vols., Wiesbaden, 1963–66, and H. Corbin (with the collaboration of S.H. Nasr and O. Yahya), *Histoire de la philosophie islamique*, vol. I, Paris, 1964. This volume covers only the period up to the death of Ibn Rushd, but Corbin completed the later periods of this history in 'Histoire de la philosophie', in *Encyclopedie de la Pléiade*, Paris, 1974. See also the other major studies of Corbin, such as *En Islam iranien*, 4 vols., Paris 1971–72; and his *La Philosophie iranienne islamique*, Paris, 1981. The work of Corbin to turn the attention of the Western

world to the integral tradition of Islamic philosophy has been followed by S.H. Nasr, T. Izutsu, M. Mohaghegh and several other scholars.

On Islamic philosophy see also M. Fakhry, *A History of Islamic Philosophy*, New York, 1970. An extensive bibliography on Ibn Sīnā and general works on Islamic philosophy is found in Nasr, *An Introduction to Islamic Cosmological Doctrines*.

33. The history of this school, like much of Islamic philosophy, remains full of unknown elements, with many texts remaining to be studied and analyzed. For a summary of what is known of the history of this school see Corbin, *Histoire . . .*, pp. 118–151.
34. On Suhrawardī see Nasr, *Three Muslim Sages*, chapter 2; Corbin, *En Islam iranien*, vol. II.
35. On these figures see Corbin, *En Islam iranien*, vol. IV: the essays by Nasr in Sharif, *op. cit.*, vol. II; and S.H. Nasr, *Ṣadr al-Dīn Shīrāzī and His Transcendent Theosophy*.
36. See our 'The Influence of Traditional Islamic Thought Upon Contemporary Muslim Intellectual Life', in R. Klibansky (ed.), *Contemporary Philosophy*, Florence, 1971, pp. 578–583.
37. See F. Copleston, *Religion and the One*, New York, 1982, chapter 5, where a leading Catholic historian of Western philosophy looks upon the significance of this problem for Islamic thought in comparison with both Eastern traditions and Western thought.
38. For a general account of the contribution of Muslims to mathematics and astronomy see E.S. Kennedy, 'The Arab Heritage in the Exact Sciences', *al-Abḥāth*, vol. XXIII, 1970, pp. 327–344; and A.I. Sabra, 'The Scientific Enterprise', in B. Lewis (ed.), *The World of Islam*, London, 1976, pp. 181–200.
39. This model has been called the 'Ṭūsī couple' by its modern discoverer E.S. Kennedy. See his, 'Late Medieval Planetary Theory', *Isis*, vol. 57, part 3, 1966, pp. 365–378.
40. On Islamic atomism see the still valuable work of S. Pines, *Beiträge zur islamischen Atomenlehre*, Berlin, 1936.
41. See S. Pines, *Nouvelles études sur Awḥad al-Zamān Abu'l – Barakāt al-Baghdādī*, Paris, 1955; Pines, 'What was Original in Arabic Science?' in A.C. Crombie (ed.), *Scientific Change*, New York, 1963, pp. 181–205. See also D.R. Hill, *The Book of Ingenious Devices by the Banu (Sons of) Musa bin Shakir*, Boston, 1979, for an analysis of a major text on mechanics which, like al-Jazarī's better known work (also translated by Hill [Al-Jazarī: *The Book of Knowledge of Ingenious Mechanical Devices*, Boston, 1974], touches upon certain problems of physics, although the discipline of mechanics (*'ilm al-ḥiyal*) belongs to another category in the Islamic classification of the sciences.
42. This work is probably the most influential single book in the history of medicine.
43. On the general survey of Islamic medicine and pharmacology see M. Ullmann, *Islamic Medicine*, Edinburgh, 1978.
44. For a historical account of the 'occult sciences' see M. Ullmann, *Die*

Natur-und Geheimwissenschaften im Islam. But the significance of these sciences, especially alchemy, cannot be discovered save in the light of the metaphysical and cosmological principles of which alchemy is a particular application. See T. Burckhardt, *Alchemy, Science of the Cosmos, Science of the Soul*, trans. W. Stoddart, Baltimore, 1971; and E. Zolla, *Le meraviglie della natura. Introduzione all' alchimia*, Milan, 1975.

45. See 'From the Alchemy of Jabir to the Chemistry of Razi', in our *Islamic Life and Thought*, Albany (N.Y.), 1981, pp. 120–123.
46. In fact no traditional civilization has ever sacrificed its vision of the Immutable for an ever-changing and accumulative science of nature which continues at the expense of the forgetting of that *scientia sacra* that is rooted in the very substance of intelligence.

Chapter Nine

The Islamic Philosophers' Views on Education

*Whoever wishes to perfect himself as a human being [*insānīya*] and reach the rank [*amr*] which is meant by 'human nature' in order to integrate his self [*li-yatimma ḍātahu*] and have the same preferences and intentions as those of the philosophers, let him acquire these two arts [*ṣinā'atain*]. I mean the theoretical and practical parts of philosophy; as a result, there will accrue to him the essential natures of things [*ḥaqā'iq al-umūr*] by means of the theoretical part, and good deeds by means of the practical part.**

(Ibn Miskawayh, *Tartīb al-sa'ādah*.)

The crisis of the contemporary Islamic world has turned many Muslim scholars to the question of education and initiated a re-examination of the traditional Islamic educational system so neglected during the past century in most Islamic countries. The principles underlying Islamic education in turn cannot be fully

*Trans. by D. Gutas in 'Paul the Persian on the Classification of the Parts of Aristotle's Philosophy: a Milestone between Alexandria and Baghdad', *Der Islam*, Band 60, Heft 2, 1983, p. 232.

understood without an appreciation of the views of Islamic philosophers concerning all aspects of education, ranging from its goal to its content and from its curriculum to its method. In recent years, however, the significance of Islamic philosophy has often been neglected and even its Islamic character denied by many of those 'fundamentalists' who, in the name of an Islam rationalistically interpreted, outwardly oppose things Western while at the same time allowing modern ideas to fill the vacuum created in their mind and soul as a result of the rejection of the Islamic intellectual tradition.

At this time, a kind of scientism has crept into the world-view of many 'fundamentalists' and 'revivalists',[1] which causes them to praise Islamic science and the men of learning who produced it but, ironically, the philosophers who formulated the world-view upon which this much praised Islamic science is based come in for attack from the same quarter. It must therefore be stated at the outset that Islamic philosophy as it developed over the centuries is Islamic in character and is an integral part of the Islamic intellectual tradition.[2] Moreover, it was the educational system which trained the Islamic philosophers that also produced the Islamic scientists; there existed a single educational system which made possible the appearance of the Muslim philosopher-scientists over the ages, of men who were at once philosophers and masters of some field of science.[3] Finally, the views of these philosopher-scientists concerning education are essential in making possible today the re-establishment of an educational system which would be at once Islamic and of a veritable intellectual character. If there is to be once again an educational system to produce an al-Bīrūnī or an Ibn Sīnā, it must at least take seriously the views which they held concerning education. For centuries Islam produced men who were at once the most devout Muslims and the foremost thinkers in various intellectual disciplines. Present-day Muslims seeking to recreate an authentic Islamic education system cannot but take into consideration the views of such men concerning the content, goal, methods and meaning of education.

Islamic philosophy is not of course confined to a single school, nor is it simply the sum of the views of individual philosophers following one after another as one finds in post-medieval European philosophy. Although there are individuals who stand out as solitary figures in the history of Islamic thought, Islamic philosophy consists essentially of perspectives or schools which have survived over the ages. To grasp in a synoptic fashion the views of the Islamic philosophers concerning education, it is necessary to turn to outstanding representatives at each school[4], while to survey the field completely would require the examination of each school as it has developed over the centuries. For the purpose of the present essay, therefore, we have chosen the Ikhwān al-Ṣafā', Ibn Sīnā, Suhrawardī and Mullā Ṣadrā, representing the Ismā'īlī and Hermetic – Pythagorean, Peripatetic (*mashshā'ī*), Illuminationist (*ishrāqī*) schools and the 'transcendent theosophy' (*al-ḥikmah al-muta'āliyah*), respectively.

Although the Ikhwān al-Ṣafā' came to be associated later with Shi'ism in general and Ismā'ilism in particular,[5] their *Rasā'il* came to be read by a wide circle of Islamic scholars and thinkers, both Sunni and Shi'ite, and including such celebrated Sunni theologians as al-Ghazzālī. The *Rasā'il*, while being a synthesis of Shi'ite learning presented in an encyclopedic fashion, possessed an educational impact that went beyond the confines of a particular school to touch the whole of the Islamic community.Likewise, while its perspective, in which Neoplatonic, Hermetic and Neopythagorean elements were integrated into Islamic esotericism, remained closely wedded to Ismā'īlī philosophy, its philosophical influence was felt widely among many different figures in later periods of Islamic history. It is enough to read the pages of the *Asfār* of Mullā Ṣadrā to realize how powerful indeed were the echoes of the *Rasā'il* some seven centuries later.

The purpose of the Ikhwān al-Ṣafā' in composing the *Rasā'il* was itself educational and the questions of education, its goal, stages, content, methods and other elements are to be found throughout the fifty-one treaties which comprise it.[6] It is, however, especially in the seventh treatise of the first volume, entitled *Fi'l-ṣanā'i' al-'ilmiyyah* (the second *Fi'l-'ilm wa'l-ma'lūm wa'l-ta'allum wa'l-ta'līm*: 'On Knowledge, the Known Teaching and Learning)', that they deal with education, while in the ninth treatise, called *Fī bayān al-akhlāq wa asbāb ikhtilāfiha . . .* ('Concerning the Description of Ethics and the Cause of Differences among its Schools . . .'), they deal with the influence of the environment, the home and the school, professors and other pertinent factors bearing upon the education of students.[7] According to the Ikhwān, the soul is a 'spiritual, celestial, luminous, living and knowing substance potentially and active by nature.'[8] The goal of education is to enable the soul to actualize these potential possibilities, thereby perfecting it and preparing it for eternal life.[9] Knowledge acquired through education is in fact the ultimate nourishment which sustains man's immortal soul, while actualization of what is potential in the soul is existence (*wujūd*) itself, the mode of existence which does not perish with death.

This process of actualization is composed of stages, of which the most important are *tahdhīb* (refinement), *tāṭhīr* (purification), *tatmīm* (completion) and *takmīl* (perfection).[10] These stages are moral as well as propedeutic; in fact the two are never separated in the view of the Ikhwān, who reassert the universal Islamic principle stated in so many *ḥadīths* to the effect that the gaining of theoretical knowledge and the purification of the soul have to be combined in order for 'science', or *'ilm*, to become rooted in the soul, transform its substance and embellish it in such a way that it will be worthy of eternal life in the Divine Presence.

The Ikhwān also consider the stages of life in which education has to be imparted to body, mind and soul. From birth to the age of four, the senses and instincts are to be strengthened. From the age of four through fifteen, the basic skills of reading, writing, mathematics etc. are to be mastered in school (*maktab*) with the help of a teacher (*mu'allim*) through the process of dictation (*imlā'*). After this age, the mental powers become more mature and the student begins to learn from a master (*ustād*) through the use of the intellect (*'aql*) by means of demonstration (*burhān*) and also through inspiration (*ilhām*).

There is a hierarchy of knowledge as there is a hierarchy of teachers. Education is based on a hierarchy which leads from the exoteric sciences to the esoteric through the instruction imparted by teachers who themselves stand in a hierarchy ranging from the *mustajīb* to the *ḥujjah* and the *imām*, the latter possessing perfect knowledge of both the exoteric and the esoteric orders.[11] The goal of education is to perfect and actualize all the possibilities of the human soul leading finally to that supreme knowledge of the Divinity which is the goal of human life. While education prepares man for felicity in this life, its ultimate goal is the abode of permanence and all education points to the permanent world of eternity (*al-ākhirah*) beyond the transient vacillations of this world of change. According to the Ikhwān, the ultimate goal of education, even while one is mastering the sciences of nature, is not to dominate the world and gain external power, but to dominate oneself in such a manner as to be able to go beyond the world of change into the abode of eternity, and to do so embellished with the ornament of knowledge combined with virtue which alone are worthy of the world into which the soul of the faithful hopes to enter at the end of this earthly journey.

Among the well-known Muslim philosophers, the first to have treated the question of education in a substantial manner was Ibn Sīnā, the foremost among the Muslim philosopher-scientists, who is the source and origin of so many basic aspects of traditional Islamic thought.[12] He deals specifically with the question of education in his *Tadbīr al-manāzil*, while also referring to this subject in several passages of the logic of the *Shifā'*, *Risālat al-siyāsah* and the *Canon*. Of course, his discussion of the nature of man and his entelechy in several of his philosophical works should also be considered as being related to the subject of education in the most general sense of the term for, whenever Ibn Sīnā deals with man, he also concerns himself with his final end and the means whereby man can attain perfection, the process of the attainment of this perfection being nothing other than education in its most universal sense.

For Ibn Sīnā, education begins at the moment of birth – and even before: at the moment that a man chooses a mate whose moral and intellectual character will deeply affect the child who is yet to be born. He also emphasizes the role of the wife and mother in the bringing up of the children and her share in their earliest education. The child is to be given discipline from the time of breast-feeding, and in fact the first steps in his learning of manners and morals, as well as the building up of character (*ta'dīb*), are to be taken in this earliest stage of human life. The teaching of the sciences, on the other hand, should begin when the body of the child begins to form fully: when the joints are becoming firm and the ears and tongue functioning properly. Ibn Sīnā insists, moreover, that each child should be given individual attention and brought up according to his or her particular make-up. In no case should there be a quantitative egalitarianism imposed upon everyone, for this would cut counter to the qualitative differences which are ingrained within the very substance of human nature and which must be nurtured and protected with the greatest care. He in fact goes so far as to assert that the consideration of human beings solely on the basis of quantitative equality leads to their destruction and perdition.[13]

In the *Canon*, Ibn Sīnā specifies the regimen from infancy to adolescence, having at once an educational and medical goal in mind. 'The great principle here is the inculcation of control of the emotions. One should take care that they do not give way to anger and fear, or be opposed by despondency, or suffer from sleeplessness. They should therefore be allowed that which is pleasing and appetizing, and one should avoid giving them anything arousing disgust.'[14] As a result, the mind becomes accustomed to positive emotions from the beginning and develops good habits, while the body also benefits from these beneficial habits of mind.

Meanwhile, the child grows to an age when, in addition to the parents and family who have been his sole teachers until now, a suitable teacher from the outside must be sought for him. 'At the age of six, he may be given tuition by a master [who is of mild and benevolent desposition], who will teach him step by step and in order [cheerfully, without constraint]. He should not be compelled to stay continuously in school. [Relaxation of the mind contributes to the growth of the body.] At this age, bathing and rest should be less frequent, and the exercise before meals should be increased.'[15] Ibn Sīnā advises that this program is to be continued until the age of thirteen, insisting that light exercise should be encouraged, while that which entails toil and hardship should be avoided between boyhood and adolescence. Meanwhile, grammar should be taught to the student, followed at the age of 14 and onwards by mathematics and then philosophy.

Ibn Sīnā distinguishes clearly between the first stage of education carried out in the home and the second carried out at school (*maktab*) under the care of a teacher (*mu'allim*). At this stage, school and home begin to complement each other in promoting the goals of early education, which are strengthening of faith, building good character, health, teaching literacy and the rudiments of correct thinking and learning a craft. The teacher should be carefully chosen for, at this stage, his influence upon the character of the pupil is as great as his influence upon his mind. Therefore, the teacher should be pious, have firm moral principles and be of gentle disposition, as well as being knowledgeable. He must be the possessor of wisdom (*ḥikmah*; *khirad*), and be able to have insight into the character of his pupils and even judge their aptitude for pursuing different fields of knowledge so as to be able to advise them which subjects to pursue in later stages of life.

As for school, it is necessary because, not only does it make possible the transmission of knowledge, but it also provides a social ambience wherein students can learn from each other and live with one another. Ibn Sīnā emphasizes the importance of healthy rivalry and competition, as well as encouragement in attaining educational goals before other students. Moreover, the presence of other students makes possible discourse and disputation, which increase understanding, and the making of friends, which helps to purify character and strengthen certain virtues.[16]

The eight-year program of the *maktab* begins with the teaching of the Quran, religious instruction and language. This is naturally followed by the teaching of ethics and then of some kind of art or craft in the light of the students' capabilities and interests and also in view of what is necessary to earn a living. Sport should also be taught and students should spend certain hours of the day participating in some form of it. At this stage, the student should begin some kind of livelihood, while those who have the appropriate mental constitution and intellectual ability should continue their education further into such fields as medicine or the other sciences.

As far as the method of instruction is concerned, Ibn Sīnā emphasizes moderation in dealing with students. The teacher should be neither excessively lenient nor harsh. He should choose a manner of instruction, whether it be through mental training, imitation, repetition, logical analysis, etc., that is in conformity with the nature of the student. Likewise, in the choice of the particular field of the arts in which the student should specialize, the capabilities and interests of the student should be taken fully into consideration.[17]

No discussion of Ibn Sīnā's views on education would be complete without mention of his doctrine of the intellect, the faculties of the soul and the hierarchy which determines the different levels of man's intellectual faculties, and the process whereby man can attain to the highest level of intellectual perfection. Education on the higher level is in fact nothing other than the process of actualization and perfection of the faculties of the theoretical and practical intellect (*al-'aql al-naẓarī* and *al-'aql al-'amalī*).

Ibn Sīnā deals with this subject in several of his works, especially

Book Six of the *Tabī'iyyāt* of the *Shifā'*, where he considers the soul and its faculties and powers.[18] A full discussion of this theory of the intellect (*'aql*) would require a separate study and in fact there have already been several works devoted to this very subject[19], but its brief mention is nevertheless necessary here because of its crucial educational significance. According to this theory, man 'possesses' both a theoretical and a practical intellect, the faculties of which he must strengthen, moderate and perfect as the case may be. Education of the mind is essentially that of the theoretical intellect,[20] while that of character involves both the theoretical and practical intellects. While the practical intellect includes all the vegetal and animal faculties (*al-quwa'l-nabātiyyah* and *al-quwa'l-ḥayawāniyyah*), including apprehension (*wahm*), imagination (*khayāl*) and fantasy (*fantasiyyah*), the theoretical intellect encompasses the levels of material intellect (or intelligence) (*al-'aql al-hayūlānī*), intellect *en habitus (al-'aql bi'l-malakah)*, intellect in act (*al-'aql bi'l-fi'l*) and finally the sacred or acquired intellect (*al-'aql al-qudsī* or *al-'aql al-mustafād*). The process of learning implies the actualization of the potentialities of the intellect through the effusion of the light of the Active Intellect. It is this separate Intellect, identified with the angelic substances, that is the real teacher of the seeker of knowledge and the illumination of the human intellect by the hierarchy of Intelligences lies at the heart of the whole process of attaining knowledge, the highest level of which is intuitive knowledge (*al-ma'rifat al-ḥadsiyyah*), attained directly from the Active Intellect.

The *Visionary Recitals* of Ibn Sīnā, in which his 'Oriental Philosophy' (*al-ḥikmat al-mashriqiyyah*) is expounded in a symbolic fashion,[21] can also be studied as a source for his philosophy of education at the highest level. In these treatises the doctrine of the intellect becomes depicted concretely in the form of angels and celestial guides who lead man to the highest degrees of Divine Knowledge. The guide in *Ḥayy ibn Yaqẓān* is the teacher *par excellence* and Avicennan angelology a key for the understanding of the master's educational philosophy.[22] In his vast philosophical synthesis, Ibn Sīnā begins the process of education with the role of the parents as the first teachers of the child and concludes with the angel who, in illuminating the soul, enables it to experience the vision of God and fulfil the ultimate goal of all education and in fact human existence itself.

It is this last strand of Ibn Sīnā's philosophy that is fully elaborated and developed by the Master of Illumination, Shaykh al-Ishrāq Shihāb al-Din Suhrawardī.[23] The founder of the school of *ishrāq* emphasizes the necessity of the education of the whole man as the goal of philosophy. For him all life is oriented toward the attainment of knowledge through a process which is none other than educational in the universal sense of the term. The beginning of this process is marked by the thirst for knowledge, when the 'student' already experiences the need for seeking knowledge, this seeking or searching being called *ṭalab*; hence, the person at this first stage of the educational process being called *ṭālib*.[24] The process continues with the development of the mental faculties or those of reason, when the student is called *ṭālib al-baḥth*, 'seeker of discursive thought'. This stage is followed by the disciplining of the passions and purifying of the soul, for according to Suhrawardī true philosophy can be attained only if the discursive faculties are perfected and also the soul is purified of its defilements and imperfections so that it can attain illumination. At this stage the seeker is called *ṭālib al-ta'alluh*, 'seeker of "theosis"', the state of becoming God-like. At a higher stage, the student becomes a seeker of both discursive knowledge and theosis, while gradually he develops into a philosopher (*ḥakīm*), well-versed first in discursive thought, then theosis and finally both. At last man becomes a theosopher (*al-ḥakīm al-ilāhī*), first of *baḥth*, then of *ta'alluh* and finally of both. Above those human stages of perfection, which are traversed by means of education understood in its *ishrāqī* sense, stands the Imam, who possesses full knowledge of metaphysical, cosmological and eschatological realities and who is both the prototype of the human state and the exemplar of the perfection that is possible for man.[25] The final goal of education is the attainment of illumination, which in turn requires the perfection of all the faculties of man, both mental and psychological, involving both the rational element and the soul in all its aspects and dimensions.

In this educational process, the angel plays a particularly central role; and in many of his treatises, such as *Qiṣṣat al-ghurbat al-gharbiyyah*[26] and *Rūzī bā jamā'at-i ṣūfiyān*[27], Suhrawardī identifies the angel with the Archangel Gabriel, who, as the instrument of the Quranic revelation, 'taught' the Prophet the Word of God. The angel is also identified with the Holy Spirit as well as with the spiritual master (*murshid*), who is the veritable teacher in that process of education which constitutes the heart of both *ishrāqī* theosophy and Sufism.

As Suhrawardī writes at the beginning of his *Rūzī bā jamā'at-i ṣūfiyān* ('Epistle on the State of Childhood'):

> When I was a child I used to play, as children do, at the edge of the village. One day, I saw some children walking along together whose meditative appearance surprised me. I went up to them and asked: 'Where are you going?' 'We are going to school to acquire Knowledge', they told me. 'What is Knowledge?' I asked. 'We do not know how to answer that,' they said to me; 'You must ask our teacher'. And with that, they went on their way.
>
> Some time later, I said to myself, 'Now, what is Knowledge? Why shouldn't I go with them to their teacher and learn from him what Knowledge is?' I started looking for them and could not find them; but I saw the shaikh standing alone in the deserted countryside. I approached and greeted him, and he returned my greeting, his whole manner towards me exhibiting the most courteous affability.
>
> Self: 'I saw a group of children on their way to school, and I asked them: "What is the point of going to school?" They told me that I should ask their teacher that question. I was not interested at the time, so they left me. But after they had gone I felt the wish to find them again, and I started looking but couldn't find them. I am still looking for traces of them. If you can't tell me anything about them, tell me at least who their teacher is'.
>
> Shaikh: 'I am their teacher'.
>
> Self: 'You must teach me something about Knowledge'.
>
> The shaikh took up a tablet on which he had written *alif*, *ba*, *ta* . . . (a, b, c,), and proceeded to teach me.
>
> Shaikh: 'Stop there for today. Tomorrow I will teach you something else, and every day a little more, until you become a Knower.'
>
> I returned home, and until next day I kept repeating, *alif*, *ba*, *ta* . . . The two following days I went back to the shaikh for another lesson, and I assimilated these new lessons as well. It went so well that I ended up going to the shaikh ten

> times a day, and each time I learned something new. Finally, I never left his presence for a single moment, and I acquired a great deal of Knowledge.[28]

Education for Suhrawardī is therefore inseparable from the spiritual life, from the illumination of the soul by the angel and the guidance provided by the angelic substances which, being themselves light, illuminate the soul with veritable knowledge that is itself light, according to the already-cited *ḥadīth*, 'Knowledge is light' (*al-'ilm^u nūr^un*), and that enables man to experience finally God who is the Light of Lights (*nūr al-anwār*).

In the field of education, as in so many other domains, the most extensive elaboration in the annals of Islamic philosophy is to be found in Mullā Ṣadrā, whose synthesis of philosophy, Sufism, *kalām* and the *Sharī'ite* sciences is fully reflected in his doctrine of the growth and development of the soul which underlies the whole question of education.[29] For Mullā Ṣadrā, the genesis, growth and perfection of man and his soul, a subject which he usually identifies as *istikmāl al-nafs*, or perfection of the soul, occupies a central position and he deals with it in many of his works. The most complete treatment of the subject is to be found in the fourth journey of his *magnum opus*, *al-Asfār al-arba'ah*[30], while others of his major works, such as *al-Mabda' wa'l-ma'ād* and *al-Shawāhid al-rubūbiyyah*, also deal extensively with the subject. Moreover, Mullā Ṣadrā returns to this theme in his works on the Quran, including his commentary upon the Light verse (*āyat al-nūr*)[31] and his *Asrār al-āyāt*[32], wherein is contained the synthesis of his doctrine of man.

Upon a vast canvas, Mullā Ṣadrā depicts the journey of man from the embryonic stage to his meeting with God and combines the curve of the life of man in this world with that in the world to come, treating these phases as parts of a single 'curve of life' stretching from the origin (*al-mabda'*) to the end (*al-ma'ād*). For him there is an organic relation between this life and the life to come, and all moments and stages of life exist in the light of that final goal, which is the encounter with God. He describes the nature, faculties and powers of man and the purpose and entelechy of his existence. This entelechy is perfect knowledge of God and the happiness which results from it. For Mullā Ṣadrā, knowledge transforms the being of the knower, so that the whole process of education is the means whereby man ascends in the scale of being and moves toward the state of perfection for which he was created.[33]

According to the principle of trans-substantial motion, the very substance of all beings in the world of generation and corruption is being continuously transformed, motion or change being not only in the categories of accidents but in the very substance of beings. In the case of man, this process is most noticeable and 'radical', the human state being central in the terrestrial domain where man stands at the foot of the vertical axis which relates all levels of being. Man is transformed through trans-substantial motion, which must not under any condition be confused with evolution in the modern sense,[34] from the mineral state to the plant, from plant to animal, from animal to the ordinary state of man, and from this stage to the angelic, and finally beyond the angelic to the domain of Divine Proximity, or, to use the Quranic image, 'the length of two bows'.[35] Up to the stage of the 'ordinary' human state, the process is carried out by both the angels and the forces of nature as God's agents in this world.

But from this stage onward, it is by means of the actualization of the potentialities of the soul and its faculties through education, that the process is carried onward. Since man is given free will, this stage of the process does not take place 'naturally' and automatically as before the existant in question entered the human state. Since the knower becomes united with the known at the moment of intellection (*ta'aqqul*), the very mode of existence of man is changed through the process of knowledge. For Mullā Ṣadrā, the process of knowing is the key to the future of man's mode of being and hence lies at the heart of the concerns of religion.

The perfection of man resides in the perfection of his soul for which Mullā Ṣadrā uses the traditional philosophical term *al-nafs al-nāṭiqah* or 'rational soul'. But the term *nāṭiqah*, although usually translated as 'rational', must not be reduced to the modern understanding of this term. This word in Arabic still contains all the meaning which such terms as *nous*, *intellectus* and even *ratio* possessed before Cartesianism and empiricism deprived reason of its connection with the intellect and reduced it for the most part to its rapport with the outer senses. For Mullā Ṣadrā the *nafs al-nāṭiqah*, which is the first perfection of the body and the faculty capable of intellection,[36] possesses two basic faculties: accepting that which descends from above (*al-quwwat al-'ālimah*) and acting upon that which is below it (*al-quwwat al-'āmilah*). The second faculty, which is the practical, is helped by and depends upon the first, which is the intellectual. The goal of education is the actualization and perfection of these faculties with the aim of fulfilling the purpose for which man was created, this purpose being the knowledge of God (*ma'rifat Allāh*).[37]

The intellectual faculty consists of stages from the 'material intellect' (*al-'aql al-hayūlānī*) to the intellect *en habitus (al-'aql bi'l-malakah*) and from there to the intellect in act (*al-'aql bi'l-fi'l*), which represents the perfection of the intellectual faculty. As for the perfection of the practical faculty, it resides in following faithfully the Islamic Divine Law (*al-sharī'at al-muḥammadiyyah*). The very process of learning (*ta'līm*) transforms the soul and enables it to be transformed from a state of potentiality to one of actuality. Education, therefore, lies at the heart of religion and is the basic concern of Islam, which in its totality, embracing both the *Sharī'ah* and the inner way or *Ṭarīqah*, consists of a vast program of education for all aspects of the human being, from the corporeal to the highest faculties of the spirit.

The most elevated kind of knowledge is the perception (*idrāk*) of God, a knowledge which, however, cannot be attained save through the possession of faith (*īmān*).[38] The strengthening of faith is therefore a prerequisite of any educational system which seeks to possess an Islamic character, while this strengthening is itself not possible without moral education and the acquisition of the virtues of purity and reverential fear of God (*taqwā*). Man is able to attain to this supreme knowledge because his archetype (*al-insān al-kāmil*), which he bears within the depth of his being, is the mirror in which is reflected the Supreme Name, *Allāh*, and hence the reality of all that is found in the world of manifestation.[39] Man is created in such a way that the Active Intellect comes at once before his *nafs* and is attained as the fruit of the perfection of the *nafs*. Through the process of education, which results in this perfection, man realizes that he is the complete book containing all the signs (*āyāt*) manifested in His creation.[40] All learning and every step in the process of education is legitimate if it contributes to man's being able to read this 'book' which he carries within himself. Moreover, to read this 'book' is to fulfil the goal of life and to attain the end for which man was created. It is the ultimate goal of Islamic education.

In present-day discussions of Islamic education, far too little attention has been paid to the views of those Islamic philosophers and sages who, over the centuries, have meditated upon the meaning of education in the light of such fundamental questions as Who is man?; What is his nature?; Where does he come from?; and, Where is he going? They proposed an educational philosophy which, while remaining faithful to the nature of man in the light of his nature and entelechy, served as background for the creation of not only Islamic philosophy but also Islamic science. The Islamic philosophers' views on education represent an important branch of that tree of the Islamic intellectual tradition whose roots are sunk in the teachings of the Quran and *Ḥadīth*. No serious concern with Islamic education today can afford to remain oblivious to this millennial heritage, nor can any account of Islamic education be considered as being complete without consideration of the remarkable depth, amplitude, universality and also practical significance of the Islamic philosophers' educational concepts and views.

Notes

1. As already mentioned it is remarkable how the so-called 'fundamentalists' share with the Islamic modernists their complete espousal of modern science and technology, indifference to Islamic sacred art, hatred of traditional wisdom and the peace and contemplation associated with the inner life, and many other aspects of traditional Islam. In many ways, Islamic 'fundamentalism' and modernism are the two sides of the same coin and share much in common on many issues while both stand opposed to traditional Islam.
2. Those who claim otherwise are influenced either by Western interpretations of Islamic philosophy which see it merely as Greek thought masquerading in Arabic dress or in that of the Islamic theological and juridical schools of thought which have traditionally opposed *falsafah*. On the Islamic character of Islamic philosophy see S.M.H. Ṭabāṭabā'ī, *Uṣūl-i falsafay-i ri'ālizm*, Tehran, 1332 (A.H. Solar), vol. I; H. Corbin (in collaboration with S.H. Nasr and O. Yahya), *Histoire de la philosophie islamique*, pp. 13ff.; and our *Three Muslim Sages*, introduction.
3. On the 'philosopher-scientists' see *Three Muslim Sages*, chapter 1.

4. This is the method we have developed in the study of Islamic philosophy in our *Three Muslim Sages* and cosmology in our *An Introduction to Islamic Cosmological Doctrines*.
5. On the identity of the Ikhwān see Nasr *ibid.*, pp. 25ff.; and I.R. Netton, *Muslim Neoplatonists*, London 1982, chapter 1, where views of various scholars and the literature of the past few years on the subject are discussed.
6. See for example *Rasā'il*, Cairo, 1928, vol. I, pp. 21 and 347; vol. II, pp. 129, 291, 348, 364 and 380; and vol. III, p. 385.
7. See L. Gardet, 'Notions et principes de l'education dans la pensée arabo-musulmane', *Revue des Etudes Islamique*, vol. 44, 1976, pp.1–13; Also A.L. Tibawi, 'Some Educational Terms in *Rasā'il* Ikhwān aṣ-Ṣafā'', *Islamic Quarterly*, vol. 5, 1959, pp. 55–60.
8. « جوهر روحانية سماوية نورانية حية علامة بالقوة فعالة بالطبع ».
   Rasā'il, vol. I, Beirut, 1957, p. 260.
9. « ونصف ايضا كيفية اخراج ما في قوة النفس من العلوم الى الفعل الذى هو الغرض الاقصى في التعاليم، وهو اصلاح جواهر النفس وتهذيب اخلاقها وتتميمها وتكميلها للبقاء في دار الآخرة التى هي دار الحيوان ».
   ibid., p. 258.
10. See Tibawi, *op. cit.*, p. 60.
11. On the Ismā'īlī understanding of these terms see H. Corbin, *Trilogie Ismaélienne*, Tehran-Paris, 1961, p. 138.
12. On Ibn Sīnā see Nasr, *Three Muslim Sages*, chapter 1; Nasr, *An Introduction to Islamic Cosmological Doctrines*, pp. 177 ff.; S. Afnan, *Avicenna, His Life and Works*, London, 1958; and W.E. Gohlman, *The Life of Ibn Sīnā*, Albany (NY), 1974.
13. Ibn Sīnā writes, 'Equality of states and proximity of measures concerning human beings leads to corruption and finally causes their annihilation and destruction'. M.N. Zanjānī, *Ibn Sīnā wa tadbīr-i manzil*, Tehran, 1319 (A.H. solar), p. 6.
14. Ibn Sīnā, *A Treatise on the Canon of Medicine*, trans. O.C. Gruner, London, 1980, p. 379.
15. *ibid.*
16. See Ibn Sīnā, *Tadbīr al-manāzil*, Baghdad, 1929.
17. For a summary of these views see I. Ṣadīq. '*Naẓariyyāt-i Ibn-i Sīnā dar bāb-i ta'līm wa tarbiyat*', *Jashn-nāma-yi Ibn Sīnā*, vol. II, Tehran 1334 (A.H. solar), pp. 149–158.
18. See *Avicenna's De Anima, Being the Psychological Part of Kitāb al-Shifā'*, ed. F. Rahman, London, 1952. See also Ibn Sīnā, *Psychologie v Jehe dile aš-Šifā'*, 2 vols., ed. and trans. J. Bakoš, Prague, 1956.
19. See for example H.A. Davison, 'Alfarabi and Avicenna on the Active Intellect', *Viator*, 3, 1972, pp. 109–178; and N. Ushida, *Etude comparative de la psychologie d'Aristote, d'Avicenne et de St. Thomas d'Aquin*, Tokyo, 1968, especially chapter V.
20. The category of 'mind' belongs to modern philosophy and is alien to Ibn Sīnā's world-view.
21. On the 'Oriental Philosophy' see Corbin, *Avicenna and the Visionary*

Recital, trans. W. Trask, Irving (Texas), 1980, pp. 36ff; and Nasr, *An Introduction to Islamic Cosmological Doctrines*, pp. 185ff.

22. One day the whole 'Oriental Philosophy' and the cycle of Visionary Recitals should be studied in detail in the light of Ibn Sīnā's philosophy of education.
23. On Suhrawardī see Corbin, *En Islam iranien*, vol.II, our *Three Muslim Sages*, chapter 2; and our 'Shihāb al-Dīn Suhrawardī', in M.M. Sharif, *A History of Muslim Philosophy*, pp. 372–398.
24. The term *ṭālib* is used with a special meaning in *ishrāqī* philosophy or wisdom (*ḥikmah*), while the term *ṭalabah*, closely related to it, has acquired in Arabic and Persian the general meaning of 'student' (especially of the religious sciences).
25. See Suhrawardī, *Ḥikmat al-ishrāq*, edited by H. Corbin, in *Oeuvres philosophiques et mystiques*, vol. II, Tehran-Paris, 1977, pp. 10–12.
26. See *Oeuvres philosophiques et mystiques*, vol. II, pp. 274–297; and W.M. Thackston (trans.), *The Mystical Visionary Treatises of Suhrawardī*, London, 1982, pp. 100–108.
27. See Suhrawardī, *Oeuvres philosophiques et mystiques*, ed. S.H. Nasr, vol. III, Tehran-Paris, 1977, pp. 241–250; and Thackston, *op. cit.*, pp. 44–50.
28. Thackston, *op. cit.*, pp. 62–63.
29. Over the past two decades a fairly extensive literature has grown around the subject of Mullā Ṣadrā and numerous studies have been devoted to him especially by Persian scholars, but there does not exist as yet any independent work concerned with his educational philosophy. On Mullā Ṣadrā see our *Ṣadr al-Dīn Shīrāzī and His Transcendent Theosophy*; our 'Ṣadr al-Dīn Shīrāzi (Mullā Ṣadrā)', M.M. Sharif, (ed.), *A History of Muslim Philosophy*, vol. II, pp. 932–960; J. Morris (trans.) *The Wisdom of the Throne – An Introduction to the Philosophy of Mullā Ṣadrā*, Princeton, 1981; Corbin, *En Islam iranien*, vol. IV, Paris, 1972, pp. 54–122; and Corbin, *La philosophie iranienne islamique aux XVIIe et XVIIIe siècles*, Paris, 1981, pp. 49–83.
30. See Nasr, *The Transcendent Theosophy of Ṣadr al-Dīn Shīrāzī*, chapter 3; and J. Muṣliḥ, *'Ilm al-nafs yā rawānshināsī-yi Ṣadr al-Muta'āllihīn*, Tehran, 1352 (A.H. solar).
31. See Mullā Ṣadrā, *Tafsīr-e-āyeh-e-nūr*, ed. by M. Khājavī, Tehran, 1362, (A.H. solar).
32. See Mullā Ṣadrā, *Asrār al-āyāt*, ed. by M. Khājavī, Tehran, 1981, *al-mashhad al-thānī*, especially, pp. 126ff.
33. Mullā Ṣadrā explains this relation between knowing and being through the two principles of the unity of the knower and the known (*ittiḥād al-'āqil wa'l-ma'qūl*) and trans-substantial motion (*al-ḥarakat al-jawhariyyah*). On these principles see our 'Ṣadr al-Dīn Shīrāzī', pp. 948ff.
34. See our *Knowledge and the Sacred*, pp. 244–245.
35. *Qāb al-qawsayn*. See the Quran, LIII; 9.
36. See Mullā Ṣadrā, *al-Mabda' wa'l-ma'ād*, trans. A. Ardakānī, ed. 'A. Nūrānī, Tehran, 1362 (A.H. solar), p. 304.
37. *ibid.*, p. 306.

38. - «انّ ادراك الحقّ تعالى بعلم مستأنف لايمكن لاحد الّا في مرآة قلب المؤمن المتّقي، و لهذا بني العالم وخلق الكون و ابداع النظام.»

Mullā Sadrā, *Tafsīr-e āyeh-e-nūr*, p. 168.

39. «وكذلك في الانسان الكامل والمظهر الجامع، يوجد جميع ما يوجد في عالم الاسماء وفي مظاهرها الآفاقيّة.»

ibid., p. 171. On the universal man see T. Burckhardt's translation of al-Jīlī *Universal Man*, Sherborne, Glos., 1983; and our *Science and Civilization in Islam*, pp. 338ff.

40. «الانسان الكامل كتاب جامع لآيات ربّه القدّوس ويحمل مطويّ فيه حقائق العقول والنفوس، ومملكة كاملة مملوّة من فنون العلم والشؤون، ونسخة مكتوبة من مثال كن فيكون...»

ibid., p. 175.

Chapter Ten

The Traditional Texts Used in the Persian *Madrasahs*

To understand the traditional Islamic educational system, not only is it necessary to consider the 'philosophy of education' underlying the system, but also to study the actual curriculum of the *madrasahs* or traditional schools. In many parts of the Islamic world, the curriculum became more and more limited from about the 8th/14th and 9th/15th centuries onward, until during this century only subjects dealing with the transmitted sciences (*al-'ulūm al-naqliyyah*) remain. The Persian *madrasahs*, however, reflected until recently, more than the *madrasahs* of many other areas, almost the full spectrum of both the transmitted (*naqlī*) and the intellectual (*'aqlī*) sciences[1] taught in Muslim universities as well as in private circles during the full flowering of educational activity in earlier centuries of Islamic history.

In Persia and certain adjoining areas, such as Iraq, Afghanistan and some of the republics which now lie within the Soviet Union, until a few generations ago there were many *madrasahs* in which, not only law and theology, but also all the other disciplines included in the traditional curriculum, ranging from medicine to astronomy, were still taught. It is only during the last hundred years that, even in this area, some of the subjects have been discontinued, while others have been changed or modified and new books of instruction introduced for their teaching.

Nearly forty years ago the Persian scholar and statesman Seyyed Hasan Taqizadeh,[2] who had himself received his early education in one of the *madrasahs* and who was much interested in the Islamic sciences, asked one of the leading Islamic scholars of the day, Muḥammad Ṭāhir Ṭabarsī, known as Mīrzā Ṭāhir Tunikābunī, to write a treatise in which the works studied in the *madrasahs* would be described for posterity before this knowledge became forgotten. Mīrzā Ṭāhir, who was one of the leading traditional philosophers of Persia during the past century, set about this task and composed a treatise, which has been published only recently after a long period of neglect.[3] It remains one of the most authoritative and complete works on the subject, reflecting the practice of Persian *madrasahs* for the several centuries which preceded the composition of the treatise in 1938.

According to Mīrzā Ṭāhir, the texts used for teaching the various sciences in the *madrasahs* of Persia and adjacent regions were as follows:

The Transmitted (*naqliyyah*) Sciences

I. The Science of Morphology (*ṣarf*)

1. *Ṣarf-i mīr* – A short treatise in Persian on the subject by Mīr Sayyid Sharīf Jurjānī, who lived in the 8th/14th century.[4]

2. *Taṣrīf-i zanjānī* with commentary – The text was written by 'Izz al-Dīn Ibrāhīm Zanjānī, who lived in the 7th/13th century, and commented on by Sa'd al-Dīn Mas'ūd ibn 'Umar Taftazānī (8th/14th century).[5]

3. *Sharḥ-i niẓām* – The text of this work is the *Shāfiyah* of Jamāl al-Dīn Abū 'Umar, known as Ibn Ḥājib al-Malikī (7th/13th century), while the commentary is by Niẓām al-Dīn Ḥasan Nayshābūrī, whose commentary is favoured over the numerous other commentaries written upon this celebrated work.

In older days, students also made use of the *Marāḥ al-arwāḥ* of Aḥmad ibn ʻAlī ibn Masʻūd, but this work lost its popularity and gradually was dropped from the list of the main texts to be studied.

II. The Science of Syntax (Grammar) (*naḥw*)

1. The *'Awāmil* of Jurjānī – The work of the 5th/11th century scholar, ʻAbd al-Qāhir Jurjānī, upon which many commentaries have been written, but it is the text itself which has remained popular throughout the centuries.

2. The *'Awāmil* of Mullā Muḥsin – Although some consider this work to be by Mullā Muḥsin Fayḍ Kāshānī, the celebrated student of Mullā Ṣadrā, most likely it is by Mullā Muḥsin Muḥammad ibn Ṭāhir Qazwīnī, who lived in the late Safavid period and who also wrote a commentary upon the *Alfiyyah* of Ibn Mālik.[6]

3. The *Ṣamadiyyah* – This celebrated treatise is by Shaykh Bahā' al-Dīn ʻAmilī[7] and was written for his nephew ʻAbd al-Ṣamad. Numerous commentaries have been written upon it of which the most famous are the major and minor commentaries by Sayyid ʻAlī Khān, who was his contemporary.

4. The *Unmūdhaj* – This is a summary by the famous 6th/12th century grammarian Jārallāh Abu'l-Qāsim al-Zamakhsharī of his own extensive grammar, which is one of the peaks of grammatical studies of Arabic.

5. The *Kāfiyah* – This is another of the important grammatical works of Ibn Ḥājib upon which numerous commentaries have been composed in Arabic and Persian, including those of Sayyid Sharīf Jurjānī and Sayyid Rukn al-Dīn Astrābādī, who was a student of Naṣīr al-Dīn Ṭūsī.

6. The *Alfiyyah* – This popular work by the 7th/13th century Andalusian grammarian, Ibn Mālik, contains a thousand verses in which the principles of *naḥw* are outlined. Of the numerous commentaries written upon it, that of Jalāl al-Dīn al-Suyūṭī is the most popular in Persia.

7. The *Mughnī al-labīb* – A work by Jamāl al-Dīn ibn Yūsuf known as Ibn Hishām, who lived in the 8th/14th century. There are several well-known commentators on this work including those of Muḥammed ibn Abī Bakr al-Damāmīnī and Jalāl al-Din al-Suyūṭī.

III. The Literary Sciences (Rhetoric (*maʻānī wa bayān*) and the Art of Metaphors (*badīʻ*))

1. *Talkhīṣ-i miftāḥ* – The most popular work in this field has been the summary made by Jalāl al-Dīn ʻAbd al-Raḥmān Qazwīnī (8th/

14th century) of the *Miftāḥ al-'ulūm* of Sirāj al-Dīn Yūsuf al-Sakkākī (7th/13th century), a work whose third section is devoted to the literary sciences. This summary is usually studied along with the two commentaries of Sa'd al-Dīn Taftazānī, the long (*Muṭawwal*) and the short (*Mukhtaṣar*).

2. *Dalā'il al-i'jāz* – This work by the 5th/11th century scholar, 'Abd al-Qāhir Jurjānī, has become popular only during the past century or two.

3. *Asrār al-balāghah* – Another fairly short work by Jurjānī.

IV. The Principles of Jurisprudence (*Uṣūl al-fiqh*)

1. The *Dharī'ah* – This famous work is by 'Alī ibn Abī Aḥmad Ḥusayn, known as Sayyid Murtaḍā as well as 'Ālam al-Hudā (5th/11th century).

2. *'Iddat al-uṣūl* – One of the most respected works on *uṣūl* by the famous 5th/11th century Shi'ite scholar Shaykh al-Ṭā'ifah Muḥammad ibn 'Alī al-Ṭūsī, usually studied with the commentary of Mullā Khalīl ibn Ghāzī Qazwīnī.

3. *Minhaj al-wuṣūl ilā 'ilm al-uṣūl* – By the 7th/13th century scholar, Najm al-Dīn Abu'l-Qāsim, known as Muḥaqqiq-i Ḥillī.

4. *Mabādī al-wuṣūl ilā 'ilm al-uṣūl* – By the well-known 'Allāmah Ḥillī (7th/13th century), upon which Miqdād ibn 'Abdallāh al-Suyūrī al-Ḥillī has written a commentary.

5. *Tahdhīb al-uṣūl* – Another well-known work on the subject by 'Allāmah Ḥillī.

6. *Ma'ālim al-dīn* – This work by Ḥasan ibn Shaykh Zayn al-Dīn, known as Shahīd-i Thānī (10th/16th century), is very popular and has been commented upon by numerous authors.

7. *Zubdat al-uṣūl* – This is one of the best-known religious works of Shaykh Bahā'al-Dīn 'Āmilī, upon which his own student, Jawād ibn Sa'dallāh al-Baghdādī, as well as Mawlā Ṣāliḥ ibn Aḥmad Sarawī, have written widely-studied commentaries.

8. The *Kitāb al-wāfiyah* – This short but masterly treatise is by Mullā 'Abdallāh ibn Ḥajj Muḥammad Tūnī Bushrawī Khurāsānī (11th/17th century). Several of the outstanding scholars of the past three centuries, including Sayyid al-Sanad Baḥr al-'Ulūm, have written commentaries upon it.

9. The *Qawānīn* – By the 13th/19th century jurisprudent Mīrzā Abu'l-Qāsim ibn Muḥammad Gīlānī.

10. The *Fuṣūl fī 'ilm al-uṣūl* – This very popular work of

Muḥammad Ḥusayn ibn ʻAbd al-Raḥīm Ṭihrānī Rāzī (13th/19th century) gained almost immediate acceptance after its composition.

11. The *Farā'id al-uṣūl* – Also known as *Rasā'il*, this work was composed a little over a century ago by the great master of *uṣūl*, Shaykh Murtaḍā ibn Aḥmad Amīn Anṣārī.

Most of these works belong to the later centuries of Islamic history. There are also several other works in *uṣūl* which were written earlier (many by Sunni rather than Shi'ite scholars) and were popular before the composition of these later works and which have continued to be studied, but not to the same extent as before.[8] Some of these works are the *al-Mustaṣfā* of Ghazzālī, the *Aḥkām fī uṣūl al-aḥkām* of Sayf al-Dīn al-Amīnī (7th/13th century), the *Mukhtaṣar al-uṣūl* of his student, Ibn Ḥājib, upon which many commentaries have been written, the *Minhaj al-wuṣūl ilā ʻilm al-uṣūl* by Qāḍī Nāṣir al-Dīn Bayḍāwī (7th/13th century), the *Maḥṣūl* of Fakhr al-Dīn Rāzī (6th/12th century) and its summary by Sirāj al-Dīn Urmawī (7th/13th century) and the *Jamʻ al-jawāmiʻ* of Tāj al-Dīn al-Subkī al-Shafti'ī (8th/14th century).

V. Jurisprudence (*fiqh*)

Among the Shi'ites, the main source of *Ḥadīth*, which includes the sayings of both the Prophet and the Imams, and which serves, after the Noble Quran, as the fountainhead for the injunctions of the *Sharīʻah*, consists of four books, which are as follows:

1. The *Kāfī* – The *Kitāb al-kāfī* comprised of both *uṣūl* (principles) and *furūʻ* (branches) by Muḥammad ibn Yaʻqūb al-Kulaynī (4th/10th century), which is the most authoritative of all these sources.[9] Numerous commentaries have been written on this work, especially upon the *uṣūl*, including those of Mīr Dāmād (10th/16th century), Mullā Ṣadrā – his being one of the most important works of Islamic philosophy – Rafīʻ al-Dīn Muḥammad Ṭabāṭabā'ī (11th/17th century) and Mullā Muḥammad Bāqir Majlisī (11th/17th century).

2. The *Man lā yaḥḍuruhu'l-faqīh* of Ibn Bābūhyah, known as Shaykh-i, Ṣadūq upon which Mullā Muḥammad Taqī Majlisī (11th/17th century) wrote two commentaries, one in Persian and the other in Arabic.

3. The *Tahdhīb* – A major authoritative source by Shaykh al-Ṭā'ifah Muḥammad al-Ṭūsī (5th/11th century).

4. The *Istibṣār* – A second work of authority by Muḥammad al-Ṭūsī.

As for books on jurisprudence itself and its basis in the Quran and *Ḥadīth*, numerous works have been written by both Sunni and Shi'ite authorities of which the following became particularly popular during the past few centuries when Persia became predominately Shi'ite:

1. *Wasā'il al-shī'ah ilā aḥkām al-sharī'ah* – By Muḥammad ibn Ḥasan, known as Shaykh Ḥurr-i 'Āmilī (11th/17th century).

2. The *Wāfī* – The *Kitāb al-wāfī*, by Mullā Muḥsin Fayḍ Kāshānī (11th/17th century), is concerned mostly with both the traditions upon which *fiqh* is based and the injunctions themselves.

3. The *Biḥār al-anwār* – This voluminous religious encyclopedia by Muḥammad Bāqir Majlisī includes nearly every branch of the religious sciences, from sacred history to jurisprudence. All parts of this work have been and still are popular in *madrasahs* throughout Persia.

4. The *Nihāyah* – By Muḥammad al-Ṭūsī, with numerous commentaries by *mujtahids* of nearly every generation.

5. The *Mabsūṭ* – Also by Muḥammad al-Ṭūsī and commented upon by numerous *mujtahids* over the ages.

6. The *Sharā'i' al-islām* – By Muḥaqqiq-i Ḥillī and usually studied along with its summary called the *Mukhtaṣar-i nāfi'*.

7. *Masālik al-afhām ilā fahm sharā'i' al-islām* – By Shaykh Zayn al-Dīn, known as Shahīd-i Thānī.

8. *Madārik al-aḥkām* – By Shams al-Dīn Muḥammad ibn 'Alī 'Āmilī (10th/16th century). Many commentaries have been written upon this work, the most famous being the *Jawāhir al-kalām* of Muḥammad Ḥassan Najafī (13th/19th century).

9. The *Irshād al-adhhān fī aḥkām al-īmān* – By Ḥasan ibn Yūsuf ibn Muṭahhar Ḥillī. Several well-known commentaries have been written upon it such as the *Ghāyat al-murād* of Jamāl al-Dīn Makkī, known as Shahīd-i Awwal (8th/14th century), and *Majma' al-fā'idah wa'l-burhān* of Aḥmad ibn Muḥammad Muqaddas-i Ardibīlī (10th/16th century).

10. The *Qawā'id al-aḥkām* – Also by Muḥaqqiq-i Ḥillī. Several important commentaries have been written upon it such as the *Īḍāḥ al-qawā'id* by the author's son, *Kanz al-fawā'id* by his nephew Sayyid 'Amīd al-Dīn, *Jāmi' al-maqāṣid fī sharḥ al-qawā'id* by Muḥaqqiq-i Thānī Nūr al-Dīn 'Alī ibn 'Abd al-'Alī Karakī (10th/

16th century), *Kashf al-lithām 'an mu'dalat qawā'id al-aḥkām* by Bahā' al-Dīn Muḥammad Iṣfahānī, known as Fāḍil-i Hindī (12th/18th century), and *Miftāḥ al-karāmah fī sharḥ qawā'id al-'Allāmah* by Sayyid Jawād 'Āmilī (12th/18th century).

11. *Lum'a-yi dimashqiyyah* – By Shahīd Awwal with commentaries by Shahīd-i Thānī.

During the last century, the *Makāsib* and *Ṭahārat* of Shaykh Murtaḍā Anṣārī, dealing with specific aspects of *fiqh*, have also become very popular and have been commented upon by some of the most celebrated *mujtahids* of this era such as Mullā Muḥammad Kāẓim Khurāsānī and Sayyid Muḥammad Kāẓim Yazdī.

VI. The Sciences of *Ḥadīth* and its History (*'ilm-i dirāyah*)

1. *Risālat al-bidāyah fī 'ilm al-dirāyah* – By Shahīd-i Thānī
2. The *Wajīzah* – By Shaykh Bahā' al-Dīn 'Āmilī
3. *Rawāshiḥ al-samāwiyyah* – By the great philosopher and founder of the school of Isfahan,[10] Mīr Dāmād, who before composing his commentary upon the *Kāfī*, wrote the *Rawāshiḥ* on the science of *Ḥadīth*.
4. *Nuzhat al-naẓar fī sharḥ nukhbat al-fikar* – Both the text and the commentary are by Ḥāfiẓ Shihāb al-Dīn 'Asqalānī (9th/15th century). The work has many other commentaries, which, however, have not become popular in Persia.
5. The *Alfiyyah* – By Jalāl al-Dīn Abū Bakr al-Suyūṭī (9th/15th century).

VII. The Quranic Sciences (*tafsīr*)

This is the crown of all the Islamic sciences and possesses many branches. As far as the science of the recitation of the Quran (*qirā'ah wa tajwīd*) is concerned, the popular treatises in Persia have been the *qaṣīdah*, *Ḥirz al-amānī wa wajh al-tahānī*, of Abū Muḥammad Qāsim al-Shāṭibī (6th/12th century), among the many commentaries upon which are the *Sirāj al-qāri'* of Ibn Qāṣiḥ (8th/14th century), which is the best known, and the *Muqaddimah* of Muḥammad ibn Muḥammad al-Jazarī (9th/15th century).

As for Quranic commentaries, both those composed by Sunni scholars and Shi'ite ones are studied, the most popular being the following:

1. The *Tafsīr* of 'Alī ibn Ibrāhīm Qummī (4th/10th century).
2. The *Majma' al-bayān* – By Abū 'Alī Faḍl ibn Ḥasan Ṭabarsī

(6th/12th century) summarized by the author himself as *Majma' al-jawāmi'*.

3. *Rawḥ al-jinān wa rūḥ al-janān* – By Abu'l-Futūḥ Rāzī (6th/12th century), a vast Persian commentary which is also a masterpiece of Persian literature.

4. *Tafsīr-i ṣāfī* – By Mullā Muḥsin Fayḍ Kāshānī, a commentary which is at once gnostic and theological.

5. The *Tafsīr* of Ṭabarī – The celebrated commentary by the 4th/10th century author Muḥammad ibn Jarīr al-Ṭabarī.

6. The *Tafsīr al-kabīr* – One of the most extensive of all Quranic commentaries by the 6th/12th century theologian Fakhr al-Dīn Rāzī.

7. The *Kashshāf* – By Jārallāh al-Zamakhsharī (6th/12th century). Numerous commentaries have been written upon it.

8. *Tafsīr anwār al-tanzīl wa asrār al-ta'wīl* – By Qāḍī Nāṣir al-Dīn al-Bayḍāwī. Many commentaries have been written upon this work.

9. *Kanz al-'irfān* – By Miqdād ibn 'Abdallāh Ḥillī (8th/14th century) dealing mostly with the Quranic basis of Shari'ite injunctions.

10. *Zubdat al-bayān* – By Aḥmad ibn Muḥammad (Muqaddas-i Ardibīlī) also dealing with the Quranic foundation of Shari'ite injunctions (*aḥkām*).

The Intellectual (*'aqliyyah*) Sciences

I. Logic (*manṭiq*)

1. *Risāla-yi kubrā* – A short treatise in Persian by Sayyid Sharīf Jurjānī.

2. The *Ḥāshiyah* of Mullā 'Abdallāh – This is one of the most popular works on logic and consists of glosses upon the *Tahdhīb al-manṭiq* of Taftāzānī by Mullā 'Abdallāh Yazdī (9th/15th century). The work has two parts, the first on logic and the second on theology (*kalām*). The first part alone became widely popular,

while the second part is studied only among the religious students of Kurdistan.

3. *Sharḥ-i shamsiyyah* – The text of the *Shamsiyyah* is by Najm al-Dīn Dabīrān Kātibī Qazwīnī (7th/13th century),[11] while the commentary is by Quṭb al-Dīn Rāzī[12] (8th/14th century) and is one of the most popular works on logic.

4. *Sharḥ-i maṭāli' al-anwār* – The text of *Maṭāli' al-anwār* is by Sirāj al-Dīn Urmawī (7th/13th century),[13] while the best-known commentary is by Sayyid Sharīf Jurjānī.

5. *Sharḥ-i manẓūmah* – Both the text and commentary are by the great Qajar philosopher and sage, Ḥājjī Mullā Hādī Sabziwārī (13th/19th century). The work includes a complete cycle of traditional philosophy starting with logic and ending with eschatology, prophetology and ethics.[14]

6. *Sharḥ-i ishārāt* – The celebrated *al-Ishārāt wa'l-tanbīhāt* of Ibn Sīnā (4th-5th/10th-11th century), with the commentaries of Fakhr al-Dīn Rāzī, Ṭūsī and Quṭb al-Dīn Rāzī, has been over the centuries one of the mainstays of the programs of study in various branches of philosophy, including logic.

7. *Jawhar al-naḍīd fī sharḥ manṭiq al-tajrīd* – The *Tajrīd* is Naṣīr al-Dīn Ṭūsī's main theological work, but the first part is devoted to logic. With the commentary of his student, 'Allāmah Ḥasan ibn Yūsuf ibn al-Muṭahhar Ḥillī, this section on logic became known as a separate work and gained popularity during the last century.

8. *al-Baṣā'ir al-naṣīriyyah* – The work by the 7th/12th century philosopher, Zayn al-Dīn 'Umar ibn Sahlān Sāwajī, was neglected until Muḥammad 'Abduh wrote a commentary upon it and began to teach it at al-Azhar University in Cairo. It then gained popularity, not only among Egyptian students, but among Persian ones as well.[15]

9. The logic of the *Ḥikmat al-ishrāq* – The whole of this masterpiece of *ishrāqī* theosophy by the founder of this school, Shaykh al-ishrāq Shihāb al-Dīn Suhrawardī (6th/12th century),[16] is extremely popular in Persia and is usually studied with the commentary of Quṭb al-Dīn Shīrāzī and the glosses of Mullā Ṣadrā. The logic, which is a departure from Peripatetic logic, is usually studied by students after they have studied the usual works on formal logic based upon the Organon and the modifications made upon it by the Islamic logicians.

10. The logic of the *Shifā'* – Because of its inaccessibility and

difficult style, the logic of the *Shifā'* of Ibn Sīnā has never become a popular work. But being the most thorough and extensive treatment of formal logic in Islamic philosophy, it could not escape the attention of the most advanced students of the subject, who usually studied it with the glosses and Mullā Ṣadrā, Sayyid Aḥmad 'Alawī and several others of the later *ḥakīms* of Persia.[17]

II. The Philosophical and Theological Sciences (*falsafah* and *kalām*)

1. *Sharḥ-i hidāyah* – The text of this celebrated work is by the 7th/13th century philosopher, Athīr al-Dīn Abharī, and consists of three parts: logic, natural philosophy and metaphysics. The section on logic was commented upon by the 9th/15th century philosopher and Sufi, Shams al-Dīn Fanārī but, while this commentary has always been popular in Turkey, Syria and Iraq, it has never become widely accepted in Persia. There are, however, numerous famous commentaries on the last two sections, those of Ḥusayn ibn Mu'īn al-Dīn Mībudī Yazdī and Mullā Ṣadrā being extremely well-known in Persia, Afghanistan and the Indian subcontinent.[18]

2. The *Tajrīd* – This work of Naṣīr al-Dīn Ṭūsī is the main text for Shi'ite *kalām* and is usually studied with the following commentaries[19]:

a) That of 'Allamah Ḥasan ibn Yūsuf al-Ḥillī.

b) The *Tasdīd al-qawā'id fī sharḥ tajrīd al-'aqa'id* of the 8th/14th century theologian Shams al-Dīn Aḥmad Iṣfahānī, to which Mīr Sayyid Sharīf Jurjānī has written important glosses.

c) The very popular commentary of the 9th/15th century scientist, philosopher and theologian, 'Alā' al-Dīn Qūshchī, which is famous throughout the Islamic world and upon which over four hundred scholars have written glosses, including Dawānī and Khafrī.

d) The *Shawāriq al-ilhām fī sharḥ tajrīd al-kalām* by 'Abd al-Razzāq Lāhījī (11th/17th century) which, although incomplete, is widely read and considered one of the most important commentaries upon the *Tajrīd*.[20]

3. *Sharḥ-i ishārāt* – As already mentioned in the section on logic, the whole of the *Ishārāt* of Ibn Sīnā, concerned not only with logic but also natural philosophy and metaphysics, as commented upon by Fakhr al-Dīn Rāzī, Ṭūsī and Quṭb al-Dīn Rāzī, has been over the

centuries and continues to be one of the basic texts of Islamic philosophy in Persia.

4. The *Ḥikmat al-ishrāq* – The *Ḥikmat al-ishrāq* of Suhrawardī along with the commentary of Quṭb al-Dīn Shīrāzī and the glosses of Mullā Ṣadrā constitutes the central work of the *ishrāqī* school and is studied by everyone who wishes to master the doctrines of this school.[21]

5. *The Sharḥ-i manẓūmah* – The already-mentioned work of Sabziwārī is as popular in the field of philosophy as it is in logic, and since the last century it has come to be taught in nearly all the *madrasahs* where philosophy forms part of the curriculum.

6. The *Asfār al-arba'ah* – The major opus of Mullā Ṣadrā consists of four 'journeys' (*safar*) and deals respectively with metaphysics, natural philosophy, psychology and eschatology.[22] This vast work is considered the most advanced treatise on philosophy in Persia and is studied only after the student has mastered all the other branches and schools of the 'intellectual' and even 'transmitted' sciences. Many commentaries have been written upon it, including those of the 13th/19th century students of Mullā Ṣadrā's school, Mullā 'Alī Nūrī, Ḥājjī Mullā Ḥādī Sabziwārī and Mullā 'Alī Zunūzī.

Several other works of Mullā Ṣadrā such as *al-Mabda' wa'l-ma'ād*, *al-Shawāhid al-rubūbiyyah*, *al-Mashā'ir*, *al-'Arshiyyah*, *Mafātīḥ al-ghayb* and *Asrār al-āyāt* have also been popular among students of *madrasahs* since the beginning of the 13th/19th century when the teachings of Mullā Ṣadrā were revived throughout Persia.

III. Sufism and gnosis (*taṣawwuf* and *'irfān*)

1. The *Kitāb al-tamhīd fī sharḥ qawā'id, al-tawḥīd* – Also called *Tawḥīd al-qawā'id*, this important treatise on the Sufism of the school of Ibn 'Arabī by Ṣā'in al-Dīn ibn Turkah (9th/15th century)[23] deals with the two poles of all Sufi doctrine: the transcendent unity of being (*waḥdat al-wujūd*) and the universal man (*al-insān al-kāmil*). It has always been very popular as a treatise on gnosis (*'irfān*) and has been commented upon by several masters including Āqā Muḥammad Riḍā Qumsha'ī.[24]

2. *Sharḥ-i fuṣūṣ al-ḥikam* – The text of this most celebrated of all works on the doctrines of Sufism is by Muḥyī al-Dīn ibn 'Arabī and numerous commentaries have been written upon it.[25] As far as Persia is concerned, the most popular commentaries over the centuries have been those of Dā'ūd Qayṣarī (8th/14th century) upon

which Āqā Muḥammad Riḍā Qumsha'ī has written extensive glosses; 'Abd al-Razzāq Kāshānī (8th/14th century); 'Abd al-Raḥmān Jāmī[26] (9th/15th century) and Bālī Afandī (10th/16th century). But these commentaries are nearly all based on that of Mu'ayyid al-Dīn Jandī which, however, has never become popular itself.[27]

3. *Sharḥ-i miftāḥ al-ghayb* – The text of this advanced work on Sufi doctrine is by Ṣadr al-Dīn al-Qunyawī (7th/13th century), the foremost expositor of Ibn 'Arabī in the East, and the commentary by Shams al-Dīn Hamzah Fanārī who has already been mentioned.[28]

IV. Medicine (*ṭibb*)

1. *Sharḥ-i nafīsī* – The text of this popular medical treatise is the *Mūjaz* by 'Alā' al-Dīn 'Alī ibn Abi'l-Ḥazm Qarashī (7th/13th century), which is itself an epitome of the *Canon* of Ibn Sīnā. The most famous commentary which has been printed with the *Mūjaz* is by Nafīs ibn 'Iwaj Kirmānī (9th/15th century). There are other commentaries upon the *Mūjaz*, such as those of Jamāl al-Dīn Aqsarā'ī and Sadīd al-Dīn Kāzirūnī, which, however, have never reached the fame of *Sharḥ-i nafīsī*.[29]

2. *Sharḥ-i asbāb* – The text of this work is the *Asbāb wa 'alāmāt* of Najīb al-Dīn Samarqandī, the well-known 7th/13th century physician and pharmacologist, and the commentary by the same Nafīs ibn 'Iwaj Kirmānī mentioned above.

3. The *Qānūn (Canon)* – This magnum opus of Ibn Sīnā, consisting of five books, is the most important work in Islamic medicine.[30] It is usually studied in Persia with the commentaries of Fakhr al-Dīn Rāzī, Quṭb al-Dīn al-Miṣrī, 'Alā' al-Dīn Qarashī and Muḥammad ibn Maḥmūd Āmulī. But the most thorough and respected commentary is that of Quṭb al-Dīn Shīrāzī which stands as a major medical work of its own.

4. *Fuṣūl-i Buqrāt* – Many of the works of Hippocrates have been popular among medical students, perhaps the foremost being the *Fuṣūl*, which, in Persia, is usually studied with the commentaries of 'Abd al-Raḥmān ibn 'Alī (known as Ibn Abī Ṣādiq), Ibn Quff and 'Alā' al-Dīn Qarashī.

V. The Mathematical Sciences (*riyāḍiyyāt*)

1. Geometry – The students of geometry relied most of all upon the *Elements* (*Uṣūl*) of Euclid in the translation, recensions and

commentaries of Ḥajjāj ibn Maṭar, Ḥunayn ibn Isḥāq, Thābit ibn Qurrah and Abū 'Uthmān al-Dimashqī until the 7th/13th century. At that time, with the appearance of the *Taḥrīr* of Naṣīr al-Dīn Ṭūsī, this work became the main text for the study of geometry along with the glosses of Mīr Sayyid Sharīf Jurjānī. This in turn was translated into Persian and commented upon by Mullā Mahdī Narāqī (12th/18th century). Actually the section on geometry in the *Durrat al-tāj* of Quṭb al-Dīn Shīrāzī is also a Persian version of Naṣīr al-Dīn's recension.

2. Arithmetic (*ḥisāb*) – In the older days the *Shamsiyyat al-ḥisāb* of Niẓām al-Dīn Ḥasan ibn Muḥammad Nayshābūrī (7th/13th century) and the *Miftāḥ al-ḥisāb* of Ghiyāth al-Dīn Jamshīd Kāshānī[31] were the most common works, but in the Safavid period they were replaced to some extent by the *Khulāṣat al-ḥisāb* of Shaykh Bahā' al-Dīn 'Āmilī (11th/17th century) with the commentary of his student, Jawād ibn Sa'dallāh Kāẓimaynī. In the Qajar period Mu'tamid al-Dawlah Farhād Mīrzā wrote another important commentary upon it which also became popular.

3. Astronomy (*hay'at*)

a) *Risāla-yi fārsī dar hay 'at* – The text is by the already mentioned 'Alā' al-Dīn Qūshchī and it is usually accompanied by the commentary of Muṣliḥ al-Dīn Lārī (11th/17th century).

b) *Sharḥ-i mulakhkhaṣ* – The *Mulakhkhaṣ* is by Maḥmūd Chagmīnī (8th/14th century) and is commented upon by Mūsā ibn Maḥmūd, known as Qāḍīzāda-yi Rūmī (9th/15th century) who composed it for Ulugh Beg. 'Abd al-'Alī Bīrjandī and Mīr Sayyid Sharīf Jurjānī have written glosses upon the commentary which are usually studied with the text and the commentary, while many other existing glosses have been forgotten.

c) The *Tadhkirah* – This is the celebrated work of Naṣīr al-Dīn Ṭūsī upon which many commentaries have been written, the most popular being that of Bīrjandī.[32]

d) The *Almagest* – Since the early Islamic period, the *Almagest* of Ptolemy was popular in the Arabic translation of Ḥajjāj ibn Maṭar, Isḥāq ibn Ḥunayn and Thābit ibn Qurrah. Later it was studied in the recension of Naṣīr al-Dīn Ṭūsī with the commentaries of Niẓām al-Dīn Nayshābūrī and 'Abd al-'Alī Bīrjandī.

But before studying the *Almagest*, several other works were studied which stood between the *Elements* and the *Almagest* and which, for this reason, were called the 'intermediate' works (*mutawassiṭāt*). They include:

a) The *Spherics* of Theodosius
b) *On the Moving Sphere* of Autolycus
c) The *Spherics* of Menelaus
d) The *Optics* of Euclid
e) The *Data* of Euclid
f) The *Phenomena* of Euclid

All of these works have been studied in the recension of Naṣīr al-Dīn Ṭūsī.

4. Other branches of the mathematical sciences.

An important branch of these sciences, which always attracted the interest of students, was the science of the astrolabe on which many works exist such as the *Kitāb al-usṭurlāb* of 'Abd al-Raḥmān Ṣūfī, whose *Ṣuwar al-kawākib* has also always been popular; the *Istī'āb fi'l-'amal bi'l-usṭurlāb* of Bīrūnī; the *Bīst bāb dar fann-i usṭurlāb* of Ṭūsī upon which 'Abd al-'Alī Bīrjandī has written a commentary; and two treatises by Shaykh Bahā' al-Dīn 'Āmilī, one in Arabic called *Ṣafīḥah* and the other in Persian entitled *Tuḥfa-yi ḥātamī*.

The description of the texts used in the *madrasahs* of Persia and adjacent areas until a couple of generations ago is an indication of the breadth of Islamic education when it was alive and embraced all the intellectual disciplines. It is true that this *madrasah* system did not come to terms with the modern scientific disciplines in the same way that Islamic thought confronted the Graeco-Hellenistic heritage. The fault lies as much with the educational authorities who sought to establish separate educational systems as with the traditional scholars in the *madrasahs* who refused to consider the challenge of modern science and learning. Today, there is educational havoc nearly everywhere throughout the Islamic world with contending and often contradictory educational systems vying for the souls and hearts of the new generation.

In this critical situation, the *madrasah* system, as reflected in the breadth of the program outlined above and as seen in the classical period when this system was at the height of its vigor, is not only the precious repository of the traditional Islamic sciences, but also the model from which any educational system claiming to be integrated within the various modes of Islamic culture, be it Persian, Arabic or

Turkish, can benefit in many basic ways. There is still a great deal that all contemporary Muslim educationalists can learn from the *madrasahs*, and these venerable institutions are of much greater importance to the future educational life of the various Islamic countries than the modern educationalists, who are enamoured of the rapidly changing pedagogical theories of the West, are willing to admit.

Notes

1. On the 'transmitted' and 'intellectual' sciences see our *Science and Civilization in Islam*, chapter 2; also our *Islamic Science – An Illustrated Study*, London, 1976, pp. 14ff.
2. On the life of Taqizadeh see the introduction of I. Afshar to his edition of *Maqālāt-i Taqizadeh*, Tehran, 1349 (A.H. solar).
3. Published by I. Afshar in *Farhange-e Īrānzamīn*, vol. 20, 1353/1975, pp. 39–82. Throughout this article, the prevalent Persian pronunciation of the names of people and books has been preserved in the case of names and well-known terms in Persian scholarly circles.
4. Mīr Sayyid Sharīf was at once theologian, philosopher and Sufi and is best known for his 'definitions' of the terminology of the Islamic sciences, the *Kitāb al-ta'rīfāt*.
5. Zanjānī's fame lies mostly in this treatise, whereas Taftāzānī, who was the chief *qāḍī* of Shiraz, is one of the leading exponents of late Ash'arism and his theological works are read extensively to this day in Sunni *madrasahs* throughout the Islamic world.
6. This extensive and well-composed commentary is called *Zīnat al-sālik fī sharḥ alfiyyah ibn Mālik*.
7. Shaykh Bahā' al-Dīn 'Āmilī, who died in 1030 (1621), was originally from the Jabal 'Amil in Lebanon, but was brought to Persia when he was only twelve years old. He became a master of both the exoteric and esoteric sciences and was at once the leading religious authority of Isfahan, probably the greatest poet of the Persian language of the period, a leading mathematician, architect and city planner as well as one of the outstanding Sufis of the age. Many of his works in various fields have become authoritative throughout Persia, the *Ṣamadiyyah* being one of the most famous of all. On Bahā' al-Dīn 'Āmilī see our *Science and Civilization in Islam*, pp. 57–58.

8. The science of *uṣūl* has received a great deal of attention during the last few centuries in Shi'ism, and the last two or three centuries must be considered its 'golden age' in which numerous essential treatises, very few of which have been studied in the outside world until now, have been written. In Sunnism, however, the most important treatises were written several centuries earlier. On Sunni *uṣūl* see B. Weiss, 'The Primacy of Revelation in Sayf al-Dīn al-Āmidī,' *Studia Islamica*, vol. LIX, 1984, pp. 79–109.
9. On this major opus and Mūlla Ṣadrā's commentary upon it see Corbin, *En Islam iranien*, vol. IV, pp. 84ff.
10. On Mīr Dāmād see Corbin, *op. cit.* pp. 9ff.; also *A History of Muslim Philosophy*, vol. II, our 'The School of Isfahan', in M.M. Sharif (ed.), pp. 914ff.
11. Najm al-Dīn Dabīrān Kātibī is one of the important philosophical figures in the circle of Naṣīr al-Dīn Ṭūsī but is not well known in the outside world. In Persia itself, however, his writings have always been widely popular.
12. Quṭb al-Dīn Rāzī is best known for his *Muḥākamāt* (*Trials*) which judges between the commentaries of Fakhr al-Dīn Rāzī and Naṣīr al-Dīn Ṭūsī upon the *Ishārāt* of Ibn Sīnā. But he has also written other important works, which have been neglected by scholars so far.
13. Sirāj al-Dīn Urmawī, the author of numerous works, including the *Laṭā'if al-ḥikmah* in Persian, was one of the main figures of the intellectual center of Qunyah during the lifetime of Mawlānā Jalāl al-Dīn Rūmī.
14. See our 'Sabziwārī' in M.M. Sharif (ed.), *A History of Modern Philosophy*, vol. II, pp. 1543ff. The text of the section on metaphysics of this major work has been edited critically by T. Izutsu and M. Mohaghegh, *Sharḥ-i manẓūmah*, Tehran, 1969. This work contains a long English introduction by Izutsu, but the text begins with the section on metaphysics and excludes logic.
15. The spread of the popularity of this work is a gauge of the intellectual relations which still existed between various *madrasahs* in the Islamic world in the 13th/19th century.
16. On Suhrawardī's criticism of Aristotelian logic see M.T. Sharī'atī, 'Barrasi-yi manṭiq-i Suhrawardī wa muqāyasa-yi ān bā manṭiq-i arisṭū'ī', *Maqālāt wa barrasīhā* (Journal of the Faculty of Theology of Tehran University), 1352, vol. 13–16, pp. 318–329.
17. For these figures see S.J. Ashtiyani and H. Corbin, *Anthologie des philosophes iraniens*, vols. I and II.
18. The commentary of Mullā Ṣadrā is so famous in India that to this day the work itself is referred to as 'Ṣadrā'. In any case, it is one of the four or five most popular works on Peripatetic philosophy.
19. The most recent major study of this work is by A. Sha'rānī, *Kashf al-murād-Sharḥ-i tajrīd al-'aqā'id*, Tehran, 1351 (A.H. solar).
20. Lāhījī is also the author of the popular Persian treatise on *kalām*, the *Gawhar-murād*. See our '*Al-Ḥikmat al-ilāhiyyah* and *Kalam*', *Studia*

Islamica vol. XXXIV, 1971, pp. 145ff; and Ashtiyani and Corbin, *Anthologie*, vol. I, pp. 117ff.

21. The lithographed edition of the *Ḥikmat al-ishrāq* contains both the commentary of Quṭb al-Dīn and the glosses of Mullā Ṣadrā, while the critical edition of Corbin, *Oeuvres philosophiques et mystiques*, vol. I, Tehran-Paris, 1977, includes the text of Suhrawardī and certain selections from Quṭb al-Dīn and Mullā Ṣadrā, as well as the lesser-known but very important commentary of Shams al-Dīn Muḥammad Shahrazūrī.
22. On the *Asfār* see our *The Transcendent Theosophy of Ṣadr al-Dīn Shīrāzī*, chapter 3.
23. On Ibn Turkah see Corbin, *En Islam iranien*, vol III, chapter III.
24. The first critical edition of this work, making use of the tradition emanating from Āqā Muḥammad Riḍā Qumsha'ī, has been edited by S.T. Ashtiyani, with Persian and English introductions by S.H. Nasr, Tehran, 1977.
25. On Ibn 'Arabī and the *Fuṣūṣ* see T. Burckhardt, *La sagesse des prophètes*, Paris, 1955 (trans. into English from the French by A. Culme-Seymour, *The Wisdom of the Prophets*, Gloucestershire (U.K.), 1975); T. Izutsu, *Sufism and Taoism*, Part I, London, 1983; and R.W.J. Austin (trans.), Ibn al-'Arabī, *The Bezels of Wisdom*, New York, 1980.

    On the commentaries upon the *Fuṣūṣ* see O. Yahya, *Histoire et classification de l'oeuvre d'Ibn 'Arabī*, 20 vols., Damascus, 1964.
26. See W. Chittick (ed.), *Naqd al-nuṣūṣ fī sharḥ naqsh al-fuṣūṣ* of Jāmī, Tehran, 1977, in whose introduction Jāmī's direct commentary upon the *Fuṣūṣ* is discussed. The *Naqd al-nuṣūṣ* itself contains what may be called an anthology of the major commentaries upon the *Fuṣūṣ*.
27. The vast commentary of Jandī upon the *Fuṣūṣ* has been edited for the first time by S.J. Ashtiyani, as *Sharḥ fuṣūṣ al-ḥikam*, Mashhad, 1982, with an English prolegomena by T. Izutsu.
28. The text of this difficult work has been partly translated and analysed in a European language for the first time by S. Ruspoli in his doctoral thesis at the Sorbonne, *La clef du monde suprasensible*, which has not yet been published.
29. Mīrzā Ṭāhir Tunikābunī, *op. cit.*, p. 54, complains of the lack of interest in the study of medicine in the *madrasahs* during his own day. The situation in fact deteriorated so rapidly afterwards that by the beginning of this century the teaching of traditional medicine in the *madrasahs* in Persia was discontinued completely. It has survived here and there only through the private instruction of individual masters of the art. See Nasr *Islamic Science – An Illustrated Study*, chapter VIII; and Elgood, *Safavid Medical Practice*, London, 1970.
30. On the *Canon* see O.C. Gruner, *A Treatise on the Canon of Medicine, Incorporating the Translation of the First Book*, London, 1930; and M. Ullmann, *Die Medizin in Islam*, Leiden, 1970, pp. 152–154.
31. The *Miftāḥ al-ḥisāb* is probably the most important Islamic work on arithmetic and has drawn a great deal of attention during the past few

decades. See A. Qurbānī, *Kāshānī-nāmah*, Tehran, 1350 (A.H. solar), part 3.

32. This important work of Ṭūsī has been studied by many historians of astronomy, including E.S. Kennedy, and is now being translated by G. Saliba.

Chapter Eleven

Philosophy in the Present-Day Islamic World

One of the arenas in which the confrontation of traditional Islam with modernism can be studied most directly is that of philosophy in its most general sense. Here ideas encounter ideas, with consequences for nearly every other field of human endeavor, from science to politics, from art to social life. The philosophic life of the Islamic world over the past few decades has been woven from many diverse strands and reflects all the tensions, contradictions, and conflicts which the encounter of tradition and modernism has brought about in all parts of the globe where tradition, Islamic or otherwise, still survives. To understand recent philosophic activity in various parts of the Islamic world, however, it is necessary to outline, albeit briefly, the underlying tradition and the general intellectual background within which, or occasionally in opposition to which, philosophical activity has taken place and continues to take place in this quarter. However, because of the vastness of the Islamic world, stretching from the southern Philippines to the coast of the Atlantic, we are forced to concentrate in these preliminary remarks on the central lands of Islam; thus, although our vision has to be extended in time, it has to be somewhat contracted spatially.

Islam was heir to the philosophical heritage of both the Mediterranean world and the Indian subcontinent. It transformed this heritage within the world-view of Islam and according to the spirit and letter of the Quran and brought into being a vast array of intellectual and philosophical schools, only some of which may be technically termed 'philosophy' (*falsafah*). But there are others, including several that did not bear the name of philosophy,[1] which have had the greatest philosophical importance according to the most authentic meaning of the term in the English language. This tradition produced such renowned intellectual figures as al-Fārābī, Ibn Sīnā, al-Ghazzālī, Suhrawardī, Ibn Rushd, Ibn 'Arabī, Mīr Dāmād, and Mullā Ṣadrā, some of whom are well known in the West and others of whom are only now becoming known outside the Islamic world.[2] In the Arab world, philosophy as a distinct discipline disappeared after the 6th/12th century and became drowned in the two seas of gnosis and theology. In Persia, the Turkish part of the Ottoman world and the Indian subcontinent, in addition to theology and gnosis, philosophy as such also continued and in fact has survived in many of those regions to our own day.[3] When the Islamic world first encountered the West in the 19th century in such countries as Egypt, Persia, Turkey and the Indian subcontinent, the existing intellectual tradition in each land reacted according to local conditions but within the general context of the universal intellectual tradition of Islam. Such figures as Sayyid Jamāl al-Dīn Astrābādī, usually known as al-Afghānī, Muḥammad 'Abduh, Rashīd Riḍā, Malkam Khān, Sir Aḥmad Khān, Zia Gökalp, and Muḥammad Iqbal[4] set out to encounter Western thought in different ways and were influenced by it to varying degrees.

The influence of Western philosophy in each part of the Islamic world depended upon the form of colonialism which happened to dominate in a particular land.[5] Modernized circles in the Indian subcontinent, for instance, became dominated by the English philosophy of the Victorian period. Modernized groups in Iran, on the other hand, who were attracted to French language and culture in order to escape British and Russian influences from the North and South, became infatuated with Descartes and later Cartesian philosophy and also with the Comtian positivism of the 19th century. Modernized Turks were attracted to German philosophy and the Westernized Egyptians to both the English and French schools depending on the experience of various individual philosophers and thinkers. Likewise, North Africa and the French-speaking parts of Islamic Africa became dominated by French modes of thought, and the English-speaking areas by English ones.

With the end of the Second World War, most Muslim countries gained political independence, but the philosophical scene, especially at the university level, continued for the most part to be dominated by Western thought. Now, however, Marxism became a new element which attracted a number of thinkers, especially in lands where an intense struggle for independence had led certain people to join politically leftist causes. The sense of Islamic identity, however, continued to assert itself, and perhaps the most important philosophical concern of the most relevant intellectuals remained the tension between Islam and modern Western civilization. Such themes as the spread of Western thought, including its Marxist version, and the interaction between science and philosophies of a positivistic nature, on the one hand, and religion and religious philosophies, on the other, became the main concern of Muslims engaged in philosophical activity. During the past few decades, although the earlier schools of European philosophy, now out of fashion in the West, have continued to survive in a surprising fashion,[6] newer modes of Western thought, such as logical positivism and analytical philosophy, existentialism, neo-Marxism and even structuralism, have begun to gain some attention.

But during this same period one can also observe another intellectual activity of the greatest importance, namely, the revival of Islamic thought in its various traditional forms, such as Sufism, theology, and philosophy itself in its technical sense as traditionally understood. A sense of disillusionment with modern Western civilization, uncertainty about the future and the need to return to the heart of religion have turned many people, especially the educated, to a re-examination of Sufism and a rekindling of interest in its teaching. This change is seen in the larger number of younger people, including many from the professional classes, drawn to Sufi orders in such countries as Egypt and Iran,[7] and the extensive spread of the teachings of such outstanding contemporary Sufi masters as Shaykh al-'Alawī.[8] One can also observe the spread of new versions of the earlier Wahhābī and Salafiyyah movements, characterized by a moral puritanism, 'return' to the norms of early Islam and, to a large extent, disdain for philosophical discourse. Finally, these same forces have guided many people to a rediscovery of Islamic philosophy itself and its subsequent revival, especially in Iran.[9] Therefore, it can be said that during the past few decades, at the same time that various forms of modern philosophy have penetrated further into the intellectual life of the Islamic world, a revival of traditional Islamic thought in its various modes has also been observable in most Islamic countries, and at the present moment an intense battle is being waged between these two trends for the minds and souls of educated Muslims.

In this brief survey, one can refer only to the most salient features of philosophical activity in that vast expanse of the earth's surface known as the Islamic world. It is only appropriate to begin with that heartland, namely the Arabic-Persian-Turkish world, which has nearly always provided the most widespread and enduring intellectual and spiritual impulses for the Islamic community as a whole. Today, the peoples in this area remain a minority within the Islamic world, but this area must still be considered as the center of that vaster world whose life and thought are determined by the Islamic revelation.

Let us begin with the Arab world and especially its eastern part. In this region, Egypt and Syria were the greatest centers of cultural and philosophical activity in the earlier decades of the 20th century and continued to hold this position after the Second World War, although Lebanon also came into prominence after its independence. In Egypt, the important institutions of philosophical activity of earlier days, such as Al-Azhar, Cairo, Ain Shams, and Alexandria universities, and the Arab Academy of Cairo, have continued to be dominant. Moreover, many of the figures who had already gained prominence before and during the Second World War, such as 'Abd al-Ḥalīm Maḥmūd (especially his earlier works), 'Uthmān Amīn, Ibrāhīm Madkour, A.A. Anawati, 'Abd al-Raḥmān Badawī, Aḥmad Fu'ād al-Ahwānī, Sulaymān Dunyā, Muḥammad Abū Rayyān, and Abu'l-'Alā'al-Afīfī, have continued to dominate the scene, some until recently and others to the present day. Almost all of these figures have been interested in the revival of Islamic philosophy as well as its encounter with Western thought. Some of them, such as Badawī, have written on such modern Western schools as existentialism more as followers than as detached students. Other scholars and philosophers who have gained fame as a result of following these earlier figures, for example, Muḥammad Abū Rīdah and Abu'l-Wafā' al-Taftazānī, have likewise combined training in Western thought with Islamic philosophy. They are best known for combining Western methods of philosophical analysis and scholarship with Islamic philosophical and mystical thought.

Since the Second World War, the aim of reviving Islamic thought has been combined with a major movement to translate Western philosophy into Arabic. There have also been major celebrations of the anniversaries of leading Islamic philosophers such as al-Kindī, al-Fārābī, Ibn Sīnā, al-Ghazzālī, Ibn Rushd, Suhrawardī, Ibn 'Arabī and Ibn Khaldūn in Egypt and often in many other countries of the Islamic world. These have led to editions of texts, preparation of bibliographies, analytical monographs, and histories.[10] As for translations of European philosophy, they have included many of the best known works of post-Renaissance philosophy, especially those of French and German philosophers such as Descartes, Voltaire, Kant and Hegel. There have also been histories of Western philosophy such as that of Luṭfī Jum'ah. Unfortunately, many of these translations have been made by scholars not fully aware of the richness of classical philosophical Arabic and in quality many of them fall far short of the earlier translations of Greek philosophical texts into Arabic.

Since the rise of the Palestinian problem, extreme Arab nationalism and the spread of leftist ideologies in Egypt, Syria and elsewhere in the region, there have also appeared many philosophical works concerned with political and economic themes rather than simply with theoretical philosophy, and these have often been influenced directly or indirectly by Marxism. Of these perhaps the most famous are those of 'Abdallah Laroui, who hails, however, from North America. Some of the thinkers of Egypt, both Muslim and Christian, became followers of the fashionable Western leftist trends of the postwar era. One can cite as an example the formation during the past few years of an 'Islamic left' (*al-yasār al-islāmī*) in Egypt and elsewhere, the best-known representative of which is Ḥasan Ḥanafī. But many of the prominent thinkers of this kind, such as Anwar 'Abd al-Malik, soon lost their infatuation with Marxism and other leftist ideologies and turned either to some form of cultural nationalism or back to Islam. This trend has thus moved in a direction parallel with the revival of Islamic thought within the traditional Islamic quarters in Egypt, such as al-Azhar, although the development of various types of secular philosophy does continue among some of the younger Arab philosophers such as Ṣādiq al-'Azm.

The revival of Islamic thought tends to be either of a puritanical vein following the Wahhabī-Salafī school of the earlier period[11] or concerned with Sufism, which has also been subject to an important revival over the past few years in Egypt. In this connection it is of interest to mention the Muslim Brotherhood (Ikhwān al-Muslimīn) which, although intellectually akin to the Wahhabī school, was structured upon the model of the Sufi orders. The leading intellectual figure of the Ikhwān, Sayyid Quṭb, although severely opposed to philosophy in its academic sense, himself produced a 'philosophy' based upon the teachings of the Quran with which he sought to combat ideologies imported from the West.[12]

In Syria, a situation similar to that of Egypt is to be observed. Earlier figures such as Jamīl Ṣalībā and Khalīl Georr have remained active. The Arab Academy of Damascus has continued its concern with creating a terminology to express modern philosophical thought. More traditional scholars, such as Sāmī al-Kiyālī and 'Ārif Tāmir, have been concerned with the revival of Islamic philosophy, while some of the Westernized intellectuals – mostly Christian but also some Muslim – have continued their earlier fascination with European philosophy, especially leftist politico-philosophical ideologies. Such men as Constantine Zurayk and Michel Aflaq, who wrote theoretical works on Arab nationalism and socialism, became fathers of political movements. Gradually, a form of Arab socialism became dominant in the name of the Ba'th party, which still rules in Syria as well as in Iraq, and which has caused many works of political philosophy to be written based on the idea of Arab socialism.

Parallel with this development there has been the revival of interest in Sufism during the last few decades. Much of this revival is closely connected with the Shādhiliyyah Order and more specifically the great Algerian saint Shaykh al-'Alawī, who had many disciples in Syria.[13] The revival has also produced works of intellectual quality, as can be seen in the case of the Sufi master from Aleppo, Shaykh 'Abd al-Qādir. In the field of Sufi metaphysics, it is also necessary to mention the extensive works of the Syrian scholar 'Uthmān Yaḥyā, who resides in Paris and also sometimes Cairo. Besides editing and studying the works of major figures of Sufism, especially Ibn 'Arabī, he has written as a philosopher living within the tradition of Islamic philosophy but concerned with contemporary problems especially those of modern man in a secularized world.

Lebanon has been the focus of a more modernized form of philosophical activity than either Syria or Egypt. In its universities, especially St. Joseph, most of the external philosophical influence has been French, as is also the case in Syria. Only in the American University of Beirut has Anglo-Saxon philosophy been present. Until the recent civil war, Lebanon was the major center for the publication of Arabic books in the region, especially in the field of philosophy, vying with Cairo for the lead in the Arab world. Up to a few years ago, Lebanon tried to play the role of a bridge between the West and the Islamic world, although it was in reality more of a beachhead for the Western assault upon Islam than a bridge connecting two worlds.

In Lebanon, several eminent Christian Arab philosophers have been active. Perhaps the most famous is Charles Malik who, despite his immersion in the world of Western liberalism, remains deeply Christian. One can also mention Archbishop Khodr, who is one of the leading Orthodox theologians of our day. During the past few decades, there have been such Lebanese scholars, both Muslim and Christian, as 'Umar Farrukh, Ḥasan Ṣa'b, Kamāl al-Yāzijī, Farīd Jabre, Albert Nader, Majīd Fakhrī, and 'Afīf 'Uṣayrān, who have been concerned with the study of Islamic philosophy, and Yusuf Ibish, who is one of the foremost contemporary students of Sufism and one of the leading exponents of the traditional point of view in the Arab world. As far as Sufism is concerned, it is also important to mention Sayyidah Fāṭimah Yashruṭiyyah, who was perhaps the most eminent female figure in Sufism until her recent death and who produced some of the most notable works on Sufism in Arabic in recent years.

With regard to Jordan and the Palestinian people, the traumatic events following the war of 1948 have turned the attention of the intellectual community of this region nearly completely to questions of a political nature, and the few Palestinians, such as 'Abd al-Laṭīf al-Ṭībāwī, who have been concerned with philosophy have been active in other countries. In Jordan, interest in philosophy is growing gradually as the University of Amman becomes interested in theological and philosophical studies, and slowly Amman is becoming a center for the publication of works in Arabic dealing, among other subjects, with philosophy.

In Iraq, until the Second World War, the British style of education went hand in hand with the activity of major Islamic centers of learning, especially the Shi'ite university in Najaf. The most notable activity during the past few decades has been the revival of scholarship in the field of Islamic philosophy, but tempered with discipline derived mostly from Anglo-Saxon, but also from other European forms of scholarship. Iraq has produced several scholars of note who have combined both forms of discipline, namely, the Islamic and European. These scholars include Bāqir al-Ṣadr, Kāmil al-Shaybī, Ḥusayn 'Alī Maḥfūẓ, and especially Muḥsin Mahdī, who has made noteworthy contributions to the study of al-Fārābī and Ibn Khaldūn. There has also been some effort to study the philosophy of Islamic education, especially by Fāḍil al-Jamālī. Moreover, in Iraq as in Syria, a number of philosophical works have appeared which deal with various forms of Arab nationalism, socialism and the like. Most of these works, however, are of a practical rather than of a purely theoretical nature.

The western region of the Arab world was a much more conservative and 'conserving' region than the Arab east until the Second World War. In this western area, embracing the region from Libya and Tunisia to the Atlantic, until the independence movements arose, traditional Islamic thought in both its metaphysical and theological aspects was very strong. Several outstanding Sufi masters dominated the spiritual and intellectual climate of the Maghrib. Disciples of Shaykh al-'Alawī have kept his presence alive in many regions, although the heart of his spiritual teachings was to travel to the Occident where it has had a profound and incalculable effect. Other masters such as Shaykh Muḥammad al-Tādilī have also contributed to the preservation of the Sufi tradition in the Maghrib.

Since the Second World War, at least two other notable tendencies have opposed Sufism in the Maghrib. The first is a crypto-Wahhābī puritanism inspired by movements of a similar nature in

Egypt and others of the eastern lands of Islam, and modern anti-traditional European philosophy. The puritanical rationalism of the Maghrib is little different from what is found among the Salafiyyah of Egypt and the neo-Wahhābism of Arabia. It has been marked by an open opposition to Sufism, especially its popular form, which in the Maghrib is known as *Maraboutism*[14] and a strong zeal for social reform, as well as engagement in political action with the aim of re-establishing the rule of Islamic sacred law (*Sharī'ah*). In this connection, it is important to mention the Istiqlal party of Morocco and its founder, 'Allāl al-Fāsī, who was one of the foremost thinkers of the Maghrib during the past few decades. He developed a political and social philosophy based upon certain traditional Islamic theses with elements akin to certain Salafī Wahhābī thinkers of the East but with a distinct Maghribi color. He is sometimes called a 'fundamentalist'. If this appellation be accepted, then he represents a form of 'fundamentalism' much closer to the traditional position than the violent 'fundamentalism' of the counter-traditional variety.

The second tendency, namely, European philosophy, is of a rather peculiar character in the Maghrib. In Egypt, the European philosophy which became influential was not limited to a single school. In the Maghrib, because of the predominant French influence and the preponderance of Marxism and an agnostic existentialism in French university circles after the War, these schools have become nearly completely dominant as far as European philosophy is concerned. In no other region of the Islamic world have Marxism and existentialism of the French school had such influence within university circles as in the Maghrib. It is also here that, over the past few years, strange attempts have been made to wed leftist ideologies emanating from 19th-century European philosophy with Islam. The result is various forms of 'Islamic socialism,' and even 'Islamic Marxism,' which can be seen especially in Algeria and Libya. This type of thought, which is usually closely related to various political interests, is also to be found in other Muslim countries even outside the Arab world, although it is usually confined to limited circles.

The Maghrib has also produced a small number of well-known thinkers who have attempted to chart a more distinct course and not simply follow Western fashions. Among this group is the Moroccan philosopher Ḥabīb Lahbabi, who has developed what he calls

'Islamic personalism' based on certain theses of Islamic thought and some of the predominant ideas of continental philosophy, especially existentialism. But he stands closer to modern thought than to the mainstream of Islamic philosophy. Another well-known figure from the Maghrib is the Algerian Muḥammad Arkoun who, after a serious study of Western thought, including Marxism, has turned to Islamic philosophy as a living reality. He has written both on traditional Islamic schools of philosophy and on the confrontation of Islamic thought with modernism. He is one of the first contemporary Sunni thinkers to interest himself in a dialogue with Shi'ism. One must also mention Ben Abboud, one of the leading thinkers of Morocco, who is much closer to traditional Islamic philosophy and Sufism, while interesting himself especially in the question of the nature of man. His interests are akin to those of the Tunisian, Ben Milād, who also seeks to apply Islamic philosophical teachings to the situation of man in the contemporary world with emphasis upon dynamism.[15]

In Iran, Islamic philosophy did not cease to exist as a living tradition after the so-called Middle Ages, but has survived to the present day. In fact, there was a major revival of Islamic philosophy during the Safavid period with the appearance of such figures as Mīr Dāmād and Mullā Ṣadrā. A second revival took place during the 13th/19th century led by Mullā 'Alī Nūrī, Ḥājjī Mullā Hādī Sabziwārī, and others,[16] and this tradition continued strong in the Islamic universities (*madrasahs*) into the Pahlavi period. From the end of the First World War, European philosophy, especially that of the French school identified with such figures as Descartes and, more recently, Bergson, became influential among the Western-educated classes, in particular at the modern universities and colleges, although acquaintance with French philosophy goes back to the Qajar period. During the past few decades, the European influence continued and in fact was extended to include the existentialist school. At the same time, there occurred a major revival of traditional Islamic philosophy, even among the modern educated classes. This marks a unique phenomenon in the contemporary Islamic world inasmuch as this revival did not merely involve interest in scholarship in the field of Islamic philosophy. It also signified that the tradition of Islamic philosophy, especially the school of Mullā Ṣadrā, was being taken seriously as a living and viable intellectual perspective capable of meeting the challenge of various schools of European thought.[17] The revival continues to this day through all the transformations which have taken place in Iran, while the study of European philosophy has become curtailed, except when presented in 'revolutionary' dress with an Islamic coloring.

Among the most active traditional figures in the revival of Islamic philosophy in Iran, one can mention Sayyid Abu'l-Ḥasan Qazwīnī, Sayyid Muḥammad Kāẓim 'Aṣṣār, Ilāhī Qumsha'ī, 'Allāmah Sayyid Muḥammad Ḥusayn Ṭabāṭabā'ī, all eminent philosophers and gnostics,[18] Murtaḍā Muṭahharī, Mahdī Ḥā'irī,[19] Sayyid Jalāl al-Dīn Āshtiyānī and Jawād Muṣliḥ. There are also those who have tried to deal with modern philosophical questions and the challenges of Western thought from the point of Islamic metaphysics and philosophy. Still others, although trained in modern universities, are concerned mostly with the editions and study of Islamic philosophical texts. This last-named group includes such scholars as M. Khwansārī, M. Moghaghegh, J. Falaturi, M.T. Danechepazhuh, M. Mo'in, and S.J. Sajjādī.

Those concerned mostly with European philosophy, its translation into Persian and exposition for the Persian world include R. Shafaq, G. Sadīghī, Y. Mahdavī, and Sharaf Khurāsānī. During the past few decades, all of these scholars have made important studies and translations of European philosophy of the earlier period. Another group, including M. Bozorgmehr, N. Daryābandarī, and M. Raḥīmī, have been concerned more with contemporary European philosophy, the first two with Anglo-Saxon philosophy and the third with French existentialism. Recently, there has also been some interest in Heidegger, whose ideas have been expounded in comparison with traditional Islamic thought by A. Fardīd and many of his colleagues and students. Likewise, some attention has been paid to various neo-Marxist modes of thought. In this connection one must mention 'A. Shari'ati, who sought to combine a populist interpretation of Islam with certain Marxist theses and who had an important philosophical and political impact during the Iranian Revolution. His philosophical interpretations were, however, opposed by most of the traditional Islamic philosophers, especially M. Muṭahharī.

As in other Islamic countries, so in Iran, the last few decades have been witness to a major rise of interest in Sufism among the educated classes. Most of the important orders, such as the

Ni'matallāhī and Dhahabī, were extremely active throughout the country until the events of 1979 and also produced many mystical works of great philosophical significance. In this context, the voluminous writings of Javād Nourbakhsh, the spiritual leader of the Ni'matallāhī order, are of particular significance. Some of his shorter tracts on various aspects of Sufism have also been rendered into English and French.

Philosophical activity in Iran is so extensive that it is not possible to describe all of its facets in this short survey. Suffice it to say that both in traditional schools and in most universities philosophy has been taught and studied, and numerous works continue to appear on the subject every year. Iran was also the first Islamic country to establish an active philosophical academy.[20]

Iran's neighboring country, Afghanistan, which shares the same philosophical tradition with it, has been distinguished during the past few decades mostly by activity in the domain of Sufism. Such scholars as G. Māyil Hirawī and M.I. Muballigh have made important contributions to the study of Jāmī and the metaphysical school of Ibn 'Arabī in general. Scholars like A.G. Rawān Farhādī have delved into the teachings of Sufism, taking into consideration the works of such European orientalists as L. Massignon. Within university circles, the philosophical scene more or less resembles that of Iran with somewhat less diversity as regards the influence of Western schools of thought.

In Turkey, the philosophical situation is similar to that in many other Islamic countries in that there has been a marked rise of interest during recent years in the study of Islamic thought and a definite Islamic revival. This revival, intellectually at least, is perhaps best exemplified by the publication of many texts of Islamic philosophy and also by the renewal of interest in the works of Sayyid Sa'īd Nūrsī. The more secular atmosphere of Turkey has also caused a wide range of philosophical works to be translated and studied in modern educational circles without reference to Islamic considerations. In these circles, the influence of German schools of thought is more marked than in other Islamic countries.

The most notable contribution of Turkish scholars to philosophy over the past few decades has been in the domains of Sufism and the history of science rather than in the more narrowly defined philosophical disciplines. In the field of Sufism, such scholars as A. Gölpinarli, A. Ateš and T. Yaziçi have brought back the reality of the Sufi tradition to contemporary Turkish society, especially to the younger generation, which is no longer familiar with the classical works of Sufism. As for the history of science, such figures as A. Sayili, E. Tekeli, and S. Unver have made major contributions to the study of Islamic science and all that it implies philosophically. There have also been some notable Turkish contributions to the study of Islamic philosophy and theology proper, as shown in the work of M. Turker, I. Choboqchi, H. Atay and others. In contemporary Turkey, there is a polarization in the domain of philosophy between traditional Islamic thought and various forms of modern philosophy and ideology, including Marxism, which is more extreme than in most other Islamic countries and which is reflected in the situation within the universities.

In the Indian subcontinent, in addition to two Islamic countries, Pakistan and Bangladesh, there are tens of millions of Muslims in India, Sri Lanka and Nepal. The philosophical situation in this part of the world is quite different from that of any other part of the Islamic world. As a result of British domination over the area, various schools of Anglo-Saxon philosophy became deeply entrenched in the philosophy departments of the major universities and continue to be dominant today. The earlier political and social 'reformers' of the subcontinent, notably Sir Aḥmad Khān and Muḥammad Iqbāl, were also much more concerned with philosophy in the Western sense of the term than were the 'reformers' of the Arab world. Philosophical institutions, such as the All-India Philosophical Congress, were carried over into the era of independence, and both the Indian and Pakistani Philosophical Congresses have been active during past decades.[21] They have served as rallying points for philosophical activity, most of which is Western, specifically British and American. One can discern ever greater interest in Islamic thought, however, as demonstrated by the monumental *A History of Muslim Philosophy* edited by the late M.M. Sharif, one of the leading intellectual figures of Pakistan.

In Pakistan, the older philosophers, including M.M. Ahmad, M.M. Sharif, A.C. Qadir, and K. 'Abd al-Ḥakīm, have focused on issues arising from European philosophy. They have also sought to find some of the answers in the Islamic tradition, particularly Sufism, to which many of them, especially M.M. Ahmad, have been devoted. There have also been a few figures, foremost among them being Mohammad Hasan Askari, who have followed the traditional point of view and have opposed completely modern European philosophy. The most active students of this older generation of philosophers have pursued nearly the same combined interest in European philosophy and Islamic thought with which they have dealt in only certain fields and subjects. B.A. Dar has published numerous works on European philosophy, including that of Kant, while making comparisons with certain schools of Islamic thought. He thus exemplifies a trend which is strong among both Muslim and Hindu scholars in the subcontinent, namely, attempting to compare and often to synthesize Western and Eastern schools of thought.[22] Saeed Shaikh, another of the younger generation of philosophers, has been interested mostly in Islamic thought, as has M.S.H. Ma'sumi, while Manzoor Ahmad has turned to the study of the philosophy of art and comparative religion.

As for the young generation attracted to tradition, those involved with the journal *Riwāyat*, which is completely dedicated to tradition and unique in the Islamic world today, should be mentioned, especially its editor, Suhayl 'Umar, and such scholars as Ja'far Qāsimi, who has written more on Sufism than philosophy.

Pakistan has produced several notable philosophical thinkers who are at the same time influential in the life of the nation. Perhaps foremost among them is A.K. Brohi who, after a long preoccupation with modern thought, has returned to the bosom of Sufism and has expounded some of the deepest aspects of Islamic thought from a Sufi perspective. This group also includes M. Ajmal, a leading educationalist and psychologist. Ajmal is one of the first in the Islamic world to have sought to create a science of the soul based on the teachings of Sufism rather than on the imitation of Western psychoanalytical techniques and theories. A word must also be said about Fazlur Rahman, who has dealt with both with the revival of classical Islamic philosophy and a modernistic interpretation of Islam based on modern Western ideas. Finally, one must mention Mawlānā Abu'l-'Alā' Mawdūdī, the founder of the *Jamā'at-i islāmī* who, although not strictly speaking a philosopher, is perhaps the most influential of all contemporary Pakistani thinkers as far as the question of the revival of the social and economic philosophy of Islam as reflected in the *Sharī'ah* is concerned.

In India, nearly the same tendencies have been observed over the past few decades. The major centers for Muslim intellectual activity during this period have been Delhi, Aligarh, Lucknow, and

Hyderabad where some have devoted themselves to the revival of Islamic thought and others to the study of Western thought. In addition, there has been special interest in comparing the Islamic and Hindu traditions, an interest which is directly related to the particular situation of the Muslim community as a religious minority in modern India. This latter interest is reflected, for example, in the writings of M.H. Askari and even of M. Mujeeb. Such Muslim scholars as R.A. Rizvi, H. 'Abidi, H.S. Khan, A. Ma'sumi and M. Abdul Haq Ansari have been concerned with editions and analysis of classical works of Islamic philosophy, including the school of Mullā Ṣadrā. Men such as Mir Valiuddin have sought to reformulate and make better known the tradition of Sufism. Others like Mir Vahiduddin, Abid Husayn and K.G. Sayidain have been involved in studies based on the confrontation between Western trends of philosophy and Islam.

In India as in Pakistan, there has been a great revival of interest in traditional Islamic medicine and its philosophy, as well as the ecological and philosophical issues involved in the confrontation between traditional and modern science. The activities of the Hamdard Institutes of Delhi and Karachi and of their founders, Hakim 'Abd al-Hamid and Hakim Muhammad Sa'id, as well as those of the ancillary institutions established by them, especially the Institute of Islamic Studies at Delhi and the Hamdard University outside Karachi, are as important for philosophy as they are for science.

With regard to Bangladesh, its philosophical life until recently was completely wedded to that of Pakistan. Since partition, however, the same trend has continued, with the remnants of the Anglo-Saxon schools of philosophy remaining strong in university circles. There is, however, a more marked interest in Islamic philosophy among younger scholars such as A.J. Mia and M. 'Abd al-Haqq.

In the Malay-Indonesian world, which includes Singapore, the last decades have been witness to an attempt to rediscover a half-lost cultural identity. In Indonesia, numerous Islamic revivalist movements have emerged, most of which have a neo-Wahhabī color reflecting the close historical contact between that area and Arabia. There have also been attempts to revive Sufism and even certain modernistic movements claiming a traditional mystical background, such as Subud, which has gained many followers in the West thirsty for spiritual experience at any cost, have come into being. As for Malaysia, it has experienced a revival of interest in Sufism, but here the more intellectual school of Ibn 'Arabī and his followers, as it developed in that region, has received the greatest amount of attention. This particular slant in the study of Sufism is due most of all to Sayyid Naquib al-'Attas, who has devoted numerous studies to this subject, especially the works of Fanṣūrī and Rānirī. Another member of the same family, Sayyid Husayn al-'Attas, who lives in Singapore, has charted a completely different course. He has tried to create an authentic school of social science based on philosophical principles derived from the traditions of Asia rather than from 19th-century European philosophy.

Finally, a word must be said about various Muslim lands of Africa, which range from the Sudan in the east to Nigeria and Senegal in the west. In these lands, philosophical activity in the universities has for the most part followed English or French schools of thought, depending upon the colonial experience that each particular country has undergone. But there are also active Sufi movements in many areas, such as Senegal, as well as Islamic revivalist movements based on a rigorous application of the *Sharī'ah* in others. In Nigeria, the Islamic universities have shown some interest in the resuscitation of Islamic philosophy, while such thinkers as Ahmadu Bo have sought to establish a form of Islamic wisdom which is at the same time profoundly African.

Since the Second World War, nearly all Islamic countries have gained their political freedom, but they are now struggling with another form of domination, one that is cultural and philosophical and that ranges from positivism to Marxism. Parallel with the spread of such forms of thinking is a revival of interest in all aspects of the Islamic tradition, comprising the *Sharī'ah*, Sufism, theology and traditional philosophy. Interest in those aspects is not the same everywhere, however. In this struggle between modern Western patterns of thought and the Islamic tradition, much remains to be done, including the achievement of a deeper understanding of the issues involved. Gradually, however, a few Muslim intellectuals have emerged who are at once profoundly Islamic and possess a truly intellectual perspective, and who are seeking to provide an Islamic answer to the challenges posed by modern philosophy and science. Despite the anti-intellectual tendency of so many politically activist 'fundamentalist' movements, their activity continues to grow and to increase in influence. The work of this group represents perhaps the most notable feature of recent philosophical activity in the Islamic world. In its hands lies the intellectual defense of the citadel of the Islamic faith, at whose heart is to be found the purest form of *ḥikmah* or *sophia*, with the appropriate means for its realization and teachings sufficient to answer all the intellectual challenges posed for Islam by the modern world.

Notes

1. We mean such schools as those of jurisprudence (*uṣūl*), theology (*kalām*), and gnosis (*'irfān* or *ma'rifah*).
2. On Islamic philosophy in general see the already cited works of Corbin, Sharif, Fakhry and Nasr. For a synopsis of the intellectual background in question see our *Islamic Life and Thought*, chapter 6.
3. See H. Corbin, 'The Force of Traditional Philosophy in Iran Today', *Studies in Comparative Religion* (Winter 1968) pp. 12–26; also our *Islamic Philosophy in Contemporary Persia: A Summary of Activity During the Past Two Decades*, Salt Lake City, 1972.
4. On these so-called reformers see A. Hourani, *Arabic Thought in the Liberal Ages*, Oxford, 1962; and K. Cragg, *Counsels in Contemporary Islam*, Edinburgh, 1965. A great deal of more genuine Islamic activity, mostly in the field of Sufism, took place, but it has received little attention until now. On the orthodox criticism of these modernistic reformers see also M. Jameelah, *Islam and Modernism*, Lahore, 1968.
5. See 'The Pertinence of Studying Islamic Philosophy Today' in our *Islamic Life and Thought*, chapter 12.
6. We have often had occasion to mention that today late 19th-century British philosophy is taken more seriously in the universities of the Indian subcontinent than in British universities themselves.
7. See M. Berger, *Islam in Egypt Today*, Cambridge, 1970, and E. Bannerth, 'Aspects de la Shadhiliyya', *Mélanges de l'Institut Dominicain des Études Orientales* (Cairo) 2 (1972) 248 ff.
8. See M. Lings, *A Sufi Saint of the Twentieth Century*.
9. Gradually all the works of the contemporary masters of traditional Islamic philosophy, such men as 'Allāmah Ṭabāṭabā'ī, are becoming known even in the West. Meanwhile, in Iran itself the renaissance of interest in traditional Islamic philosophy, especially the school of

Mullā Ṣadrā, continues and has spread to some degree to Pakistan and India.

10. Perhaps the most extensive celebrations were those held in 1952 and 1953 in Egypt, Iraq, Iran, India and several other lands on the occasion of the millennium of Ibn Sīnā. It was responsible for hundreds of books and articles concerning this master of Muslim Peripatetics. As far as Iran and Iraq are concerned see *Millenaire d'Avicenne, Congrès de Baghdad*, Cairo, 1952, Z. Safa (ed.). *Le Livre du millénaire d'Avicenne*, 4 vols., Tehran, 1953. For accounts of these activities, especially in Egypt, see the numerous studies of A.A. Anawati in the *Mélanges de l'Institute Dominicain*. On philosophical activity in the Arab world during the past century see also *Al-fikr al-falsafī fī ma'at 'ām*, published by the American University of Beirut, 1962.
11. On the Wahhabī-Salafī line of thought and its background see L. Gardet and M.M. Anawati, *Introduction à la théologie musulmane*, Paris, 1948, especially pp. 447ff., which deals with the theological aspects of this movement; and H. Laoust, *Essai sur les doctrines sociales et politiques de Taḳi-al-Din Aḥmad B. Taimiyah*, Cairo, 1939. On more recent developments see M. Imara, *Ṭayārāt al-fikr al-islāmī*, Cairo, 1984.
12. On the Muslim Brethren see I.M. Husaini, *The Muslim Brethren*, Beirut, 1956; and R.P. Mitchell, *The Society of the Muslim Brothers*, London, 1969.
13. On this remarkable figure see M. Lings, *A Sufi Saint of the Twentieth Century*.
14. On Maraboutism in the Maghrib, see O. Dupont and X. Copolani, *Les Confrérie religieuses musulmanes*, Algiers, 1897; and E. Dermenghem, *Le Culte des saints dans l'Islam maghrébin*, Paris, 1954.
15. The efforts of Corbin, Izutsu, Nasr and others are finally becoming fruitful in directing the attention of not only Westerners but other Muslims to the significance of this later school of Islamic philosophy.
16. In addition to the works cited in the previous chapter, see M. Mohaghegh and T. Izutsu, *The Metaphysics of Sabzavari*, Delmar (N.Y.), 1977.
17. See our *Islamic Philosophy in Contemporary Persia*.
18. See the introduction to S.M.H. Ṭabāṭabā'ī, *Shi'ite Islam*, trans. by S.H. Nasr, Albany (N.Y.), 1975.
19. He is perhaps the only master of Islamic philosophy trained originally in a traditional school who is also completely familiar with Western philosophy. See his *Knowledge by Presence*, Tehran, 1983.
20. The Imperial Iranian Academy of Philosophy, besides publishing numerous works on Islamic thought, comparative philosophy and such-like, also published the biannual *Sophia Perennis* and an annual bibliography of works on philosophy published in Iran. After the Revolution, the publication of the journal ceased but a series of books has continued to appear under the new name of the Iranian Academy of Islamic Philosophy.

21. See R.V. De Smet, *Philosophical Activity in Pakistan*, Lahore, 1961.
22. Some of these attempts have been, to put it mildly, far from successful. See our 'Metaphysics and Philosophy East and West', in *Islam and the Plight of Modern Man*, pp, 27–36.
    It is important to mention once again the writings of Maryam Jameelah who, although of American origin, belongs to the Pakistani scene. Her writings are among the most rigorous criticisms of the West to come out of the contemporary Islamic world. They stand diametrically opposed to the facile comparisons and so-called syntheses of Eastern and Western thought which pollute the intellectual atmosphere of so much of the Islamic world.

Chapter Twelve

Teaching Philosophy in the Light of the Islamic Educational Ethos

In the confusing philosophical scene depicted in the previous chapter, the question of teaching philosophy in the Islamic world looms large upon the horizon. Before discussing how philosophy should be taught, however, it is important to deal with the question of whether it should be taught at all, because there are many within the Islamic world, even in positions of educational responsibility, who doubt the usefulness of teaching such a subject – or who even oppose it completely. If by 'philosophy' we mean modern, Western philosophy, then it is of course very much open to debate whether this subject should be taught at all to Muslim students especially to students who have had no grounding in the Islamic philosophical tradition. But remembering that 'philosophy' is a polysemic term (a word with many meanings), it can be confidently asserted that it is not possible to have an educational system without some kind of philosophy being taught, even if the subject is never mentioned as such by name. One cannot teach modern physics or chemistry without accepting certain assumptions concerning the nature of reality which are intimately related to 17th-century European philosophy, nor biology without teaching the student at the same time certain very hypothetical ideas about change, process and so-called evolution which are all related to 19th-century European philosophy. Nor can one study even classical Islamic theology without a basic knowledge of logic. In fact, even in classical Islamic education, all students were taught some kind of philosophy, understood here in the sense both of world-view and of a method of thinking applicable to various sciences, including jurisprudence (*fiqh*). It must, therefore, be accepted that one cannot impart knowledge and have a formal educational system without having some kind of philosophy in these meanings of the term. The question, therefore, is not whether one should teach philosophy to Muslim students but rather *what kind* or *kinds* of philosophy should be taught and how the subject should be approached. Lack of attention to this crucial question has caused innumerable problems in educational institutions throughout the Islamic world and has been one of the main causes for the inability of contemporary Islam to create a proper Islamic educational system which would be fully Islamic and yet not shun the philosophical questions which the modern world poses for Muslims.

If philosophy is to be taught, then one must first decide what is meant by 'philosophy' and what kind of philosophy or philosophies one should teach. For most modernized and educated Muslims the term simply implies *Western philosophy*, especially its main current from Descartes, Leibnitz and Malebranche through Locke, Hume, Kant and Hegel to the various modern schools of existentialism, positivism and Marxism. Most Western-educated Muslims have also heard of al-Fārābī or Ibn Sīnā, without knowing exactly what they really said. For many traditional Muslims not yet touched by modern education, the term still implies wisdom, *al-ḥikmah*, which they associated with the prophets as well as with the Muslim saints. As for the learned among the traditional segment of Islamic society, those not influenced by the rationalizing movements of the 12th/18th and 13th/19th centuries associated with the name of 'Abd al-Wahhāb and others, philosophy is simply associated with the traditional *falsafah*, towards which they have the same traditional attitude as in older days. But few are aware of the fact that, in the context of present-day education and the current understanding of philosophy, not only is *falsafah* truly philosophy, but that there is also 'philosophy' in many other Islamic sciences such as *tafsīr*, *Ḥadīth*, *kalām*, *uṣūl*, *al-fiqh* and *taṣawwuf*, as well as of course in the natural and mathematical sciences, all of which are rooted in principle in the Quran, which is of course the fountain of *ḥikmah* or wisdom.

In order to define what we mean by 'philosophy', it is necessary to go beyond this polarization. One cannot consider philosophy as simply modern Western philosophy or accept the appraisal of even the most knowledgeable of Muslim 'reformers' in philosophical matters, that is, Muḥammad Iqbāl, when he took certain strands of European philosophy so seriously that in his *Jāvīd-nāmah*, where Rūmī is guiding him in paradise, he comes upon Nietzsche and asserts:–

I said to Rūmī, 'Who is this madman?'
He said, 'This is the Wise Man of Germany.'

Nor can one be completely successful and honest, intellectually speaking, by simply rejecting philosophy as *kufr* and refusing to understand it, although most of modern philosophy is in fact *kufr* from the Islamic point of view. This cannot be done because Western philosophical ideas will simply creep in through the back door in a thousand different ways and students will then be much less prepared to confront them since they will not have been properly inoculated against them through a vigorous study and refutation of their false theses. What must be done, therefore, is to define philosophy itself from the Islamic point of view and then to re-appraise the current meaning or meanings of philosophy in the light of the Islamic perspective.

It is true that the Islamic intellectual tradition is too rich and diversified to provide just one meaning for the Quranic term *al-ḥikmah*, but it is also true that the several intellectual perspectives that have been cultivated in Islam all conform to the doctrine of unity (*al-tawḥīd*), and one can therefore come to understand the term 'philosophy' as implying knowledge of the nature of things based upon and leading to *al-tawḥīd*, therefore profoundly Islamic even if issuing originally from non-Islamic sources. The view of traditional Islamic philosophers that 'philosophy originates from the lamp of prophecy',[1] derives directly from their using *al-tawḥīd* as the criterion for the Islamicity of a particular teaching. In any case, 'philosophy' could be redefined according to Islamic standards to preserve its intellectual vigor but at the same time remain attached to the revelation and its central doctrine, which is none other than unity.[2] From the very beginning, the currently prevailing idea of philosophy as scepticism and doubt, as an individualistic activity of man as a being who has rebelled against God and as the objectivization of the limitations of the particular kind of human being called 'philosopher', should be removed from the minds of students. It should be replaced by the idea of wisdom, universality, certitude and the supra-individual character of, not only the Truth as such, but also its major traditional formulations and crystallizations, so that philosophy becomes identified with an enduring intellectual perspective, as it has always been in the East, rather than with an individualistic interpretation of reality, as has been the case in Western philosophy since Descartes.

The teaching of philosophy to Muslim students should begin, not only with an Islamic understanding of the meaning of philosophy, but also with a thorough study of the whole of the Islamic intellectual tradition. Before the student is exposed to Descartes and Kant, or even Plato and Aristotle as seen through the eyes of modern Western philosophy, he or she should receive a thorough grounding in Islamic philosophy and the other related disciplines. Those devising curricula should possess as wide a perspective as possible and go beyond the debilitating attacks of the past century upon the Islamic tradition itself, which would reduce the great wealth of the tapestry that is the intellectual life of Islam to simply one of its strands. Whether the planners or the teachers sympathize with the jurisprudents or theologians, the philosophers in the technical sense of *falāsifah* or the Sufis, with the critics of logical discourse or its supporters is really beside the point. If there is to be a successful program of philosophy enabling the Muslim student to confront modern disciplines, ideologies and points of view without losing his spiritual orientation, then the full force of the Islamic intellectual tradition must be brought into play and a narrowing of perspective carefully avoided.

Even great debates between various Islamic schools of philosophy and thought in general, such as those which were carried out between Ibn Sīnā and al-Bīrūnī,[3] al-Ghāzzālī and Ibn Rushd,[4] Naṣīr al-Dīn Ṭūsī and Ṣadr al-Dīn al-Qunyawī[5] and many others, must be made known and their significance fully brought out. After all, during the periods of Islamic history, when Muslims produced world-famous scientists and thinkers, such as al-Fārābī, Ibn Sīnā, or al-Bīrūnī, debates between various perspectives were held without Islam being harmed in any way since they were all carried out within the context of the world-view of the Islamic tradition. The student should be encouraged to know something of this rich intellectual background and not be presented with a picture of the Islamic intellectual tradition as a monolithic structure amenable only to one level of interpretation. Such a perspective only deadens the mind and creates a passivity which makes the penetration of foreign ideas into the Islamic world so much easier.

The Islamic intellectual tradition should also be taught in its fullness and as it developed throughout Islamic history. Nothing has been more detrimental to an authentic revival of Islamic thought than the fallacious notion that it decayed at the end of the 'Abbasid period. This interpretation of Islamic history was originally the work of orientalists who could accept Islamic civilization only as a phase in the development of their own civilization. The adoption of this view by certain Muslims is, therefore, even more surprising since it does so much injustice to the grandeur of Islamic civilization and, even more importantly, is manifestly false. It was adopted in certain circles for nationalistic reasons or for political opportunism but surely cannot be entertained today.[6] How can a civilization which created the Sultan Aḥmad Mosque or the Shaykh Luṭfallāh Mosque be decadent? Or, on the intellectual plane, can one call a Mīr Dāmād or Mullā Ṣadrā a less serious metaphysician than any of their contemporaries anywhere else in the world? The presentation of the Islamic intellectual tradition should definitely cover the period up to the present day, categorically brushing aside this false notion of decadence derived from European historical studies of the 19th and early 20th centuries. But even so this presentation *should* include discussions of periods when there was a lack of intellectual activity, if such indeed was really the case. Those parts of the Islamic world where Muslims were actually 'sleeping over treasures', to quote a contemporary metaphysician and master of Islamic intellectuality, should be mentioned; but so also should such figures as Shaykh al-Darqāwī, Hājjī Mullā Hādī Sabziwārī or the philosophers of Farangī Maḥal, all of whom rekindled various schools of traditional Islamic intellectuality in different parts of the Islamic world during the past two centuries. In fact, the so-called Muslim reformers, about whom so much has been written, should be reappraised in the light of a full knowledge of the Islamic intellectual tradition.

Having gained a thorough ground-knowledge of the Islamic intellectual tradition in its general features, if not in its details, the Muslim student should then be introduced to other schools of philosophy, not only Western but also Oriental ones. No better antidote can be found for the scepticism inherent in much of modern Western philosophy than the traditional doctrines of the Orient which, like Islamic philosophy itself, are philosophy only in the sense of *wisdom* because they all are based upon the Absolute and the means of attaining the Absolute. They are, in a sense, various forms of commentary upon the Quranic verse, 'Verily we come from God and unto Him is our return' (II:156). The Muslim student should in fact be made aware that, besides the Islamic world and the all-powerful Western philosophies and ideologies, there are other civilizations with their own profound intellectual traditions.

Besides the Orient, ancient Greek philosophy and its antecedents in Egypt and Mesopotamia should be taught, not as a part of Western thought, but independently as Muslim thinkers have always considered them. It is strange that most Islamic modernists have seen Greek philosophy almost completely through the eyes of its modern Western interpreters.[7] When Iqbal calls Plato 'one of the sheep', he is following Nietzsche's interpretation of Platonism rather than that of those Islamic philosophers who saw in Plato and Pythagoras a confirmation of the Islamic doctrine of *al-tawḥīd*. The study of Greek thought according to the Islamic intellectual tradition and independent of its Western interpretation is in fact crucial for the Islamic confrontation with modern Western philosophy itself, whether it be the thought of men like Jaspers and Heidegger, who have dealt extensively with the Greeks, or positivists who do not consider anything before Kant, or at best Hume, as being philosophy at all.

The study of non-Islamic schools of thought should also emphasize Christian and Jewish philosophy in the European Middle Ages and their later continuation. Not only should such medieval figures as St. Bonaventure, St. Thomas, Duns Scotus, Maimonides and Ibn

Gabirol, who were also very close to Islamic thought, be well known to Muslim students, but much more attention should be paid in philosophy courses in the Islamic world to the later continuation of these schools. Instead of just relegating the Christian and Jewish philosophy to the medieval period and following immediately with secularized modern philosophy, as is the case today, more emphasis should be placed upon the continuation of these schools, not only through Suarez and Spinoza but into the 20th century with such figures as E. Gilson and J. Maritain, and H.A. Wolfson and D. Hartman.[8] The purpose of this exercise would be to demonstrate to the Muslim student, who might be carried off his feet rapidly as a result of his encounter with modern Western philosophy, how, despite the weakening of religion in the West, religious or 'prophetic' philosophy in many ways similar to the Islamic and based upon God and revelation has continued to this day. Of course in such an enterprise thoroughly anti-traditional but outwardly 'Christian' philosophies, such as Teilhardism, should also be exposed for what they are.

Finally, as far as the development of Western philosophy is concerned, emphasis should be placed upon what has been called the 'anti-history of anti-philosophy', namely, those more traditional schools of philosophy which remained on the margin of European thought and which are not usually discussed in standard texts on the history of Western philosophy employed in both Western universities or those of the Islamic world. The research of the past few decades has revealed that certain forms of non-rationalistic philosophy, such as Hermeticism, survived much more in the Renaissance and even the 17th and 18th centuries than had been thought before, and that such schools as the Kabbalah, the Rosicrucian movement, Hermeticism and the like were even influential in the rise of experimental science to a degree hitherto unsuspected.[9] Giordano Bruno, Paracelsus, Basil Valentine, Robert Fludd and many similar figures are seen to be of much greater significance even from the point of view of science than the rationalistic interpretations of earlier days had led everyone to believe. It is important to make Muslim students aware of these elements since such philosophies are both akin in structure and related through historical sources to various schools of Islamic thought.

As for later centuries, more should be said about such figures as Jacob Böhme, Goethe as a philosopher, Schelling, von Baader,

St. Martin and many other figures, who are also attracting much attention in the contemporary West itself as part of the quest for that lost *sophia* which much of its own so-called philosophy denies or abhors.[10]

Since it is primarily modern Western thought which is the source of doubt and scepticism for the educated Muslim, it is essential to acquaint the Muslim student fully with the criticisms made against this thought in the West itself. It has always been said that the cure for a snake bite is the poison of the snake itself. In the same way, the best antidote for the errors which constitute the essence – though not necessarily all of the accidents – of that which is characteristically modern, in contrast to contemporary, thought, can be found in the criticisms made in the West itself. To be sure, certain profound criticisms have come from the East, but for the most part Orientals have been either too enfeebled as a result of the process of Westernization itself to stand totally on their own ground or else have been unable to get to the heart of the problem involved as a result of a lack of knowledge of the inner workings of Western thought. The few profound criticisms from the East, such as those of that incomparable Indian metaphysician and scholar, A.K. Coomaraswamy, have been the exception rather than the rule.[11]

From the West, however, has come a total and complete criticism of the very structure of modern thought. These criticisms include magisterial expositions based on traditional authority and grounded in thorough knowledge of traditional metaphysics and philosophy, such as the *Oriental Metaphysics* of R. Guénon and the *Logic and Transcendence* of F. Schuon[12], as well as a description of the 'malaise' inherent in modern philosophy and thought by a large number of notable thinkers seeking to rediscover the Truth: a task from which many critics believe the mainstream of European philosophy to have departed since the Renaissance. These include philosophers as well as scientists and men of letters: such figures as E. Zolla in Italy, H. Corbin, G. Durand and A. Faivre in France, H. Smith and Th. Roszak in America and many others. They also include those, such as E. Gilson, who have written histories of Western philosophy from the point of view of Thomist ontology and epistemology and who have detected in the history of Western thought a gradual fall in the role of philosophy from being the study of Being itself, or of the One who alone *is*, in the absolute sense, to the study of logic alone.[13] The Muslim student should be presented with these criticisms while at the same time studying the history of Western thought so that he is able to acquire certain intellectual concepts necessary to protect himself from the withering effects of the agnosticism and doubt associated with so much of modern philosophy.

In teaching philosophy, then, traditional Islamic philosophy should be made central and other schools of philosophy taught in relation to it. It must be remembered, however, that by 'Islamic philosophy' we do not mean only its history. The method of reducing philosophy to the history of philosophy is itself something completely modern and non-Islamic. Nor in fact does this method conform to the perspective of any of the other major traditional civilizations. In such civilizations, philosophy is not identified with an individual who gives his name to a particular philosophical mode of thought, which is then called, for example, Cartesianism, Hegelianism, etc., but which is almost immediately criticized and rejected by a subsequent philosopher. Rather, philosophy is identified with an intellectual perspective which lasts over the centuries and which, far from being a barrier to creativity, remains a viable means of access to the Truth within the particular tradition in question. Men who give their names to traditional schools of thought are seen more as 'intellectual functions' than mere individuals. Such a situation was also found in the West when it was Christian; for centuries, people followed the Augustinian, Thomistic or Palamite schools of theology and philosophy, and these schools were seen, and still continue to be seen to the extent that Christian philosophy is alive, as intellectual perspectives transcending the individualistic order. In traditional India and China, the situation has of course always been of this kind; namely, wisdom or philosophy has been identified with the name of a great sage, whether he be a historical or a mythical figure, who has opened up an intellectual perspective of a supra-individualistic order surviving over the centuries far beyond the life span of the founder himself or his immediate disciples.

Islamic philosophy should be taught in a morphological manner as schools rather than as a continuous history of individual philosophers and their philosophies, as has been the case even in many books written by Muslims themselves but completely emulating Western models. Islamic intellectual life should be divided into its traditional schools of *uṣūl*, *kalām*, *mashshā'ī* (Peripatetic) philosophy, *ishrāq* (the School of Illumination), *ma'rifah* or *'irfān* (theoretical and doctrinal Sufism) and, finally, the later school of *al-ḥikmat al-muta'āliyah* (the Transcendent Theosophy) associated with the name of Ṣadr al-Dīn Shīrāzī. Then each of these schools should be subdivided according to their traditional divisions, such as Sunni and Shi'ite *uṣūl*, Mu'tazilite, Ash'arite, Ithnā 'Asharī and Ismā'īlī *kalām*, eastern and western schools of *mashshā'ī* philosophy, etc.

Also each school should be taught according to its own traditional methods; that is, beginning with principles which are always related to the Quran and *Ḥadīth* and followed by the application and development of these principles. Only after the intellectual structure is made known should a historical account be given of each school, a historical account which should come up to the present day, if that school has survived until now, as is in fact the case for nearly all Islamic intellectual disciplines, provided the whole of the Islamic world is considered and not only its central lands. For example, once the Mu'tazilite school is presented in its doctrinal and philosophical aspects, its historical unfolding should be taught, not ending with Qāḍī 'Abd al-Jabbār in the 5th/11th century, but also including the whole later development of this school among the Zaydis of the Yemen up to modern times and, finally, its revival among certain of the theologians of al-Azhar during this century.

In the same manner, the development of *mashshā'ī* philosophy should not stop with Ibn Rushd, as is usually the case, following Western sources for which Islamic philosophy ends with him, but include the later Turkish criticisms of his *Tahāfut al-tahāfut* during the Ottoman period, the revival of *mashshā'ī* philosophy in the East by Naṣīr al-Dīn Ṭūsī and Quṭb al-Dīn Shīrāzī and the continuation of the school of Ibn Sīnā up to our own times, when major philosophical commentaries and analyses of his work have continued to appear in Persia, Pakistan and India. The same could be said of the other schools.

Of course, this task is not an easy one because of the state of present-day knowledge of Islamic intellectual life in its totality. The detailed development of every one of these schools remains unknown if the whole of the Islamic world is considered. There may be Malay scholars who know how *kalām* developed in their part of the Islamic world, as there may still be scholars in Morocco who can provide knowledge for the development of the metaphysics of the school of Ibn 'Arabī in that region. But there is no single work nor any one center of research where all of this knowledge has been brought together. Yet, once it is realized how important it is to provide a total and complete map of Islamic intellectual life in both space and time for current Muslim students, it would not be difficult to provide the means to carry out the task of studying these schools, beginning with the traditional method of presenting first their principles, then their branches and various other details, and only later their development in history, a method which would help to avoid the relativization of the truth and the reduction of all permanence to becoming that are inevitably implied by the methods whereby philosophy has been studied and taught in the West. Of course, even here the anti-historicism of certain current Western thinkers can be of help in preventing Muslims from falling into the trap of historicism without at the same time being in any way against historical facts. After all, al-Bīrūnī and Ibn Khaldūn were able to be very keen historians without reducing all truths to their history and all permanence to becoming.

The traditional conflict between the various schools of Islamic thought should also be taught as conflicts between so many different perspectives converging upon the Truth, conflicts which are of a very different nature from those found between contending philosophical schools in the modern world because, in the first case, there are always the transcendent principles of the Islamic tradition which ultimately unify, whereas, in the second case, such unifying principles are missing. It is true that the Ash'arites opposed the Mu'tazilites, that the *mutakallimun* in general were against the *mashshā'ī* philosophers, that Suhrawardī, the founder of the school of *ishrāq*, criticized Peripatetic logic and metaphysics, that Ibn Taymiyyah wrote against formal logic and Sufism, etc. But had these conflicts been like those of modern thought, the Islamic tradition would not have survived. There was, however, always the unifying principle of *al-tawḥīd*, and a sense of hierarchy within the Islamic tradition itself which allowed intellectual figures to appear from time to time who were at once *mutakallim*, philosophers and metaphysicians of the gnostic school (*al-ma'rifah*), and who realized the inner unity of these perspectives within their own being. The fact that there were many and not just one school of thought should not therefore be taught to students as a sign of either chaos or weakness, but as the result of the richness of the Islamic tradition, which was able to cater to the needs of different intellectual types and therefore to keep within its fold so many human beings of differing backgrounds and intellectual abilities. The diversity should be taught as the consequence of so many applications of the teachings of Islam, some more partial and some more complete, yet all formulated so as to prevent men with different mental abilities and attitudes from seeking knowledge and the quenching of their thirst for answers to certain questions outside the structure of the Islamic tradition itself, as was to happen in the Christian West during the Renaissance. This profusion and diversity of schools, which were different but which all drew from the fountain-head of the Quranic revelation and *al-tawḥīd*, was the means whereby Islam succeeded in preserving the sacred character of knowledge while at the same time creating a vast civilization in which the development of various modes of knowledge and different sciences was a necessity.

The study of Islamic philosophy in this manner should be complemented by the study of the different philosophical questions and themes with which the contemporary student is usually faced. For students of different disciplines, such as law, medicine and the like, questions such as the nature of the world, causality, the relation between creation and God, etc. could be fitted into a general program for the study of philosophy within the matrix of the different schools cited above. But for those who study philosophy itself, or the religious sciences on the one hand and certain of the sciences, such as physics, on the other, it would be very helpful and perhaps even necessary to deal with these subjects separately and morphologically. Even in the Western philosophical syllabus, students study logic, aesthetics, ethics, social and political philosophy and, in many places, metaphysics, cosmology and philosophical psychology by themselves.

From a pedagogical point of view, it is important to deal separately with these disciplines for particular groups of students concerned with the subjects mentioned above along with general courses on Islamic intellectual life on the lines described already. It is also obviously essential to teach Islamic political philosophy in a more fully developed and thorough manner to students of political science, the philosophy of art and aesthetics to students of art and architecture, the Islamic philosophy of science to students of all the different natural and mathematic sciences, and so on. In such cases, each discipline should be taught from the Islamic point of view and then the views of Western or non-Islamic Eastern schools also presented and, when in contradiction to Islamic teachings, criticized and explained. In nearly every branch of philosophy, the Islamic tradition is rich beyond belief, if only its sources were made known. This is especially true of metaphysics. Here Islamic metaphysics should be presented as the science of Ultimate Reality, which is the One (*al-Aḥad*) or Allah, who has revealed Himself in the Quran. There has been no Islamic school whose teachings are not based on the doctrine of the One who is both Absolute and Infinite. In the study of this Sublime Principle, the Muslim sages developed several languages of discourse, some based on the consideration of the One as Pure Being with an ensuing ontology conforming to that view but always seeing Pure Being, not as the first link in the 'great chain of being', but as the Source which transcends existence altogether. Others saw the One as Light (*al-nūr*) according to the Quranic verse, 'God is the Light of the Heavens and the earth' – (XXIV:35); and yet others as the Truth (*al-Ḥaqq*) which transcends even Pure Being, as the supra-ontological Principle whose first determination or act is in fact Being, for God said *be* (*kun*) and *there was*. It is the Western scholars of Islamic philosophy who have called Ibn Sīnā 'the first philosopher of being'; without any exaggeration or chauvinism, one could say that, in a sense, the development of ontology in the West is a commentary or footnote to Ibn Sīnā, but one which moves towards an ever more limited understanding of Being until finally it results in either the neglect of ontology or a parody of it. Even the present-day *Existenz Philosophie*, identified with men like Heidegger, seems like a rudimentary discussion of love by someone who has never experienced it when compared to the philosophy of Being of a figure like Ṣadr al-Dīn Shīrāzī, who writes about Being only after having drowned in the Ocean of Pure Being and who, after purification, has been endowed with the sanctified intellect which alone can speak of this Ocean.

In other philosophical subjects also, such as logic and epistemology, the Islamic tradition presents an immense richness which should be first resuscitated and then taught to the students. Only then should the various modern schools of logic and discussions of the question of knowing be presented. These are, of course, certain problems of contemporary concern which have no antecedents in Islamic thought and it would be a falsification of the truth, in fact a betrayal of the Islamic tradition, to read them and their solutions back into the Islamic sources and find there allusions to cybernetics, Riemanian space or modern information theory when in actuality none exists. But even in these cases, a mind disciplined in the Islamic sciences would be able to approach such subjects from the point of view of Islamic thought rather than as a *tabula rasa*. There are, of course, other concerns of a particularly modern nature, such as semantics and the question of causality, in which the Islamic tradition is remarkably rich. In such instances, the Islamic teachings could be presented first and only then the current – and of course ever-changing – modern theories and views taught to students who have to be concerned with such fields.

The modern world does not possess a cosmology in the real sense of the term, but there are many theories about the Universe based on the generalization of contemporary physics. In Islamic civilization, however, several forms of cosmology were developed, all related to the basic teachings of the Quran concerning the creation of the world by God, the higher planes of being associated with *malakūt* in the Quran, etc.[14] These cosmologies, which are of an eminently symbolic character and cannot be negated by any form of modern physics and astronomy, should first be taught to the students along with their full metaphysical and religious significance which would also explain such events as the nocturnal ascension (*al-mi'rāj*) of the Blessed Prophet.[15] Only after the student is made to have a 'feeling' for and an intellectual appreciation of the Islamic universe should he be exposed to various modern forms of so-called cosmology, all of which should be presented for exactly what they are, namely theories based upon certain questionable and usually empirically unprovable assumptions.

The student should also be taught about the various schools of the Islamic 'philosophy of nature', which are closely related to cosmology. These schools have views concerning time, space, matter, change, cause and effect and many other subjects which form the basis of the natural sciences and which in fact have attracted the attention of several important contemporary Western scientists and philosophers of science. With modern physics being in quest of a new 'philosophy of nature', the Islamic teachings on this subject are of the utmost importance for Muslim students of the sciences, and perhaps even in the development of a new type of physics or science of nature sought by many perceptive minds today. The same could be said of Islamic works on the philosophy of mathematics which have hardly been studied in modern times.

Likewise in philosophical psychology, the Islamic sources are replete with teachings which are of great value in the confrontation of questions posed in psychology today. In this field, material can be drawn all the way from Quranic commentaries and the *Ḥadīth* to Sufi ethical and psychological tracts, not to speak of the philosophical psychology of the philosophers themselves, such as Ibn Sīnā, and works of Islamic medicine.

In the philosophy of art or aesthetics, the teaching of the Islamic perspective is important not only from the educational point of view but also because of the effect that the training of Muslim students of art and architecture in Western ways has upon the destruction of the Islamic character of cities and the way of life of the people within the Islamic world. Islamic art is not accidentally Islamic; rather, it is a direct crystallization of the spirit and form of the Islamic revelation complementing the *Sharī'ah*. One supplies the Islamic mode of action and the other the Islamic environment in which the spirit of Islam breathes and which provides the necessary background for an Islamic way of life. If Islamic art were only accidentally related to Islam, one could not observe and feel the unmistakable fragrance of the Islamic revelation in the mosques or handicrafts of lands as far apart as East Bengal (Bangladesh) and Senegal.

Until recently oral traditions and the homogeneity of the Islamic environment did not necessitate an explicit formulation of the Islamic philosophy of art. But now, along with the teaching of the techniques of Islamic art, it is essential to formulate and teach the principles of the philosophy or wisdom (*al-ḥikmah*)[16] which underlies Islamic art, remembering that this form of art is the fruit of the marriage between technique (*al-fann*) and wisdom (*al-ḥikmah*). This is especially necessary today, since modern theories of art and aesthetics, and works based upon them, have engulfed much of the Islamic world and corrode the soul and weaken the faith of Muslims in a direct manner that is often more insidious and pervasive than the effect of anti-religious ideologies. Many Muslims are in fact painfully unaware of the religious danger of anti-traditional art-forms and therefore display a remarkable passivity towards them.[17]

In the practical aspects of philosophy, such as the political and social ones and ethics, Islamic sources once again possess an immense richness. Here, as before, the various schools should be presented as so many elaborations upon the themes of the Quran and the *Ḥadīth*. For example, Islamic ethics is of course itself based upon these twin sources of Islamic revelation; but there are elaborations of ethics as a science or as a branch of philosophy in works as different as *al-Risālat al-qushayriyyah* of Imam al-Qushayrī, sections of *al-Mughnī* of Qāḍī 'Abd al-Jabbār dealing with ethics, many works of Islamic literature, such as the *Kalīlah wa Dimnah* and the *Gulistān* of Sa'dī, the *Iḥyā' 'ulūm al-dīn* of al-Ghazzālī and the *Akhlāq-i nāṣirī* of Naṣīr al-Dīn Ṭūsī, all of which aim to inculcate within the soul of man the virtues taught in Islam, but each providing a different type of ethical theory and method and emphasizing different aspects of ethics. In a domain such as this, it is even easier than in the other fields mentioned above to teach firstly the ideas of the different schools of Islamic ethics and only then the current ethical theories of Western philosophers, or even Confucian and Buddhist ethical ideas for that matter, which should also be definitely studied.

As for political and social philosophies, there too the Islamic sources are very diverse, embracing not only books of philosophy in the strict sense of the term, but also those dealing with history and literature, as well as of course works of jurisprudence (*fiqh*) and the different branches of the Law. In these fields, a certain amount of work has already been done towards presenting students with the views of the various Islamic schools before embarking upon the teaching of Western theories. Unfortunately, however, in many cases, instead of presenting the different Islamic schools objectively in all their diversity and richness, local political conditions have often been chosen as criteria for what schools should be taught as being genuinely Islamic, and even among Western ideologies, only those are studied which are closest to the political stance of the particular Muslim state in question, whereas all the different Western schools of political and social philosophy which have been or are still of any consequence should be studied and criticized from the stance of the Islamic tradition. In this way, the student will feel secure within his own tradition, no matter which type of modern philosophy he confronts. For example, if the *laissez-faire* type of social and political philosophy is studied and rejected from the Islamic point of view but the Marxist passed over in silence, the

Muslim student may be completely unequipped intellectually when confronted with it and consequently unable to defend his position before its arguments or the arguments of those pseudo-syntheses which would try to combine the Islamic and Marxist views, as if ice and fire could be made to exist harmoniously side by side.

The implementation of the program outlined above requires of course educational planning, the training of qualified individuals as both teachers and research scholars, the collection of manuscripts and the composition of books and monographs on various levels. As far as educational planning is concerned, it must be said at the outset that obviously Islamic philosophy should be taught to students who have already studied the principles of Islam, the Quran, *Ḥadīth*, the sacred history of Islam and at least some aspects of *fiqh* and *uṣūl al-fiqh*, even if only in rudimentary fashion. In this way, the mind of the student would be impregnated with Islamic values and norms and he could confront alien ideas and ideologies accordingly. But if philosophy is taught in the manner outlined above, this function will also be performed by the various schools of Islamic philosophy themselves. Ibn Sīnā was already thoroughly educated in the purely Islamic disciplines before confronting Aristotelian metaphysics; therefore his works can help the student and strengthen his Islamic intellectual formation before he faces the works of a Hegel or Heidegger with which classical Islamic philosophy was not familiar for obvious reasons. But if the Islamic intellectual tradition is put aside and the student is presented with only the Quran and *Ḥadīth*, from which he is expected to deduce his own 'philosophy of Islam', then such an enterprise can never succeed. A student thus educated would at best shy away from problems posed by modern thought in order to protect his faith, and at worst would be overcome by what, for an untrained person, is an overwhelming challenge. As a result, he would either lose his faith, develop an anti-intellectual attitude which would substitute intoxicating fury for intellectual response, or end up with some kind of a pseudo-synthesis of Islam and different modern ideologies, which is often more insidious and dangerous than complete loss of faith.

As far as educational programming for the teaching of Islamic philosophy is concerned, it must begin on the secondary – or even on the elementary – level and not be limited solely to the university. From the earliest grades, references in the textbooks of Muslim children should be primarily to Muslim men of learning. Biographies of great sages and thinkers, such as al-Ghazzālī, ʻAbd al-Qādir al-Jīlānī, al-Fārābī, Ibn Sīnā, al-Bīrūnī, Ibn Khaldūn, etc., should impregnate the history and cultural programs established for the earlier years of education, following directly upon the study of the life of the Prophet, the Companions, the imams of the *madhāhib* and, for Shiʻism, the Shiʻite Imams, etc. Moreover, the vast popular literature concerning many Islamic intellectual figures should be included.

In the later years of secondary education, the names of the major books of Islamic thought and a few of the basic ideas and debates, such as those mentioned above, should be added. Finally, for the last two years, programs comprising metaphysics and ethics, a brief intellectual history of the various schools, etc., should be devised on thoroughly Islamic lines as, for example, the French and German educational systems have done for the *lycée* and the *gymnasium*, though there on purely European lines. Only then should something be mentioned in the program for Muslim students about Western and possibly even Oriental philosophies. But the treatment of Western thought, although very elementary at this stage, should still be critical and not either apologetic or defensive.

As for university education, there must be several types of programs: one for those majoring in philosophy; one for those whose field is close to philosophy, such as theology, Islamic Law, comparative religion or one of the other religious disciplines; one for those majoring in the theoretical sciences, such as physics and mathematics; one for those majoring in one of the descriptive sciences, such as biology, ecology or geology; one for students of the social sciences; another for the arts; and so on. The details of such programs need careful study and cannot be provided in this chapter, but the general aim of Islamizing the educational system by making its intellectual perspective and world-view totally Islamic can be pointed out and emphasized even before studying the actual details of the implementation of such a program.

The training of personnel for such a program poses a major problem at the present moment but not one that is insurmountable. Today, only a handful of the traditional masters of Islamic philosophy who connect the present generation to the days of Suhrawardī and Ibn Sīnā continue to survive. The oral traditions which they still possess and which complement the written texts are a most precious treasure of Islamic intellectual life. Before such people disappear from the surface of the earth altogether, it is essential to choose a number of gifted students and provide the means for both teachers and students to make this vital training and transmission possible. Furthermore, scholars with a more contemporary training but also expert in the Islamic intellectual disciplines are very limited in number. There are not enough people to staff even the major universities of the Islamic world. Therefore, every effort should be made to create several institutes, academic societies, etc., which would bring such experts together with qualified students. To train such students, it is necessary to create both the atmosphere and the minimum number of qualified teachers who would in fact attract good students through their own presence. Efforts by the writer of these lines in this direction have produced satisfactory results in the past. With all the funds available in the Islamic world today, it should not be difficult to finance a few such centers whose students could later become university professors training men and women who would in turn later teach on both the secondary and elementary levels.

An urgent and highly important task for promoting a fuller understanding of the various dimensions and the immense richness of Islamic thought is the collection and preservation of manuscripts relating to Islamic philosophy, metaphysics and allied subjects. Most of these manuscripts are in Arabic, but a large number are also in Persian and a few in other Islamic languages, such as Turkish, Urdu and Malay. Despite the laudable efforts of various public and semi-public libraries, especially in Turkey and Iran, as well as the Arab League Center for Arabic Manuscripts in Cairo and the collection on Islamic medicine and related sciences being assembled by the Hamdard Foundations in Delhi and Karachi, a great deal needs to be accomplished in collecting manuscripts still in private collections which are in danger of being lost or destroyed. This is especially a problem in the Indo-Pakistani subcontinent, which is extremely rich in Islamic manuscripts but at the same time possesses a warm and humid climate which causes manuscripts to decay and fall apart very rapidly if they are not well-stored and cared for. Parallel with this effort, copies should be made of manuscripts dealing with Islamic philosophy and related subjects, and collected in the few centers created for the advanced study of Islamic philosophy and thought in general.

As far as books and monographs are concerned, so much needs to be done that a separate study would be required to even outline the work involved. Here it suffices to point out some of the major projects which need to be undertaken. First of all, the work of the mixed group of Muslim and Western scholars who have performed the thankless task of editing the actual texts of Islamic thought must be continued in force so that within a few years complete critical editions or *opera omnia* of at least the major Islamic intellectual figures, such as al-Ghazzālī, Ibn Sīnā and Ibn Khaldūn, will be available. Islamic civilization lags far behind others, like those of Japan and India, in this respect and even today there is not a single major Islamic intellectual figure all of whose writings can be found in a critical edition.

Parallel with this effort, dictionaries must be compiled of philosophical and scientific terminology in Islamic languages. To this end, there must be greater cooperation between the scholars of these languages than has been the case until now. Some activity in this field has take place under the auspices of the Arab Academy and several Iranian organizations, but much remains to be accomplished before philosophy, including Western thought, can be taught to Muslim students in their own languages in a way which would remain faithful to the genius of that language and its traditional roots. The secularization of thought is always closely related to the secularization of language.

The question of language is so essential that it is necessary in some cases to rewrite classical works in a contemporary medium, especially for students, while preserving the classical technical vocabulary to the largest extent possible. Not only is there an urgent need to translate the major masterpieces of Islamic metaphysics and philosophy, such as the *Kitāb al-ḥurūf* of al-Fārābī, *al-Najāt* of Ibn Sīnā, *Tahāfut al-falāsifah* of al-Ghazzālī, *Ḥikmat al-ishrāq* of Suhrawardī, *Fuṣūṣ al-ḥikam* of Ibn 'Arabī, *al-Insān al-kāmil* of 'Abd al-Karīm al-Jīlī and *al-Shawāhid al-rubūbiyyah* of Ṣadr al-Dīn Shīrāzī, from Arabic into various Islamic languages (some of this task has already been accomplished with varying degrees of success), but such works should be 'rewritten' in contemporary Arabic in such a way as to preserve their original technical vocabulary and at the same time make their content more accessible to the contemporary Arab student. Many classical recensions in fact performed the same task for people of other centuries.

The teaching of philosophy also requires that works be composed on the basis of these traditional sources, but dealing with more specific subjects, such as metaphysics, ethics, aesthetics, etc. Such treatises, written from the Islamic point of view, are rare indeed, although a few fine examples may be found in Arabic, Persian, and even Urdu. Treatises of this kind must be written on different levels so as to reach the whole spectrum of students. In the more advanced works of this kind, comparisons can also be made with non-Islamic thought, although separate works on 'comparative philosophy' remain essential.

The Muslims have been somewhat more successful in writing histories of philosophy if one judges by numbers. Such works, emulating mostly Western models, range from the large two-volume history edited by M.M. Sharif[18] and sponsored by the Pakistani Government to individual efforts of much more modest dimensions. Still, the Islamic world has not been able to produce such definitive and thorough works on the history of Islamic thought as those produced by Indian, Chinese and Japanese scholars on their own traditions. What is needed in the case of Islamic thought is many more monograph studies, which would make known so many areas of learning that remain still *terra incognita*. A few years ago one could hardly have imagined that the anthology prepared by H. Corbin and S.J. Ashtiyani which dealt with Islamic philosophy in Persia alone and only since the Safavid period would run to some seven weighty volumes. Even so, many basic selections had to be left out because of the unmanageable size of each volume.[19]

Finally, the teaching of Islamic philosophy requires the preparation of encyclopedias and philosophical dictionaries[20], such as those available for not only Western but also the Indian and Japanese traditions. At the present moment, knowledge about many facets of Islamic thought is not easily accessible and certainly beyond the means of most students even if they are advanced. Considering that Muslims were accustomed to composing encyclopedias dealing with various subjects, such as the Mu'tazlilite encyclopedia *al-Mughnī* of Qāḍī 'Abd al-Jabbār, the *Shifā'* of Ibn Sīnā on Peripatetic philosophy, or the *Biḥār al-anwār* of Mullā Muḥammad Bāqir Majlisī on Shi'ism, it is even more difficult to understand why this tradition has not been pursued in our own day. In various fields of intellectual life, certainly, such encyclopedias, presented in a contemporary manner and in such a way as to be easily accessible, are badly needed.

Of course, the Islamic world cannot wait until all these tasks are accomplished before its philosophy is taught seriously in the educational system. Time is in fact a most important factor because the withering influence of secularizing ideologies and false philosophies continues to erode the foundations of the Islamic tradition before our very eyes. Every effort should therefore be made to do what is possible here and now. It must always be remembered that the greatest obligation of the Muslim is towards the Truth (*al-Ḥaqq*), which is another name of Allah. From this Truth, or *al-Ḥaqīqah*, has issued, not only a Sacred Law which guarantees human felicity on the plane of action, but also a wisdom which alone is the guarantee of correct knowledge. The loss of this wisdom cannot but affect the understanding and mode of attachment of men to the Sacred Law. The teaching of Islamic philosophy in the sense defined above is the means of protecting the Truth and providing ways for repelling the attacks which are made against it from all sides. Its teaching in the correct manner is, therefore, in a sense a religious duty, for any step taken in the understanding of *al-Ḥaqīqah*, as well as in providing means to protect it from profanation, distortion, and obliteration, lies at the heart of the concerns of Islam as the message and the embodiment of the Truth for whose sake alone human beings were created and placed as vicegerents of God on earth.

Notes

1. Yanba‘ al-ḥikmah min mishkāt al-nubuwwah.
2. See our 'The Meaning and Role of "Philosophy" in Islam', *Studia Islamica*, vol. 36, 1973, pp. 57–89.
3. See Ibn Sīnā and al-Bīrūnī, *al-As'ilah wa'l-ajwibah*, ed. by S.H. Nasr and M. Mohaghegh, Tehran, 1973, especially our English introduction, which was also published as 'al-Bīrūnī versus Avicenna in the Bout of the Century,' *Courier*, June 1974, pp. 27–29.

4. See Ibn Rushd, *Tahāfut al-tahāfut*, trans. by S. van der Bergh, London, 1954.
5. See W. Chittick, 'Mysticism vs. Philosophy in Earlier Islamic History: The al-Ṭūsī, al-Qunawī Correspondence', *Religious Studies*, vol. XVII, 1981, pp. 87–104.
6. It is very difficult to remove error once it becomes embedded in the generally accepted view of history. Despite all the works of Corbin, Izutsu, Nasr and others about post-Ibn Rushd Islamic philosophy, the idea of the decadence of Islamic thought and philosophy after the Abbasid period continues to persist.
7. Strangely enough, this is also true of many of the 'fundamentalist' thinkers whose evaluation of Greek thought is based almost completely upon modern Western interpretations of this legacy rather than upon the traditional Islamic view. Here again the modernist and 'fundamentalist' camps meet, while they both stand opposed to the traditional perspective.
8. It is strange that there are as yet so few works on the history of European philosophy written in any Islamic language and from the Islamic point of view rather than being more or less translations from European sources.
9. Works by such scholars as W. Pagel, F. Yates, A. Debus and A. Faivre have cast new light on this subject and must be carefully studied by any Muslim scholar seriously interested in the appraisal of the philosophic and more generally intellectual history of the post-medieval West.
10. See our *Knowledge and the Sacred*, pp. 93ff.
11. On Coomaraswamy see R. Lipsey, *Coomaraswamy, His Life and Works*, Princeton, 1977.
12. See also Schuon's *Light in the Ancient World*, trans. Lord Northbourne, Bloomington (Indiana), 1984; and S.H. Nasr (ed.), *The Writings of Frithjof Schuon – A Basic Reader*, Warwick (N.Y.), 1986.
13. *The Unity of Philosophical Experience* of Gilson is particularly important as far as this subject is concerned.
14. See our *An Introduction to Islamic Cosmological Doctrines*.
15. See our *Muḥammad – Man of Allah*, London, 1982, pp. 14ff.
16. T. Burckhardt, who was the first contemporary scholar to formulate the principles of the Islamic philosophy of art, has dealt with this issue in many of his works especially *The Art of Islam*. See also our *Islamic Art and Spirituality*.
17. See chapters 13 and 14 of this work as far as Islamic architecture is concerned.
18. We have already referred several times to this important reference source, which has recently been translated into Persian.
19. Unfortunately, since the death of Corbin and recent events in Iran, the publication of this *magnum opus* has become interrupted. Only the first four volumes have been printed, the last without the extensive French prolegomena of Corbin, which was such an important element of each of the first three volumes. These three prolegomena were printed

separately after Corbin's death as *La Philosophie iranienne islamique*, to which we have already referred.

20. An important step in this direction is the four-volume work of S.J. Sajjādī, *Farhang-i maʿārif-i islāmī*, Tehran, 1357 (A.H. solar).

Chapter Thirteen

The Architectural Transformation of the Urban Environment in the Islamic World

The same tensions and conflicts that were observed in the domain of ideas can also be seen displayed in the most tangible and visible manner in the architecture and urban environment that surround Muslims living in the modernized parts of the Islamic world. If in the intellectual field, German, French or English philosophies are contending with traditional Islamic thought, in the field of architecture one observes German or French styles in one area, American ones in another, and Italian in yet a third area. These vie with traditional Islamic architecture for every foot of space in various Muslim urban centers in a struggle which, until quite recently at least, nearly always went in favor of the foreign styles in question. The result has been the creation of disorder and chaos in the urban setting that directly reflect the tensions created in the mind and soul of so many Muslims as a result of the confrontation between traditional Islam and modernism.

Surely one can hardly deny the fact that the major modern urban environments of the Islamic world are suffering from a crisis which is most directly reflected in their ugliness. This stands in stark contrast to the serenity and beauty of the traditional Islamic city.[1] Islamic architecture has in fact been eclipsed by a conglomeration of often hideous styles, or at best bland ones, which imitate foreign models in the pretence of universality and world-wide applicability. The crisis within Islamic architecture and the modern Islamic cities hardly needs to be underlined. Nor is it necessary to elaborate here the principles and values of traditional Islamic architecture and city planning, the forgetting of which has brought the present crisis into being.[2] Our task is to study the transformations which have taken place within the mind and soul of the contemporary Muslim and which have brought about that inner chaos whose externalization is to be seen in the architectural creations of much of the contemporary Islamic world. The external environment which man creates for himself is no more than a reflection of his inner state. As the saying goes, 'As within, so without'.

What transformations have overcome the contemporary Muslim, who is responsible for the prevailing architectural and urban crises within the Islamic world? Perhaps, such a question should not be directed at all contemporary Muslims but only at the members of the small Westernized minority which possesses economic and social influence far exceeding its numbers, a minority which represents in fact an elite (*khawāṣṣ*) in reverse. One must remember that Latin proverb *corruptio optimi pessima* ('corruption of the best is the worst') and, the well-known Arabic and Persian proverb that states that the fish begins to stink from its head.[3] The changes which affect this small yet influential Westernized minority as far as architecture and city planning are concerned, also have an effect upon the intellectual, emotional and artistic aspects of life. They bear upon the intelligence as well as upon the imagination and sensitivity.

To understand this process of change and transformation fully, it is necessary to review the two major effects that Westernization has upon Muslims. The first is the spread of secularization; and the second, related to both internal and external factors, is the narrowing of the tradition (*al-dīn*) to include only the principles of human action as embodied in the *Sharī'ah*, not the principles of wisdom (*ḥikmah*) and the norms of making things which are contained in the principles and methods of Islamic art.

As far as secularization is concerned, the effect of Westernization has been to reduce the Islamic conception of *'ilm*, according to which all knowledge, including mathematics, is considered as sacred, to the conception of science as a purely profane form of knowledge. The traditional architect, who is entitled *mi'mār* ('he who builds': [*'umrān*] in the traditional sense) or *muhandis* ('he who is a geometer', again according to the traditional conception of geometry similar to that found in the Pythagorean tradition), becomes transformed into the modern architect with fancy offices filled with the latest gadgets, a person who now deals with profane mathematics and engineering techniques divorced from both wisdom and craftsmanship. Often, notable exceptions notwithstanding, the change also implies a loss of humility and dignity on the part of the traditional architect and the rise of a sense of egotism and worldliness that is usually associated with the 'international' architect and businessman. It implies a weakening of moral fibre and in some cases even a divorce from ethical considerations in one's professional work.

This intellectual change has also been depleting such fundamental realities and concepts as space, light, rhythm, form and matter of their sacred content. They are transformed into post-Cartesian Western concepts bearing the same name, and are experienced on only a limited material level. Space is then no longer the symbol of Divine Presence, nor Light of the Divine Intellect. Architectural rhythms which reintegrate multiplicity into Unity are forgotten. Form loses its symbolic value, and material substance becomes simply the dead, inert matter of Newtonian physics, far removed from the concept and experience of 'matter' entertained in traditional Islamic cosmology.[4]

Moreover, these changes are taking place within the minds, not only of most of the modern-trained Muslim architects, but also of most of their major clients, who are either drawn from the ranks of the rich or government authorities, and who order most of the new modern architecture in the Islamic world. In fact, for some people the transformation has been so rapid and abrupt that they do not even realize that the vast majority of the Muslim peoples for whom they are building still entertain different notions of space, light, form and matter from those that the modernized classes have learned in modern universities, whether these schools are located geographically in the Occident or in the Islamic world itself. It is of much interest to note that, while knowledge of traditional Islamic architecture still survives in the craft guilds and 'in the breast' (*ṣadr*) of certain individuals, there is not a single school of architecture in the universities of the Islamic world where this traditional Islamic architecture and its principles are taught in a serious manner.[5]

As far as the imagination is concerned, a nearly identical process of desacralization is to be observed. The imagination of the traditional Muslim is determined by forms and symbols drawn mostly from the Noble Quran; his soul consists essentially of the intertwining of certain basic formulas of the Holy Book, which imbue his inner being with fundamental attitudes *vis-à-vis* God and His creation.[6] In Islamic cosmology, the world of imagination occupies an intermediate region in the hierarchy of cosmic existence between the material and purely spiritual worlds. Its forms, sounds and colors have an objective reality, and its ontological reality serves to give human imagination a function above and beyond profane imagination as understood in the modern world. It is this imagination which Ibn 'Arabī refers to so often in his work, speaking of its creative power,[7] and which has been translated as *mundus imaginalis* to prevent its being confused with the profane use of the term 'imagination' in modern parlance.[8] The imagination of the traditional Muslim artist was constantly nourished by the Islamicized cosmic sector of this world, and of course more directly by the central theophany of the Islamic revelation, which is the Quran. The modern Muslim has, on the contrary, been deprived of this celestial sustenance, so that even where there is a degree of creativity on the part of some modernized Muslim architects, the fruit of this creativity has hardly anything to do with Islamic art and architecture. There are of course exceptions, but we speak of the majority, not of isolated cases.

Finally, the sensibility of those Muslims affected by the withering influence of Westernization has been deeply changed. In fact, in this domain, even those Muslims who still live within the traditional Islamic world suffer from the same problem when it comes to the judgement of art-forms outside their own traditional world. In Islamic art, beauty is considered to be a reflection of the Divine Beauty: as the famous prophetic *ḥadīth* asserts, 'God is beautiful and loves beauty'.[9] Moreover, beauty is an intrinsic dimension of the Truth and its manifestations, and it is therefore a necessary component of every legitimate artistic creation. Islam never separates beauty from utility, or art from making, as must have been the case in the traditional West when art meant *ars* and technology was still related to *techne*. The change of sensibility due to modernization has caused many Muslims to lose this inner sense of beauty, dignity, harmony and nobility, which characterizes Islamic art as indeed it does all authentic manifestations of the Islamic spirit. The modernized Muslim can hardly be conceived to be the descendant of those who built the Sultan Ḥasan Mosque at Cairo or the Maydān-i Naqsh-i Jahān at Isfahan.

Likewise, traditional Islamic sensibility saw the world in its transient aspect; it was aware of the negation or *lā* of the *shahādah* (*Lā ilāha illā'Llāh* – 'there is no divinity but God') which reduces everything to nothingness before the Immutable Majesty of Allah. Hence, architecture sought to avoid the grandiose and the worldly, and aimed to preserve and substantiate the basic intuition of the ephemerality of the world, which the spiritualized form of Semitic nomadism, propagated by Islam, accentuated and strengthened. The traditional Muslim looked at the city with full awareness of its passing, transient quality with respect both to God Himself and to virgin nature, the handiwork of God. Moreover, he saw the city as the extension of the natural environment in harmony rather than in discord with it.

Islamic architecture remained faithful to simple building materials and employed the elemental forces of nature such as light and wind for its sources of energy. It brought nature into the city by recreating the calmness, harmony and peace of virgin nature within the courtyards of the mosque and of the home. The modernized Muslim, whose spiritual sense has become dulled by the force of secularization, has forgotten the ephemeral quality of human life on earth and the peace and harmony pervading nature. Like the modern Westerner whom he emulates, he wants to build homes as if he were going to live forever and construct cities whose very existence is based upon defiance of nature, the violation of her rhythms and the depletion of her resources. The wish of modern man, including the secularized Muslim, is to create an ambience in which God is forgotten. This means creating an urban environment in total disequilibrium with that natural environment which is created by God and which, being itself a reminder of the Divine, gives the lie to the very notion of secularism.

In addition to the transformations brought about on the levels of intelligence, imagination and sensibility in modernized Muslims, there is also a general loss of the sense of unity and integration of life which directly affects architecture and city planning. Islam is based upon Unity (*al-tawḥīd*) and is the means toward the integration of human life, and in fact of all multiplicity, into Unity.[10] Every authentic manifestation of the Islamic spirit reflects the doctrine of *al-tawḥīd*. This doctrine is the principle of all the Islamic arts and sciences, as well as of the *Sharī'ah*, which integrates all human action and prepares man to return to the One in the mold of the perfection that is found on the highest level in the Blessed Prophet in the mold which could be called 'The Muḥammadan Perfection,' i.e., the *uswah*, the model which Muslims follow.

The traditional Islamic city reflected this unity directly. Since there is no distinction in Islam between the sacred and profane, a unity pervaded the architecture of the city which related the architecture of the home and even of the palace and other municipal buildings to that of the mosque. This unity made the space within the Muslim home an extension of the space within the mosque, which in fact it is from a ritual as well as an artistic point of view. The all-embracing nature of the *Sharī'ah*, which includes worship (*'ibādāt*) as well as transactions (*mu'āmalāt*), made possible the integration of all forms of activity. In the heart of the Islamic city, spaces designed for worship became interconnected with those designed for education, the making of things and business transactions, as well as for private living and cultural activity. The heart of many Islamic cities today still displays this remarkable unity of space and function within the mosque, *madrasah*, bazaar, private homes and the like. Needless to say, secularism destroys this vision of unity and the integration of all human activity within a divine norm and pattern. The loss of this unity, at least on a more external level,[11] is one of the primary factors responsible for the plight of the modern city within the Islamic world. It becomes even more marked by the fact that the vast majority of Muslims still live with a unified world-view and cannot bear the compartmentalized form of life imposed upon them by the mind and will of the minority who build for them according to models of architecture and city planning based, not on unity, but on the segmentation and separation of the various domains of human activity.

The second effect of contact with the West is the narrowing down of religion to embrace only the laws pertaining to human action. The *Sharī'ah* includes a series of complex factors some of which are related to forces within Islamic society and some to contact with the West. It is not possible to deal here with the how and why of the spread of puritanical, rationalistic movements such as various forms of Neo-Wahhabism and different so-called reformist movements associated with groups like the Salafiyyah, the Ikhwān al-muslimīn, the Deoband movement and the Jamā'at-i islāmī, and the reason for their indifference to Islamic art. What is important for the present discussion is that these movements, in their attempt to revive the *Sharī'ah* and the Islamic practices associated with daily life, have for the most part neglected Islamic art and the metaphysical and philosophical principles underlying it. Moreover, they have made possible the appearance of later forms of violent 'fundamentalism' which, as mentioned at the beginning of this book, are as indifferent and even opposed to Islamic art as are the partisans of the modernist camp.

When this type of religiosity is combined with modernistic tendencies, it creates an atmosphere in which the only thing that matters is the juridical aspect of the religion and not its artistic dimension. At best, God is remembered as Truth, at least on a certain level, but He is forgotten as Presence. Hence, beauty becomes incidental and the Islamic character of architecture and city planning is of total inconsequence. What matters is that the new city development has a mosque or two somewhere. It matters little if the rest of the city resembles the secularized and inhuman urban spaces of modern Western cities or their suburbs, where either inhuman regimentation or a rugged individualism dominates. In such places, the only question that is never considered is the wholeness of life and the integration of human society.

Despite the religious character of this type of reform movement and its reaction to many Western things on the level of ideas, the transformation it brings about in the mind and soul of the contemporary Muslim fortifies the secularizing tendency in its effect on architecture and city planning. These factors alienate the Muslim from those aspects of the Islamic tradition which bear most directly upon art and architecture; that is, the wisdom or *sapientia* always associated with Islamic esotericism and the cosmology which issues from it, also the principles governing Islamic art itself. The secularizing tendency causes certain Muslims to become completely indifferent to their own religion, whether reflected in the *Sharī'ah* itself or in its sapiental teachings. The reformist tendency reduces religion for the most part to its juridical aspect. Through its belittling of and even disdain for wisdom (*ḥikmah*), it accepts the secularization of both art and nature and makes inaccessible those very elements of the Islamic tradition of which Muslims are most direly in need in order to recreate an authentic Islamic ambience. The atrocious destruction of so much Islamic architecture and even of sanctuaries and holy cities by apparently devout Muslims is proof, if proof is necessary, of the significance of the loss of that divine wisdom which contains the principles of Islamic art. This is true whether the loss comes from a lack of interest in religion as such through secularism, or by means of the narrowing down of religion to only one of its dimensions and the consequent forgetting of the sacramental character of traditional Islamic art as an integral aspect of the Islamic revelation.

Of course, besides these spiritual and intellectual factors, there are important social, political and economic elements with which the present chapter is not concerned. But one cannot avoid at least mentioning that most nations of the Islamic world suffer from an inferiority complex before the West. They seek to create Western forms of architecture, often as prestige projects in order to become acceptable, even if, for example, it is not economically feasible to manage a highrise building covered with glass in the middle of a desert. Likewise, the great wealth of some Islamic countries provides just the right background for the greed of many Western contractors and planners, who operate with the help of their Muslim counterparts to present plans and projects which manage to be most costly and yet not create what is most Islamic. Of course, a few arches are usually added to give the impression of conformity with the local culture, but the real intentions remain hidden only to those who are unaware of the nature of Islamic architecture. However, those people, unfortunately, are often the very persons asked to judge the validity of these projects. One wonders what would happen to many of the new urban developments within the Islamic world if architects continued to build as if the energy crisis did not exist. There is certainly no excuse for the Muslim countries to repeat the errors of Western urban development. The fact that an error may gain world-wide acceptance for a short time does not turn it into a truth.

To remedy this serious situation, one cannot suggest a more obvious first step than the training of Islamic architects, men and women who are committed to specifically Islamic architecture, rather than those who practice Western architecture with the claim that it is international and who happen to be named Muḥammad, Aḥmad or 'Alī. To train Islamic architects, in turn, requires certain essential resources for education in this field being made available. Fortunately, traditional Islamic architecture is still alive in the villages and smaller towns of many Islamic countries, and secret documents are still preserved in some of the guilds. Where modern architects and their imitators do not interfere, the architecture continues to be at once beautiful and functional. Moreover, the vast majority of the Islamic people are still drawn to the authentic expressions of architecture. Advantage can be taken of these factors to create schools of Islamic architecture to train architects and city planners who can build the cities, public monuments, housing projects and other major developments which have been necessitated by the population explosion, migration to cities, changes in ways of production and other factors. These projects are now usually carried out by people trained in Western architecture, whether they happen to be citizens of Western or Islamic countries.

The establishment of such schools and institutions[12] requires the revival of the Islamic arts and sciences and the rediscovery of their spiritual and metaphysical principles. This means that, ultimately, Islamic architecture cannot be revived unless the contemporary Muslim is reborn and the shackles of Western cultural and philosophical domination overthrown. The external world cannot be adorned with the beauty which is the theophany of the Divine Beauty unless the inner man is adorned with those virtues (*faḍā'il*) and forms of wisdom which have always characterized the creative scholars and artists within Islamic civilization. The task remains a vast one, but one can always begin with the training of a few.[13] One can hope and pray that their personal example, and the beauty of works they create according to Islamic principles, will serve as a light which will transform the darkness. With the help of authentic Islamic art and architecture, it is still possible to transform the chaos and darkness that pervades much of the urban environment of the

Islamic world into that harmony of light, space and form that has always characterized the traditional Islamic city and town.

Notes

1. The urban crisis is of course world-wide. Much that is taking place in the Islamic world is related to, and is a consequence of, this world-wide crisis. The fact that this is so indicates the passive nature of much of the Islamic world *vis-à-vis* the West and is itself an indication of this crisis. In any case, inasmuch as our main concern in this chapter is with the Islamic world, we shall limit ourselves to the architectural and urban problems of this region, although many of our comments also apply elsewhere.
2. We shall deal with some of these principles in the next chapter. See also our *Islamic Art and Spirituality*, chapter IV.
3. See F. Schuon, *Spiritual Perspectives and Human Facts*, trans. D.M. Matheson, London, 1953, part I.
4. See our *An Introduction to Islamic Cosmological Doctrines*, pp. 58–59 and pp. 218–226.
5. During the past decade some attempt has been made to rectify the situation, thanks mostly to the efforts of Hasan Fathy, the notable Egyptian architect, and some of his students. Recently the Aga Khan program of Islamic architecture has even begun a degree program in Islamic architecture at Harvard and M.I.T. One hopes that the program will be based on the Islamic principles of Islamic architecture rather than on that which some people associated with the program until now have considered as good Islamic architecture, namely 'good' architecture in the Islamic world. One wonders what criteria determine the meaning of 'good' in such statements.
6. See F. Schuon, pp. 66ff.
7. See H. Corbin, *Creative Imagination in the Sufism of Ibn 'Arabi*, trans. from French by R. Manheim, Princeton, 1969.
8. See H. Corbin, *En Islam Iranien*, vol. I, pp. 120ff.
9. Ibn Ḥanbal, *Musnad*, Book 4, v. 133–134.
10. See Schuon, *op.cit.*, chapter 1.
11. On a more external level, because inwardly the One shines like a never-setting sun at the heart of all things and most of all of man, who is the complete and central theophany of the One in this world.
12. One must not forget that these schools must in turn be based on Islamic

models that would allow long periods of apprenticeship, personal dedication to a teacher or master and the possibility of training the student morally as well as technically.

13. A few such architects are in fact beginning to appear in the Islamic world, such men as Abd al-Wahid El-Wakil and Omar Farooq.

Chapter Fourteen

The Principles of Islamic Architecture and Contemporary Urban Problems

It is important to mention once again at the outset that the principles of Islamic art, including especially Islamic architecture and city planning, are related to the Islamic revelation. Moreover this nexus exists in two different ways, one direct and the other indirect. These principles derive directly from the inner dimension of the Quranic revelation and the sacred science contained therein. They derive from the Divine Word as contained in the Quran and echoing in the hearts of men and throughout the Islamic city, determining the space in which they live and function. They derive from an aspect of the soul of the Prophet, the recipient of the Word, from a prophetic presence which embraces and, one might say, enshrouds the traditional Islamic city in a kind of beatific purity of spiritual death within whose bosom is to be found the fountain of the spiritual life.

Indirectly, Islamic architecture and city planning are related to and influenced by the Divine Law or *Sharīʿah*, which molds the life of the individual Muslim as well as that of the Islamic community and society as a whole. The Divine Law itself issues from the Islamic revelation and, although it does not create architecture or city planning, it does provide the social and human background for that architecture which, in its sacred form, is of a supra-human origin. Islamic architecture and city planning in their traditional form are, therefore, created, molded and influenced by the Islamic religion in their inner principles, symbolic language and intellectual basis, as well as by the human and social setting for which they serve as the external cadre.

It might then be asked what pertinence can such an architecture or city planning have for the Western world and the present-day urban crisis which modern civilization faces, not only in the West which gave rise to modernism, but wherever modernism has spread, whether it be in Asia, Africa or America. One might claim that Muslims, many of whose present-day cities are not at all traditional Islamic cities, can make use of the principles of their architecture to overcome the terrible problems they now encounter. One might assert that, at least theoretically, they possess this ability because they have access to these principles and also still live within a society in which the *Sharīʿah* is functioning, albeit partially, and in which it can be revived and strengthened because faith in Islam is still strong in the hearts of men and women.[1] But how can these principles be of interest or possibly help to solve problems relating to urban settings in the West where the vast majority of the population is non-Muslim and in many cases even disinterested in any form of religion? The answer is that, first of all, there are certain universal elements in man and in his relation to the natural environment. These elements make possible the introduction of such principles even in settings that are alien to the particular religious world from which those principles issued in the first place. Secondly, the dominant religion of the West, namely Christianity, which gave birth to European civilization, belongs to the same religious family as Islam and certain principles, norms or ideas drawn from Islam can always evoke a sympathetic response in the mind and soul of a European, the very strands of whose being are woven by centuries of experience of Christian religion and culture, even if he now consciously rejects this tradition.[2] Thirdly, Islam is in a sense a return to the primordial religion of Divine Unity and possesses a message at once simple and universal which can appeal to that primordial nature that lies, often hidden and only in a latent state, in the heart and indeed the very substance of all human beings.[3] Its principles and teachings, even when pertaining to the domain of architecture and city planning, can therefore be of significance and interest even in a world where its tenets are not practiced. In the light of these considerations, it is perhaps of some value to discuss certain of the principles of Islamic architecture and then see how they can be applied to contemporary urban problems.

As in other aspects of Islam, so in architecture the principle of Unity (*al-tawḥīd*) is of central importance. While in the domains of metaphysics and religion, this principle implies the unity of the Divine Principle, the interrelation of all things and their utter ontological dependence upon the One, as well as the total dedication of the individual to the Will of the One, in architecture unity implies integration of the elements of architecture, interrelation of the functions and purposes of space and the ubiquitous presence of the sacred in all forms of architecture in such a way as to remove the very notion of the secular as a category in opposition to the sacred. It implies realization of the One in the buildings created by human hands in the same way that virgin nature reflects its Unique Creator through the harmony, equilibrium and interrelation which characterize its manifold forms and phenomena. Since *al-tawḥīd* in Arabic means both 'oneness' and 'making one' (or 'integration'), the principle of Unity in architecture implies at once the state of oneness reflected through the peace, tranquility and harmony of Islamic architecture and the act of making one or integration which interconnects the elements of a single edifice, and in fact a whole village or urban setting, creating ever greater degrees of unity leading to Unity as such.[4] One could in fact say that in the same way that an Arabic treatise is in reality one long sentence, the Islamic town or city is one single edifice which integrates all its parts into a whole that transcends those parts; that is, comes before them in both conception and execution and bestows upon them sense and order. Likewise on a smaller scale, the whole of a single edifice precedes its parts, unity always predominating over multiplicity and the whole over the parts.[5]

This principle of unity can be seen in the interrelation of various types of architecture. Religious and secular architecture do not in reality exist as two distinct domains; rather the whole of Islamic architecture in fact grows out of the mosque and is its extension in the same way as any action or rite that is performed in the mosque can also be accomplished in the home or the bazaar. Something of the grace of the Quran and the soul of the Prophet spread over the whole ambience of the Islamic city, much as the call to prayers penetrates into every architectural space or the rain of mercy from Heaven falls upon the roof of every building, whether it be private house, mosque or school. The same techniques, architectural symbols, use of light, space and forms found in the mosque are also to be found in the palace or the house, except of course such distinct architectural features as the minaret or prayer niche (*miḥrāb*), which belong solely to the mosque.

The mosque, the palace, the bazaar, the school and the home are intertwined by virtue of that very organic unity which links their architectural space. In a traditional Islamic city such as Fez[6] or Isfahan, the mosque is not only itself the community center as well as the locus of religious activity, but opens into the area of economic activity, private homes, schools and palaces in such a way as to link them all together. The architecture thus reflects the unity of traditional Islamic life while itself facilitating the living of an integrated life.

The principle of unity is also to be seen in the manner in which Islamic architecture treats the outside of an edifice, the inside spaces and the landscaping. In modern architecture, these three features are distinguished and in fact different persons are usually trained as specialists in each. A modern architect usually leaves the interior decoration of a building to a decorator and the area surrounding it to a landscape architect. In Islamic architecture, on the contrary, these three components are three facets of a single reality usually conceived and executed by the same master mason or group of masons. When one contemplates the Court of Lions in the Alhambra or the garden pavilions of the Fīn Garden in Kashan or the Shālīmār in Lahore, one realizes that all these facets of architecture comprise the same reality and possess a unity which enables them to become organically integrated into a single experience embracing the interior spaces, the architecture itself in the modern Western sense and the landscape surrounding the edifice.

The principle of unity is also to be seen in the multiple functions which the spaces of traditional Islamic architecture, especially those of the home, usually serve. In contrast to modern architecture, where functions for various spaces are first defined and then a building created which sees the whole as the aggregation of those well-defined component parts, in Islamic architecture the different components of the space created are born from the conception of the structure as a whole and possess a plasticity of usage derived from the multiple functions which most spaces serve. A room in the traditional Muslim home can serve during a single day as bedroom, dining room, guest room and also place of worship, the lack of fixed furniture in the modern sense aiding greatly in facilitating such multiple usage. In older days, one hardly ever ordered a three- or four-bedroom house. The traditional architecture would create a whole out of which the spaces necessary for everyday life would grow in such a way that wholeness always dominated over the living space of the family or families in question, in much the same way as the town or city possessed a wholeness which predominated over its parts. There were, to be sure, distinct components, elements, and features, ranging from a single house to a quarter of the city, but unity always predominated over multiplicity and prevented the parts from becoming realities independent of the whole. In the same way that all the living spaces of the traditional Islamic city seem to have but a single roof, unity in both a metaphysical and architectural sense has always dominated over the parts, allowing the growth of the parts but always in relation to and in harmony with the whole.

The principle of unity is also directly related to the combining of beauty and function or utility so characteristic of all Islamic art and especially architecture. Islam emphasizes the importance of beauty as the aura of the truth for, as the already-quoted *ḥadīth* states, God is both beautiful in Himself and loves beauty. Furthermore, to quote another *ḥadīth*, 'God has "written" the mark of beauty upon all things.' The need for beauty is innate in human nature and as necessary for ultimate survival as the air that one breathes. Far from being a luxury, beauty is a human necessity. To be beautiful is to be 'useful' in the deepest sense of the word; that is, in fulfilling a basic need of man. Functionality and utility are therefore not juxtaposed against beauty but complement it. To have a total and complete image of man as being at once a body, soul and spirit, at once a creature of this earth but created for immortality and the eternal life, is to realize that no authentic functionality and utility can be divorced from beauty, for what is ugly is ultimately 'useless': it is false and finally against man's deepest interests. In the Muslim mind, not only is beauty identified with truth and goodness, but ugliness is regarded as the other face: falsehood and evil. One could even say that inasmuch as in Arabic *al-Ḥaqq*, one of the Names of God, means at once Truth and Reality (and is therefore also beautiful), ugliness is, by token of the same association, unreality and separation from the One who is at once Reality, Truth and Beauty. To speak of the functionality of architecture as separate from beauty, which is then relegated to the trivial category of luxury, is to forget the most fundamental metaphysical teachings of the Quran and *Ḥadīth* which repeatedly identify beauty with the source of all reality and truth.

The unity of beauty and functionality is also related to what one might call the principle of 'realism' in Islamic art and architecture.[7] In using 'realism' here, we do not intend its modern philosophical meaning, but rather have in mind that point of view which considers the reality of each being on its own level and sees things 'as they are' in an objective mode based on both the dicta of the Islamic revelation and the power of intelligence to be able to know and to discern, the intelligence which Islam emphasizes so often in its definition of man and which is central to an understanding of the traditional *homo islamicus*.[8] In art, this realism means to treat each material as it is, not as what it might appear to be or be made to appear to be. Brick should be used as brick and should be seen as brick, and stone as stone. Even the physical forces and laws which govern the material with which architecture is concerned should be treated and respected in such a way as to bring out their character as parts of God's creation and therefore participating in that structuring of harmony and beauty which characterize creation.

This view of the nature of materials and the manner of treating them is related in depth to the emphasis upon mathematics in Islamic architecture, which always tends to accentuate purity of geometric forms and patterns. The Muslim mind sees in geometric forms and patterns, not just quantities but a reflection of the archetypal and intelligible world[9]; one might speak of a kind of 'Abrahamic Pythagoreanism' which found a haven in the Islamic universe.[10] If Islamic sacred architecture is of a highly geometric character both in its definition of space and in the treatment of its surfaces, it is because the intelligible world (or *'ālam al-ma'qūlāt*) with which the Muslim mind identifies the origin of geometric forms and patterns, as well as mathematical rhythms, is none other than the angelic world. Through this world of the Spirit, the sacred space created by this architecture leads to the sun of Unity, whose brilliance is too dazzling to be depicted directly but to which allusion is made by all the regular geometrical forms and patterns which are generated by that Point that is everywhere and nowhere.

The emphasis in Islamic architecture upon the treatment of surfaces of buildings and especially mosques, Sufi centers, and the like, which are often covered with calligraphy, geometric patterns and arabesque forms, must not be confused with mere decoration or cosmetics in the modern sense. This treatment might be called 'cosmetic' if only one were to remember the original significance of this word as meaning 'to make cosmic-like', or 'to bring out the correspondence of something with the cosmos and cosmic harmony'. Although apparently limited to the surface of an edifice, the patterns of Islamic architecture reflect the deepest structures of physical reality, bringing out the mathematical order and harmony which underlie the appearance of the corporeal world.

In accordance with the primordial character of the Islamic revelation and its re-establishment of harmony between man and nature, Islamic architecture and city planning have always emphasized the integration of architecture and natural setting. Nature in a sense permeates and penetrates the traditional Islamic city and its buildings. The mosque itself is not a holy space separated from natural space but an extension into a man-made environment of the space of virgin nature which, because it is created by God, is sacred in itself and still echoes its original paradisal perfection. Light and air enter easily into the mosque and other buildings, and birds even fly around within the edifice during the most solemn moments of a religious ceremony. The countryside is always near by, and the rhythms of desert and mountain penetrate into the city.

Not only does one observe the absence of any opposition between the forces and elements of nature and the traditional Islamic urban ambience; but every attempt has been made in Islamic architecture to make maximum use of the forces of nature, of light, wind, shade, etc. In short the architecture has never set itself up as being against the natural order or in defiance of the rhythms and harmony of nature. Even most materials used, such as mud walls or soft brick, have been treated in such a way as to allow a building to be reabsorbed into the bosom of nature once it is abandoned by its human inhabitants. Muslim towns and even large cities were built in such a way that had they remained in their traditional form they could in principle have survived indefinitely without bringing about the ecological catastrophes with which the modern world is only too familiar. The traditional Muslim, like other traditional peoples, saw himself as the custodian of nature whose laws and rhythms he respected, even if he built some of the largest towns and cities known to mankind before modern times.

In building such urban areas where architecture of monumental proportions is to be found, as well as in the construction of more humble units in small towns and villages, Muslims never distinguished between technology and the crafts, or between the crafts and art. The arts, the crafts and technology were in fact considered as the same thing and even the same terms, such as the Arabic *ṣināʿah*, were used for them all. To make and to make beautifully in conformity with the work and the material being used were synonymous.[11] The master architects were also well versed in the technology of the material with which they dealt such as the baking of brick or the making of tiles. The people who performed the technological tasks, often of a remarkable nature even according to the standards of the modern world, which takes such great pride in its technology, the artists who designed patterns of great beauty and the architects who created the buildings were often the same people or members of a group so closely knit that their work came out as if accomplished by but one person. As a result of master-disciple relationships which made possible, not only the teaching of architectural and artisanal techniques but also the spiritual discipline transcending the individual, an anonymity was achieved which, far from destroying individual creativity, elevated this creativity to a level above and beyond individual idiosyncrasies. Unity permitted co-operation on such a scale and with such intimacy that works of universal significance were created, and even more humble and transient works of architecture came into being through the efforts of men who took great joy in working without having to assert their egotistical tendencies. In fact, the work made possible the control of the ego, leading to a joy which can never be experienced within the confinement of the prison of individualistic passions and egotistical impulses.

Islamic architecture also made possible the integration of the various facets of everyday life, such as work, leisure, play, etc., while being itself the result of such an integrated view of everyday life. As already mentioned earlier in this work, in the traditional Islamic pattern of life work is never separated from leisure, which is always integrated with worship or study. To this day, wherever such a pattern has survived, for example in certain bazaar areas, one can observe a craftsman or a shopkeeper spending some twelve to fourteen hours away from his home in what would be called his place of work, which is usually near by. But in that place of work and during those hours which appear to be long, he spends a good deal of time praying, eating, talking to friends or even going to a near-by mosque or traditional school (*madrasah*) for an hour or two of worship or study. When he comes home in the evening, he is not more tired than a worker who has spent eight hours in an office or a factory and who must seek his leisure, rest and culture, as well as his educational and religious activities elsewhere. Traditional Islamic architecture and city planning are based on such an integrated concept of life and also themselves make possible and facilitate such a pattern of life. They create spaces which, through their interconnection, proximity and multi-faceted use, enable men to experience this intertwining of work and leisure, of making a living and perfecting one's mind and soul through study and worship. In this as in so many other ways, Islamic architecture and city planning reflect the principle of unity which, being at the heart of the Islamic revelation, is more than any other factor responsible for the distinctive architecture and urban design characteristics of the world created by that revelation.

The application of the principles of Islamic architecture, some of which have been described, to urban problems in the contemporary world depends not only upon the nature of these principles, but also upon the conditions prevailing in the world in which they are to be applied. Although some of the problems existing in urban environments today, such problems as pollution and environmental decay, are world-wide, the question of applying these principles to the contemporary Islamic world differs somewhat from the West, which is the main concern of this chapter. It has already been mentioned that most of the cities of the Islamic world are suffering from terrible urban upheaval and decay caused by overcrowding, excessively rapid growth, intrusion of alien life-styles and inappropriate architecture. They are faced with social and economic problems complicated by cultural and religious dislocations. These cities are furthermore faced with the strange situation that, in numerous cases, most of the population now residing in them are from rural areas and are without experience of living in a traditional Islamic urban environment. Yet, the population for the most part still follows the *Sharī'ah* in its everyday life, and if the inner dimensions of the Islamic tradition were to be revived and applied rather than suppressed by those in power in the name of political reassertion[12], the principles of Islamic art and architecture could be reapplied to solve many of the horrendous problems that many Muslim cities face today.

In the Western world, however, the social structure of society is very different from the one based on the Islamic *Sharī'ah*, as is the religious as well as the secular ethos which together, in a combination dominated by the secular component, determine the value system of modern Western man in both its ethical and aesthetic aspects. Nevertheless, the nature of man being what it is, the inner nexus between Islam, Christianity and Judaism being of such a comprehensive nature, and the crisis of the modern urban environment being of such intensity, a situation is created whereby the principles of Islamic architecture and urban design have become worthy of serious consideration by Westerners concerned with the future of their own towns and cities.

The modern Western city suffers from excessive segmentation; disequilibrium *vis-à-vis* the natural environment; its being economically and ecologically unsound, particularly in its use of energy resources; and from the spread of a blanket of ugliness in the name of economic necessity with the result that beauty appears as luxury and is divorced from utility. The Islamic emphasis upon the unity of the facets of life as reflected in different architectural spaces, upon harmony between man and the natural environment, upon the wedding between beauty and utility, as well as many other related principles, far from being of significance only for the Islamic world, cannot but be of interest to those in the West who are genuinely concerned with the future of urban life beyond immediate considerations of fame or greed. While Islam has over the centuries appeared as the 'other' to the Christian and even 'post-Christian'

West, its architectural philosophy, based on its conception of man in his primordial harmony with the world of creation, can play a role in this dark hour of human history in the creation of an ambience, at once cultural and architectural, which can reflect man's true nature and remind him of who he is and why he is undertaking this earthly journey. Although these principles cannot bring such a transformation about without the transformation of man himself and his society, their application in architecture and urban design can at least aid in that transformation which can finally only come from within the heart and soul of man.

Notes

1. The methods and means of applying traditional principles of Islamic architecture and city planning to problems of contemporary Islamic society are therefore different from the methods needed for applying these principles to the situation of urban environments in the West. In this essay, we are concerned only with this latter problem. Concerning the contemporary Islamic world see A. El-Wakil, 'Identity, Tradition and Architecture', in *Arab Architecture: Past and Present*, Durham, 1984, pp. 26–29.
2. Because of the inner or transcendent unity of religions, such actions and reactions can take place across any religious frontier, but this possibility becomes stronger when the religions belong to the same family. In the case of Christianity and Islam, the family proximity has of course also caused the severest reactions and oppositions over the ages, especially from the side of Christian theology, which has until now repudiated the authenticity of the Islamic revelation. But this historical confrontation does not negate the possibility of positive interactions across religious frontiers today, as was the case in medieval Spain and Sicily. On the inner relation between Christianity and Islam and religions in general see F. Schuon, *The Transcendent Unity of Religions*, trans. P. Townsend, London, 1975; *Formes et substance dans les religions*, Paris, 1975; *Christianity/Islam*; and *Das Ewige im Vergänglichen*, Weilheim, 1970.
3. See Nasr, *Ideals and Realities of Islam*, chapter 1.
4. On these levels of unity in Islamic architecture see N. Ardalan and

L. Bakhtiyar, *The Sense of Unity, The Sufi Tradition in Persian Architecture*, London, 1973.

5. The training of the traditional Muslim architect reflects this principle clearly, for he is taught always to conceive of the whole and then descend to the parts rather than learning to conceive and draw the parts of the building or complex of buildings and then weld them together as a whole as is the case with modern students of architecture.
6. For a unique study which relates the principle of unity to both the architecture and social, intellectual and artistic life of Fez see T. Burckhardt, *Fez-Stadt des Islam*, Olten, 1960.
7. These questions have been dealt with in a masterly fashion by T. Burckhardt in his many writings on Islamic art already cited. In this connection see especially his 'The Spirit of Islamic Art', *Islamic Quarterly*, Dec. 1954, pp. 212–218.
8. See F. Schuon, *Understanding Islam*, pp. 13ff; also our *Knowledge and the Sacred*, chapter 5.
9. See K. Critchlow, *Islamic Patterns*, London, 1976.
10. On the question of the Islamic conception of number and geometric form see S.H. Nasr, *An Introduction to Islamic Cosmological Doctrines*, chapter 2; on the universal significance of numbers in their qualitative aspect see F. Schuon, *Esoterism As Principle and As Way*, pp. 65–78.
11. See T. Burckhardt, 'Perennial Values in Islamic art', in C. Malik (al.), *God and Man in Contemporary Islamic Thought*, Beirut, 1972, p. 129; and J.L. Michon, 'Education in the Traditional Arts and Crafts and the Cultural Heritage of Islam', in S.H. Nasr (ed.), *Philosophy, Literature and Fine Arts – Islamic Education Series*, Sevenoaks, 1982, pp. 49–62.
12. On the forgetting by the 'fundamentalists' of the inner dimensions of Islam from which the principles of Islamic art and architecture issue see our *Islamic Art and Spirituality*, chapter 1.

Part Four
Western Interpreters of the Islamic Tradition

Chapter Fifteen

In Commemoration of Louis Massignon: Catholic Scholar, Islamicist and Mystic

A dimension of the presence of traditional Islam in the modern world that has not as yet been considered in this work is that which embraces the works and thought of those scholars of Western origin who have discovered, in an authentic fashion, aspects of the Islamic tradition and presented it to the modern world. Despite the deviations observable in the writings of so many orientalists, there have been some figures who belong to the above category; that is, scholars whose love and knowledge of Islam have been genuine, if not always complete and total. In the chapters which constitute the present section of this work, I shall deal with three of the major figures of Western origin who have discovered and made known the Islamic tradition to the modern world and whom I have known personally. The first, Louis Massignon, I was to encounter in my student days and I continued my contact with him until his death. The second, Henry Corbin, I met upon my return to Tehran from America in 1958, and collaborated with him closely for twenty years in teaching and producing various works on Islamic thought. The third, Titus Burckhardt, I also met in my student days and was deeply influenced by both his works and his saintly presence, as well as by the luminosity of his thought. We met over the years on several continents, but most of all in the world of the spirit, in the 'garden of the Truth', which stands above and beyond all spatial and temporal determinations.

And so I shall begin with Massignon, perhaps the greatest academic scholar of Islam that the West has ever produced. It would be appropriate to cite by way of prelude a poem by Rūmī, which in a sense recapitulates on a particular level the spiritual and intellectual destiny of Massignon:

Regard the world as full of ecstasy,
The dominion of the 'Victorious'.
If thou wishest to be 'victorious'
Be impaled upon the gibbet,
Be impaled upon the gibbet.

This poem, which, over three centuries after the death of Ḥallāj, echoes the singular significance of the martyrdom of the great saint, is in fact also the echo which dominated the life of Massignon. It is therefore quite significant that we view the life of Massignon through this unique experience of the spiritual reality of Ḥallāj, an experience which transformed him as a human being in his youth, which dominated the horizon of his life to its end and which produced his most important work that Herbert Mason has spent twenty years translating into the English language, thus rendering a very major service to the cause of scholarship.

The choice of Ḥallāj has a particular significance within the perspective adopted here, that is, the perspective of the Sufi tradition itself. I cannot do justice to Massignon otherwise; here I write not only as a scholar, for I wish to speak about certain subjects that are not merely scholarly but which nevertheless need to be said. The fact that Ḥallāj in a sense 'visited' Massignon inwardly is not at all an academic question; rather, it is a providential event. Ḥallāj represents within Sufism the special grace of Christ as it manifests itself in the Islamic universe. He is a Christic Sufi, if we can use such a term; that is, he manifests *al-barakat al-'īsawiyyah* (to use the Arabic term) within himself. It is not that he was influenced by Christianity in a historical sense. This type of manifestation has nothing to do with the presence of Christianity as another religion. Rather, the structure of Islam is such that, within the Islamic tradition there is a possibility of 'the shining forth of the ray' of the founders of other religions, especially of Judaism and Christianity. It is possible to have a spirituality which is Abrahamic, Mosaic, or Christic. That is why I use the word 'Christic' and not 'Christian'. In the case of Ḥallāj, he represents a Christic embodiment within the Muḥammadan universe of spirituality. And the fact that he, rather than the great early masters like Junayd or Abū Yazīd al-Basṭāmī or other Sufis of Khorasan, happened to have been chosen by Massignon (or, more accurately, Massignon having been chosen by them) is very far from being an accident from the point of view of the spiritual economy of the universe within which we live. For the Ḥallājian perspective represents in fact the most accessible opening towards Sufism for the West, which is fundamentally Christian in its spiritual attitudes. Even if it tries to leave its traditional religion behind, it has nevertheless for the most part a Christian perspective upon the reality of Sufism in general and, of course, that of Islam, of which Sufism is the heart. Therefore the choice of Ḥallāj for Massignon or of Massignon for Ḥallāj, far from being an accident, represents in fact a providential event in the encounter between Islam and Christianity in the modern world.

Now, the man who was the vehicle of such a vision, namely Massignon, whose 100th anniversary was celebrated in both the Islamic world and the West recently, needs to be studied at length precisely because of his significance as a bridge between the two religions. In fact, a number of biographies of him have already been written. Here, it is important to recapitulate in a few words the main features of the contour of his life. He was a person who loved to speak of *'la courbe de la vie,'* literally 'the curve of one's life'; that is, the moments whose traces delineate the significant features of a life. Let me very quickly summarize those moments for you. This question touches me personally because Massignon was the first Western scholar about whom I ever heard from my very first teacher, my father, when I was only four or five years old.

Born in 1883 in the French town of Nogent-sur-Marne, Massignon entered the University of Paris in 1900. During the next year, he journeyed for the first time to the Islamic world: to Algeria, which was then part of France. In 1902, he finished his *licence* at the University of Paris. In 1904, he made his first journey to Morocco, which had an important effect on the whole future of that country, because it was he more than anyone else who advised Maréchal Lyautey not to destroy the old medinas of Morocco in order to build new quarters but instead to build new cities next to the medinas. The consequences of that decision for Islamic architecture in the 20th century is of course immense. The fact that we have the whole structure of the medinas in North Africa, and especially in Fez and Meknes, preserved to this day goes back to the role of Massignon in advising the powerful French official not to remodel the cities from within but to take the *villes*, the French cities, outside and thereby preserve the structure of the traditional cities. This all-important choice is the result of the very first visit of the young Massignon to Morocco.

Then in 1907, a special event took place in the life of Massignon which is quite mysterious. Even his son and other members of his family considered it to be a mystical moment in his life. The event was his discovery of Ḥallāj, a discovery which was not of a scholarly character but of an inner and spiritual nature, one which in fact left an indelible mark upon the whole of his later life and brought him back to the fold of that Christianity which he had taken very lightly until then. From 1907 to 1909, he did archaeology in Iraq, and from 1912 to 1913 he was a professor in the University of Cairo. With the exceptional command that he had of Arabic, he was able to deliver his lectures there in that language. In 1914, he married and, in 1922, after the First World War, he defended his great theses on Ḥallāj as his principal thesis, while his auxiliary thesis, that is, *Eassai sur les origines de la lexique de la mystique musulmane*, was itself to become established as one of the major scholarly works on Sufism. These two works made him immediately famous and established him as one of the leading Islamicists in France. As a result, he was in 1926 chosen as a professor at the Collège de France. From 1933 onwards, he also held the chair of Islamic Studies at the Ecole des Hautes Etudes. He held both positions until 1954 when he retired.

After the Second World War, in 1945 and 1946, he was the envoy of France to various Arab countries, seeking to revive cultural relationships between France and the Arab world. In 1952, he came for the first time as visiting professor to America and in fact spent some time at Harvard. He retired in 1954 and in 1962 passed away in the middle of the Algerian war of independence when a very bitter struggle was going on between France and Algeria. In this battle, Massignon took the side of Algeria very strongly and therefore encountered much difficulty *vis-à-vis* the authorities in France.

It is of some interest to mention the following episode which demonstrates Massignon's concern with the situation of that period, especially as it related to the Algerian Question. In fact, the last time that I met Massignon was a few months before his death at the beginning of 1962, when I was on my way from Tehran to Boston, where I was to be a visiting professor at Harvard. A night or two before, we had been at the house of Gaston Berger, the famous French author, with Henry Corbin. We were coming into the street when Corbin asked me, 'Do you have your passport with you?' I said, 'No.' He said, 'Because of the Algerian War, the police are searching everyone. If you have no passport you'll have to spend the night in the police station, then the following morning you can go to your hotel and fetch your passport.' So we retraced our tracks to the building and I made my way to a back alley and so finally got safely back to my hotel. Later, when I went to Massignon's house, upon departure he accompanied me down to the first floor and also asked, 'Do you have your passport with you? If not, you're going to have trouble with the police.' I said, 'Well, you're very perceptive as to how foreigners, especially ones looking like me, are treated at the moment; but fortunately I've already had the experience of what this involves.' He laughed and said, 'This is a very good thing, because we don't have any back alleys you can go through and you'd probably have to spend the night at the police station!'

Anyway, this is briefly the contour of Massignon's life, which it was necessary to describe at the outset before turning to his intellectual concerns. It is essential to remember, first of all, that it was as a result of his encounter with the mysterious figure of the 'Stranger', that is, Ḥallāj, in the spiritual world – and not only through scholarship – that Massignon became a leading Catholic intellectual. It was this 'converted' Massignon who became deeply involved with the whole life of the country and especially with the intellectual life of the Catholics of France for a period of over fifty years, from 1910 to

1960, almost to the moment of his death. He knew such philosophers as Jacques Maritain and Etienne Gilson intimately. The latter was in fact his colleague at the Collège de France. He was very close to the circle of such French literary figures as Paul Claudel and François Mauriac, and he exchanged letters with many of these and other major intellectual and literary figures. He was also very close to certain Catholic spiritual figures, who themselves were interested in rapprochement with Islam. In this domain the most important person was Charles de Foucauld.

For those who are not familiar with him, one should mention that Charles de Foucauld was a devout Catholic contemplative who founded a new religious order in North Africa, but who lived actually in the Muslim world all his life and, rather than try to convert the Muslims, he tried to become a kind of witness to Christianity to them and to befriend them as people following another version of his religion and the message that comes from God. He had an important role to play, not only for Catholicism, but for the whole of the Christian tradition in its relationship with Islam and the initiation of the first stages of serious dialogue between these two great religious traditions. Because he lived a life of simplicity and saintly piety, he was very close to the simple bedouin of the deserts of North Africa. Massignon's relationship with Foucauld is connected with one of the important functions that he, Massignon, had within Catholic circles in France and North Africa in the first decades of this century. When Foucauld died, a beautiful poem was composed which needs to be quoted because it recapitulates Massignon's sentiments towards Charles de Foucauld in relation with his own inner quest:

> Une consolation je l'ai cherchée, à ma douleur;
> et ma douleur a fini par devenir pour moi cette consolation;
> Une preuve, je l'ai cherchée pour mon origine, – et mon origine a fini par devenir pour moi cette preuve.
> A droite et à gauche, j'ai cherché a voir ou était le visage de l'Ami;
> Mais j'étais au dehors, et Lui, c'est tout au fond de mon âme qu'Il est.

This poem in itself reveals the profundity of the experience of

Massignon, not only as a scholar but as a person of spiritual attainment.

Parallel with this concern with the Catholic/Christian world of France, Massignon began to enjoy a very wide circle of acquaintances in the Islamic world, both in Arab and non-Arab countries. In Iran, he had very close rapport with such scholars and statesmen as Mohammad Ali Foroughi, who later became Prime Minister, Badi' al-Zamān Forouzanfar, the great scholar of Jalāl al-Dīn Rūmī, and Reza-Zadeh Shafaq, a major scholar of history from Tabriz. In the Arab world, he befriended especially the scholars of al-Azhar University in Egypt, as well as those of Morocco and Algeria that, along with Iraq, which he knew particularly well because of his love for Ḥallāj, were the main centers of his contact. He also had a number of Arab students who later became famous scholars.

I recall clearly sensing Massignon's presence at the tomb of Ḥallāj the last time I was able to visit it in 1978. The tomb had been among a cluster of beautiful tombs of Sufis of the third and fourth Islamic centuries, situated in an old cemetery that was becoming part of an ugly urban development. Because of the pressure that Massignon had put upon Iraqi authorities, although that whole area had been taken over for construction of a new quarter, one small room was built on to the tomb of Ḥallāj to protect it. Although a pathetic sight, the fact that the tomb is still there is nevertheless proof of the efforts that Massignon made and of his success in turning the attention of authorities in Baghdad towards its preservation. Without his efforts, the very site of the tomb might have been lost or covered by an unmarked structure, as has happened in so many places in the Islamic world during past decades.

As for Massignon's intellectual activity, at the center of it resides, of course, Ḥallāj through whom he saw the whole of the Islamic tradition. Perhaps the greatest service that Massignon rendered to the cause of Islamic studies was that, through the study of Ḥallāj, he demonstrated that Sufism has its roots in the Quran. Far from being a heretic, Ḥallāj was the epitome of orthodoxy, for only the saint is orthodox in the most universal sense of the term. He stands at the Center and, from the traditional perspective, everyone else is located at a point which is peripheral *vis-à-vis* that Center. Massignon realized that meditation upon verses of the Quran, emulation of the Prophet and the grace issuing from the Quranic revelation constituted the origin and substance of Sufism. And at the moment when everyone in orientalist circles considered Sufism to be a kind of alien tree planted in the soil of the Islamic world by extraneous forces – and there were those series of external influences which like fashions in ladies' dress, rotated every few years, from Indian to Christian to Neoplatonic and so forth – only Massignon, with great courage, came forward and defended the Islamic origin of Sufism. Fortunately, after half a century this truth has finally become accepted in scholarly circles in the West. Today there are not too many serious scholars, despite R.C. Zaehner and a few who have continued to write against this view, who would not defend the thesis of the Islamic origin of Sufism first presented in academic circles by Massignon and, later on, by Margoliouth and several other well-known Islamicists of the early decades of this century.

Through the figure of Ḥallāj, and by virtue of his inner 'guidance', Massignon drew the attention of the Western audience for the first time to numerous Sufis, such as Ibn 'Aṭā'allāh and 'Alī Shūshtarī; also Ibn Sab'īn, the great Sufi/philosopher of Spain, who journeyed to Maccah and there committed suicide, severing a vein before the House of God in order to die in ecstasy – quite a remarkable act considering the fact that in Islam suicide is forbidden by Islamic Law! The establishment in the West of the study of Sufism – both of its history as well as its spiritual teaching and language – as a major discipline within Islamic studies goes back to Massignon. All later histories of Sufism, of which in fact there are a few, such as *La mystique musulmane* of Gardet and Anawati, or Nwyia's books on the Shādhiliyyah order though not as yet definitive, follow the path opened by Massignon and are extensions of his research. To this day, most of the substantial work on the history of Sufism rests to his credit despite all the works produced by those who have followed his lead during the past half century.

Massignon was also much interested in what he called 'technical vocabulary', *la lexique technique*, which is so important for present-day scholarship in Islamic studies because there are so many scholars, especially in America, who are considered as experts on things Islamic, but who cannot read technical texts in Arabic or Persian. Massignon insisted that to be able to do serious scholarship one has to understand the language in depth, and more particularly it is the technical language of Sufism which provides the key for the understanding of the teachings of Sufism. If one studies Sufism, or in fact any science traditionally, one must spend many years with a master studying texts pertaining to the discipline in question. At the end, one becomes what we call in Persian *ahl-i iṣṭilāḥ*, that is, a person who knows the technical vocabulary. This is the end of the road of formal education, not its beginning. By mastering the language in depth one comes to know the subject itself. It is like it was in India in the old days, when one spent sixteen years studying Sanskrit, but after that did not study anything any more because having learned that language one had also learned the traditional sciences which are written in it. Massignon was really rendering an exceptional service when he opened the eyes of Western scholars to the significance of the actual technical vocabulary of Arabic texts. Otherwise those scholars would have remained satisfied with floating in the air, talking about great ideas without being able to relate them to a text, let alone being able to take an actual text and expand upon its various philosophical, mystical or theological interpretations.

Massignon was very much interested in bibliographies, and he prepared three important ones, all of which would, from the point of view of Islamic studies, appear to us to concern far-fetched subjects: the first being on the Nuṣayris, who did not rule at that time over Syria and so did not attract much attention; the second on the Qarāmiṭah, who created a violent and revolutionary movement in Southern Arabia and the Persian Gulf area and whom few scholars considered to be of importance when Massignon wrote about them; and thirdly, perhaps his most important bibliography, which concerned Hermetic writings in Islam, later published by Festugière in his four-volume *La Révélation d'Hermès Trismégiste*. This bibliography is an important work of research, which introduced Western scholarship to the significance of Islamic writings, both Arabic and Persian, on Hermeticism.

Massignon was very much concerned with the genius of the Arabic language. He was not as great a scholar in Persian as he was in Arabic, although he was very much interested in things Persian. But what really corresponded to his own special destiny, the inner structure of his soul, was the understanding of the spiritual contribution of the Semitic people, both Jew and Arab, through Judaism and Islam, and also Christianity, which is essentially a Semitic form of spirituality, as distinct from the Graeco-Hellenistic and Roman, as well as from other major religions of the world. What Massignon wrote on the genius of the Arabic language is, I think, among his most important contributions to scholarship.

Massignon was also much interested in Shi'ism, especially in Arabic Shi'ism. Not that he did not write on Persian Shi'ism, but he made major contributions to the study of Arabic Shi'ism. In the world of Shi'ism, two figures always attracted his attention. One was Fāṭimah, the daughter of the Prophet. No-one in the West has written in the same sensitive manner about her as has Massignon. In fact, this domain represents one of the incredible lacunae in the efforts of Western scholars, for there is not a single fully-fledged biography on her in any Western language. So many minor figures have a number of books and articles devoted to them, but the person who plays such an important role in Islamic spirituality as it concerns women has never had a full study devoted to her by western Islamicists. If one wants to study Fāṭimah now in a European language, where does one go? One has to refer back to the articles of Massignon. These studies also have a particular significance for comparative religious studies for Massignon studied the relationship between Fāṭimah and the Virgin Mary and pointed to the fact that they really represent the same archetype, the same spiritual reality, on different levels, and that there is a kind of homologous relation between them, especially in those parts of the Islamic world, like Syria, where Christianity and Islam live side by side. Many Arab women in Syria, for example, pray to God through both Fāṭimah and the Virgin when one of their children is ill. In their minds, the sanctity of Mary and Fāṭimah are related and even identified.

The second figure in whom Massignon was especially interested was Salmān-i Fārsī, or Salmān-i Pāk, whose tomb near Ctesiphon he visited and whose significance for the Islamization of Persia and its culture he brought out in an unparalleled fashion. As far as Persia is concerned, perhaps the most important single work of Massignon is in fact that profound article entitled 'Salmān Pāk et les prémices spirituelles de l'Islam iranien'. Here he unveils the symbolic and historic significance of Salmān, whose life marks the beginning of the attachment of the Iranian world to the new revelation. By adopting Salmān as a member of his family (*ahl al-bayt*), the Prophet of Islam in a sense adopted the Iranian people as an essential component of his 'people', or *ummah*.

Outside of these intellectual concerns, Massignon's main preoccupation in the world around him was on two levels. One concerned religious dialogue to which many of his biographers have alluded. Massignon was without doubt the first of the major Catholic scholars and thinkers who opened up dialogue with the Islamic world. Today it is too easy to be ecumenical, as this term is being currently understood in so many religious circles. When one does not have to believe in anything firmly, it is easy to open the doors to dialogue with other religions. I will never forget the lesson that a great traditional teacher of mine in Persia once taught me. He said, 'It is wonderful to have an open mind; it is like opening up the windows of a room. It is good to have the windows of a room open but only provided, of course, the room has walls. If you take a couple of windows into the middle of the desert, it does not matter whether you keep them open or closed, since there are no walls!' Today everyone talks of ecumenism and openness in religious dialogue, but in most cases this exercise does little to produce better understanding among religions because one is asked to sacrifice or dilute the principles and doctrines of each religion in order to carry on dialogue. There is, however, little about which one can have a dialogue when there are no principles to be defended.

Massignon began his dialogue with Islam at a time when the Catholic Church was most serious in defending its traditional principles and teachings. The atmosphere in which he then had to speak was therefore very different from that of today. He had to display exceptional courage and fortitude. But he persevered and, to achieve his goal of promoting better mutual understanding between Christianity and Islam, he propagated the cause of Charles de Foucauld, visited many Muslim centers and wrote incessantly about Islamic-Christian relations. In fact, most of his Catholic followers, like Moubarak, Bassetti-Sani and others who have written works on him in French, Italian and other languages, have also written on Muslim-Christian dialogue. Massignon is thus a sort of guiding light for a whole later generation of Catholics interested in Christian-Muslim relations. When, some years ago, I led a delegation of Persian Muslim scholars to the Vatican to meet the late Cardinal Pignedoli and discuss problems of mutual concern for Islam and Christianity with a group of Catholic scholars, the name and thought of Massignon often came up as the basis or setting for the debates that were to follow.

Massignon's second level of concern involved contemporary social and political issues endowed with a religious dimension. He was deeply involved in the actual everyday world about him and was not at all a person who lived in an ivory tower. This saintly and aristocratic man was not only an outstanding scholar but played a part in the world of action and especially engaged in Islamic causes, even with such events as the coronation of the Arab king of Syria, which he attended as a representative of France. He met Lawrence of Arabia, and was deeply concerned with the partition of the Arab world and later with the cause of the Palestinians after their displacement from their homeland. He was keenly interested in the future of France's North African colonies, especially Morocco and Algeria. His concern with the social aspect of human life and the questions of war and peace are also to be seen in his espousal of the cause of Mahatma Gandhi with whom he corresponded.

I cannot but in all frankness and honesty seize every opportunity possible to bring out this aspect of Massignon's activities because one finds today in the West a kind of occasional interest in the Islamic world and the question of human rights in that world which resembles a kind of malarial fever: it comes once in a while and then, after a chill, goes away completely and only returns at a much later date. Meanwhile nations are turned upside down thanks to a large extent to this hypocritical and selective interest in human rights. The study of Massignon's concern with the Islamic world reveals, by contrast, the incredible hypocrisy displayed by so many other scholars in the field of Islamic studies today. Massignon did not function in such a way. He did not bow with the wind. Whether General de Gaulle was in power in France, or, before him, the socialist government, or the government after the armistice, Massignon's concern for the Islamic world and its problems was a steady and constant one. He had a passion for the lands of Islam which was based, not upon opportunism or the desire to be invited to the next major conference or to get a scholarship to go to a country regardless of its form of government, but rather upon certain principles.

I think that the disservice rendered in the last few years by so many Western scholars of Islamic studies to the Islamic world, and to the lives of nearly a billion people, indeed to the whole future relationship of the West with the Islamic world, and therefore to the West itself, is so immense and the fog of purposeful distortion in the name of short-range interests so thick, that the career of Massignon and the way he went about dealing with the Islamic world stand as a great lesson to everyone. It is interesting to note that those who have held the memory of Massignon dearest have been those who have been least culpable of this sin of hypocrisy. This assertion is one which I would very gladly defend without mentioning names, but if one reads the list of scholars who one day shout about their love of humanity and the next day do not care about what is happening to the very people they were shouting about only the day before, who then go back to their daily routines as if they had never concerned themselves with human rights or been touched by love for humanity, one will see that the students of Massignon are not usually among them. That is a notable and positive moral feature of the influence that he imparted, either through his writings or through his personality upon his students.

Now, who were the students whom Massignon influenced in this way? In France, the whole later generation of Islamicists, such as Regis Blachère, Roger Arnaldez and similar important figures were either directly the students of Massignon or were his students indirectly; that is, they were deeply influenced by him. In this latter category, one can mention a scholar of the stature of Louis Gardet. But among them there is one person whom I must mention, whom I consider to be without doubt the greatest French student of Louis Massignon and his scholarly complement, namely Henry Corbin, to whom I shall turn in the next chapter. Corbin did for Persia what Massignon accomplished essentially for the Arab world; and the influence of Massignon on Corbin was immense. Corbin was one of my closest scholarly friends in France. In fact, the first time that I lectured at the Sorbonne, I found that it was in the very chair in which for twenty years Massignon had taught at the Ecole des Hautes Etudes. Corbin was then the chairman of the session, and we had a memorable afternoon during which I spoke of later Islamic philosophy.

As far as Massignon's influence upon Corbin's own formation is concerned, I must recount this story, which is quite interesting yet does not seem to have been recorded anywhere else. I once asked Corbin, 'How did you become interested in Suhrawardī?', having in mind the fact that no-one has rendered greater service to the knowledge of Suhrawardī and later Islamic philosophy in the West than Corbin. He said, 'For several years I was studying Martin

Heidegger and the German *Existenz-philosophie* and had gone several times to Freiburg to meet Heidegger but his philosophy did not quite satisfy me. I knew that I was looking for something else. One day when I was a young student sitting in the front row of a class at the Sorbonne, Massignon came in with an old book, the cover of which was very tarnished (old Persian lithograph editions were like that), and he said, "Take this book and read it. That is what you are looking for." And that was the lithograph edition of the *Ḥikmat al-ishrāq*, published in Tehran in the late Qajar period, the old edition.' Corbin added, 'I took that book home and read it. That event changed my whole life. Henceforth I put Heidegger aside on the shelf and became interested in serious philosophy.' In fact, he devoted the rest of his life to this 'serious philosophy'. This fact itself – I mean the possibility of training and influencing a man like Corbin, who did an immense amount for Islamic studies – speaks of the great impact that Massignon had on the French intellectual world.

But this impact was not of course limited to French students. He also had many students in the Arab world, some of whom are still alive. In fact, some of the best-known intellectual figures in the Arab world were either directly his students or were influenced by him. I need mention only two names: 'Abd al-Raḥmān Badawī, perhaps the most famous Egyptian scholar of Islamic philosophy, and the late 'Abd al-Ḥalīm Maḥmūd, the Grand Shaykh of al-Azhar University, who died several years ago. It might appear strange that the person who occupied the most important religious position in the Sunni world spoke excellent French, and, in fact, had been a student of Massignon. There were many other notable students of Massignon. I will not take up time here by naming them all but only mention that in the United States several of the most competent of the scholars of Islamic studies, such as George Makdisi, Herbert Mason and James Kritzeck, were directly his students.

Despite these facts and despite the grandeur of the figure of Massignon, he did not, obviously, go without criticism. He was, in fact very severely criticized in many circles, and it would require another chapter to analyze all the criticisms that have been made of him. But there are three or four points which must be mentioned. There are those who criticize Massignon for his overemphasis of the question of suffering in Islam. Now this is a very complex question.

There is no doubt that the idea of redemption through suffering in Christ does not exist in the same way in Islam as it does in Christianity. But it is also true that Muslims suffer, as all human beings do simply by virtue of being born into this world. One cannot live in this world without suffering for this world is not paradise. Therefore suffering, like every other human experience, has a spiritual significance. To belittle the element of suffering as if it did not exist is to misunderstand a whole facet of Islam, including of course Twelve-Imam Shiʿism.

We live in a very strange world: on the one hand, one reads criticism of Massignon's over-emphasis of the importance of suffering in Islam; on the other hand, one encounters articles where people who are supposed to be professors of Iranian and Islamic studies claim that all Persians want to suffer and be martyred because Shiʿism is based on this idea. There seems to be little moderation in going from the extreme of denying any significance to the meaning of suffering in Islam to going to the opposite extreme and making it the central concern of Islam, at least in its Shiʿite form. In defense of the position of Massignon, one can only point out that anyone who has had actual contact with Islamic piety, not only in the Shiʿite world but also in the Sunni world, realizes that although there is in Islam no central image of the cross on which Christ suffers and bleeds, the idea does exist of the presence of suffering in human life and the importance of the spiritual transformation that suffering brings about. And that is what, really, Massignon wanted to bring out.

Another criticism made of Massignon by many scholars, including even his student Corbin, who debated this issue with Massignon a great deal, is his lack of interest in later Sufism. It has often been said that Massignon was interested only in early Sufism, and that he did not pay attention to the significance of such figures as Ibn ʿArabī, ʿAbd al-Karīm al-Jīlī, Maḥmūd Shabistarī and other later Sufis of the school of *waḥdat al-wujūd* or the 'transcendent unity of Being'. As a person who in fact follows that school and is very sympathetic to this interpretation of Sufism, I believe that Massignon had every right not to be interested in this school. Sufism does not have only one dimension or one interpretation. There are many great Sufis who have not accepted this interpretation, and who have not shown interest in the question of *waḥdat al-wujūd*, or at least have not spoken about it, choosing rather another language for the exposition of the teachings of Sufism. This is to be seen to some degree even in Jalāl al-Dīn Rūmī, who complements Ibn 'Arabī in many ways and who lived nearly at the same time. But in fact Rūmī's formulation of this doctrine is very different from that of Ibn 'Arabī. Massignon should therefore not be criticized on the ground that his sympathies lay with earlier interpretations of Sufism and that he did not devote much attention to the Ibn 'Arabian school. Moreover, later in life, in his second edition of *La Passion d'al-Ḥallāj* which Massignon brought out a few years before his death, he displays a shift in his position and shows greater sympathy for the school of Ibn 'Arabī. That he loved Ḥallāj more than, let us say, Qunyawī or Jīlī cannot be criticized as a weakness or shortcoming on his part even from the point of view of a person like myself, who has spent much of his life studying Ibn 'Arabī and his school and who was one of the first persons to write about him in the English language and to defend him against his orientalist critics.

The third criticism levelled against Massignon which I wish to consider here is somewhat more problematic. It is the criticism made by those who could not accept the authenticity and seriousness of the concern for the spiritual and mystical aspects of Islam that Massignon shows. This type of criticism came first of all from the ranks of official orientalists in Europe and America who thought that they should study Islamic philosophy and history but strongly opposed Massignon's concern for Islam and Sufism as living spirituality. Massignon received a great deal of scathing criticism from those who did not want to accept this kind of 'existential concern' with a tradition under study, especially if this tradition happened to be Islam. Massignon was a kind of pioneer in making Islamic studies serious from a religious and spiritual point of view, not merely as philology and history. Not that everyone accepted his view or that many people do so now. Nevertheless, he was a pioneer in this type of Islamic study which combines religious and spiritual concerns, a type of study which has many more followers now than when Massignon took up his study of Islam at the beginning of this century.

Secondly, one group of Massignon's critics included many possessing a theological education and coming from a certain type of Protestant background which was opposed to the mystical dimension that he emphasized so much, scholars like W.C. Smith and others who have been themselves deeply engaged in the theological implications of Islam but who nevertheless have not been particularly interested in the mystical aspect of things. This kind of criticism still goes on in an invisible manner today, often indulged in by respected historians of Islam who believe that Massignon exaggerated the spiritual and mystical aspects in his interpretation of certain aspects of Islamic history and thought. Even the great historian of Islam, Sir Hamilton Gibb, who was a very close friend of Massignon, criticized Massignon from time to time for jumping to certain conclusions because of what Gibb considered to be Massignon's excessive emphasis upon the mystical elements in Islam. Needless to say, certain of Massignon's conclusions are inevitably open to criticism, for he was not omniscient; but his shortcomings as a historian of Islamic thought cannot be blamed upon his love and understanding of Islamic mysticism. On the contrary, it is this understanding of and sympathy for the inner dimension of Islam which enabled him to comprehend certain basic aspects of Islamic thought and history as well as their inner dynamics which had been veiled from other scholars in the field before him and remained so even afterwards.

Massignon had a method of studying texts to which Corbin alluded in a kind of facetious way as 'the helicopter method of textual scholarship'. What he meant by that characterization was that Massignon would 'descend' from above upon a text, make a sort of reconnaissance study of it and then take off again and go somewhere else. He did not go through most of the manuscript material with which he dealt in a step by step manner. There is no doubt an element of truth about this observation by Corbin and others. Massignon had a glimpse of many manuscripts, which he discovered in Istanbul or some other city, and wrote about them without fully knowing the whole text. As a result, there were certain misinterpretations on his part. For example, in his classification of the works of Suhrawardī, he made mistakes; nevertheless, he was the first to classify these writings and that fact in itself is remarkable. Both Corbin and I have given classifications of the writings of the great Master of the school of *ishrāq* which are based on a long period of study of Suhrawardī's works; they are different from that of Massignon, yet we have been indebted to him.

This sort of 'helicopter method' of textual study carried out by Massignon, although open to criticism, nevertheless made many texts known which would otherwise not have been known. What is astounding is not the errors committed in this process but the number of works discovered by Massignon during relatively short periods of stay in Istanbul and other cities where major collections of Arabic and Persian manuscripts are to be found. It is certainly amazing that Massignon was able to discover, during a short period of time, the treatise of Ibn al-Nafīs, which changed the history of medicine, and many of the treatises of al-Kindī, a discovery which has altered our conception of the early history of Islamic philosophy, not to speak of the significance of al-Kindī himself.

So much for the criticisms, which I wanted to answer before proceeding to evaluate the significance of Massignon now that a century has passed since his birth and twenty-one years since his death. How should we now characterize him? I suppose each scholar would do so in a different way, but if I were asked to summarize the salient features of Massignon, I would say that, first of all, he had a profound and universal appreciation of things spiritual. He really was a spiritual being. In the modern intellectual and scholarly realms, that is certainly a very rare quality. The modern world is in fact characterized by its inability to combine intelligence with piety. People are so often intelligent but not very pious or else pious but not very intelligent. But to combine the two, that is, deep piety with penetrating intelligence, is a rare quality in our time but one which Massignon possessed to an eminent degree. He was not only able to penetrate the spiritual significance of the Christian and Islamic worlds, which were his own, but also distant worlds, such as Shintoism, which he experienced on the island of Ise and about which he wrote the remarkable passage known to the students of his writings.

In addition to this quality, Massignon was a person who possessed great nobility of soul. He was a truly noble person, at once a saintly man and a genuine aristocrat in the traditional sense of the word. He was very shy to the extent that it was difficult to photograph him. I remember in 1957 when I journeyed from America to Morocco for the first time to take part in a month-long seminar with Massignon in the Atlas Mountains, I did everything possible to try to photograph him, but he would not allow it. I finally had to hide behind a wall and then managed to take some remarkable photos of him, but they have now unfortunately been lost. This quality of shyness came from a kind of spiritual concentration and inwardness. He did not want to over-expose himself and, when he did, the exposure of his face was always intimate and directly personal.

As already mentioned, Massignon had a genuine concern for the rights of Muslims and, in fact, of all human beings, including of course the people of Europe itself. He also had a special role to play in the creation of Islamic-Christian dialogue. All these qualities make him, I think, both as a scholar and as a human being, an example fully worthy of emulation by those in the modern world who pursue Islamic studies in more than just the academic sense and who also aspire to act as bridges connecting the West with the Islamic world.

For Massignon, everything that he did was done with great passion, in the positive sense of the term, and with great love. He was in fact totally involved in everything that he did. Once when he gave a lecture at Harvard University, a graduate student bent on quantifying everything asked, 'How many Sufis are there in the Islamic world?' Massignon smiled and replied, 'How many lovers are there in Cambridge? Sufism is a matter of love. You tell me how many lovers there are in Cambridge and I shall tell you how many Sufis there are in the Islamic world.' An excellent answer to such a question: an answer which could only come from an exceptional scholar.

Let me conclude by recounting an unforgettable moment which has always remained in my memory. It was actually late one morning in 1958 at the Dominican monastery of Tioumliline at the top of the Atlas Mountains which had been chosen as the site for an Islamic-Christian dialogue: a conference in which Gardet, Gibb, Northrop and many other distinguished scholars were taking part. Massignon was the last speaker and he spoke about the permanence of Divine Love and everything that involves the spiritual. I could never forget the silhouette of this striking face with the small amount of white hair that he still had blowing gently in the breeze. He suddenly paused and quoted a poem in Persian, although that was not his major language. He recited it from memory and concluded his talk on that day in this abrupt manner. I also wish to conclude this brief discourse on Massignon with that poem, a poem which all those who have studied Persian literature know, the verses being those of Ḥāfiẓ, who says:

هرگز نمیرد آنکه دلش زنده شد به عشق   ثبت است در جریدهٔ عالم دوام ما

He whose heart is brought to life through love never dies.
Our perpetuity is recorded in the pages of the cosmic book.

That is how Massignon will be remembered as long as there are men and women who study Islam, Christianity and their intertwined destinies, and who are also concerned with matters of the spirit.

Chapter Sixteen

Henry Corbin: The Life and Works of the Occidental Exile in Quest of the Orient of Light

Rarely has the West produced a figure who is at once a philosopher, in the traditional and still honored sense of the term and a master both of the major Islamic languages and of the intellectual sources written in these languages. Such a happy conjunction took place in the being of Henry Corbin and made him the foremost Occidental exponent of the integral tradition of Islamic philosophy and the leading hermeneutic interpreter to the contemporary world of the Islamic tradition as it has blossomed in Persia. In order to achieve this task of interpreting the vast treasures of the Islamic and, more particularly, of the Iranian worlds in a way that was at once scholarly and yet spiritually, theologically and philosophically significant as well, there had to exist in Corbin from the earliest period of his intellectual life both a love for detailed scholarly research in manuscripts and printed works of great philological complexity and difficulty, and the ability to fly into the world of traditional philosophical and spiritual speculation and meditation: to have his feet firmly grounded in a traditional metaphysical work associated with a particular historical figure or school and his eyes gazing away to the horizons of a trans-historical reality. These two often apparently contradictory characteristics were to attract him from the beginning to both the disciplines of Oriental as well as Occidental philology and philosophy. Referring to his own experience as a philologist, a connoisseur of Islamic books and as a philosopher Corbin writes,

> On peut être un orientaliste, et l'on peut être en même temps un philosophe, de formation rigoureusement et techniquement philosophique. Ce sont même les deux disciplines qui se trouvent beaucoup trop rarement conjugées dans le même homme, si rarement même du moins concernant l'Islam, que tout un secteur de l'orientalisme est longtemps resté en friche, et que simultanément les philosophes sont restés dans l'ignorance de l'une de leurs plus belles provinces. Mais que l'on soit l'homme de toute autre specialité, il reste que la participation aux travaux que comporte la marche d'une grande bibliothèque, confine une expérience dans laquelle nous verrions volontiers un complement de formation indispensable à tout chercheur.[1]

The man in whom these two strains were to meet to produce so many important works was born in Paris on April 14, 1903. After early religious studies, he was as a very young man already drawn to the mystical and gnostic doctrines which he identified at that time with some of the leading Protestant figures of the Renaissance and the 17th century, such as Jacob Böhme, for whom he continued to profess a special love to the end of his life. The particular intellectual and spiritual bent of Corbin was to lead him to the Sorbonne rather than to the strictly religious education of a seminary. He thus embarked upon a long period of formal university education in such institutions as the Sorbonne (Licence des Lettres 1925-diplôme d'études supérieures de l'Ecole Pratique des Hautes Etudes – diplôme de la section des sciences religieuses 1928) and l'Ecole Nationale des Langues Orientales (diplôme 1929). The result was a mastery of not only the classical languages (Greek and Latin) but also of the two major intellectual languages of the Islamic world, namely Arabic and Persian. Corbin was also deeply drawn to the German philosophical scene, spent considerable time in Germany and was able to master philosophical as well as literary German perfectly.

Corbin entered the arena of intellectual life in France at a moment when several important currents dealing with traditional philosophy were becoming felt, some in academic circles and others elsewhere. There were first of all the magisterial works of René Guénon, followed soon in time by those of Frithjof Schuon, which exposed traditional metaphysics in all its amplitude and depth for the first time in the modern West and which criticized mercilessly the errors of what is called 'philosophy' in the West today. Then there was the revival of medieval European philosophy which, in the figure of Etienne Gilson, was in full sway in the 1920's and 1930's. Finally, certain aspects of Islamic esotericism were being presented in the West for the first time by a number of orientalists, especially Massignon. Moreover, outside France and mostly in Germany, the school of phenomenology and *Existenz Philosophie* was attracting certain thinkers to a re-examination of the meaning of the relation between the outward and the inward, and also to the hermeneutic interpretation of the sacred texts of religion as well as to that grand book of theophanies which is nature itself.

Corbin was sensitive to all these currents and personally became closely associated with the last three. He studied directly with Gilson, who taught him the method of interpreting traditional philosophy upon the basis of an established text, a method which Corbin was to apply to the major texts of Islamic philosophy as Gilson has done for Latin works of Christian Patristic and Scholastic philosophy.

As already mentioned, Corbin was also able to study directly with Massignon, who opened new vistas into the world of Sufism as well as Shi'ism for the young student. It was in fact Massignon who acted as a major instrument of Providence in charting the course of Corbin's destiny by turning his attention, through Suhrawardī, to that Orient which is not merely geographical but which symbolizes the world of illumination.

After finishing his formal studies, Corbin began to work at the Bibliothèque Nationale in the section for Oriental manuscripts and even spent a year in Berlin, from 1935 to 1936, in order to continue his research in the rich collections of Arabic and Persian manuscripts in that city. But Corbin's relation with the German scene was mostly with the philosophical circles connected with the names of Scheler, Husserl and especially Heidegger, whose writings he studied avidly. In fact, it was Corbin who, in 1939, translated a major work of Heidegger, *Qu'est-ce que la métaphysique?* for the first time into French and who in fact was instrumental in the rise of interest in Heidegger among such figures as Jean-Paul Sartre. But, as he was to tell me when we visited St. Odile on the Franco-German border on the occasion of the first Western colloquium on Shi'ism held at the University of Strasbourg in 1966, his discovery of Suhrawardī and the 'Orient of Light' made it no longer necessary for him to cross this historic pass in order to seek knowledge at the feet of the *Existenz* philosophers. As he was to show later in his masterly comparison of the ontology of Mullā Ṣadrā with that of Heidegger,[2] the discovery of an authentic metaphysics reveals how limited and truncated the discussions which occupy the main currents of Western philosophy really are.

In any case, in 1939, Corbin left the Occident for Istanbul to gain closer knowledge of the unpublished texts of Islamic philosophy, little aware of the fact that the Second World War was to force him to remain nearly six years in the unique libraries of the old Ottoman capital, far from the intellectual and academic circles of Paris. During this period, Corbin gained an unparalleled acquaintance with manuscripts on philosophy and Sufism in the almost inexhaustible libraries of that city. Moreover, he mastered the technique of editing and correcting Arabic and Persian manuscripts developed by Hellmut Ritter and used it in his edition of the metaphysical section of Suhrawardī's *Talwīḥāt*, *Muqāwamāt* and *Muṭāraḥāt*, which appeared in Istanbul in 1945 as the first volume of Suhrawardī's *Opera Metaphysica et Mystica* (vol. II edited by Corbin, Téhéran-Paris, 1952, and vol. III edited by S.H. Nasr, Téhéran-Paris, 1970).[3] This first major work of Corbin on Islamic philosophy was to establish him immediately in the West as a notable scholar and was to lead, in 1954, to his appointment as director of Islamic studies (directeur d'études islamiques – la Section des Sciences religieuses de l'Ecole Pratique des Hautes Etudes), to occupy the chair of his old mentor, Massignon.

The plenary discovery of Suhrawardī made possible by his long stay in Istanbul attracted Corbin to Iran where Suhrawardī was born and where his school is still alive. The 'Master of Illumination' almost literally took the hands of his Occidental interpreter and guided him to the land to whose ancient culture Corbin had been already attracted as a young man and whose rich intellectual life during the Islamic period he was to discover through his love for the 'Theosophy of the Orient of Light'. In 1945, Corbin made his first journey to Iran where he immediately discovered his spiritual home. In 1946, he was appointed by the department of cultural relations of the French government to organize the department of Iranian studies at the newly created Institut Franco-iranien in Tehran and to begin the series of publications entitled *Bibliothèque iranienne* (continued later by the Imperial Iranian Academy of Philosophy until 1979), which has presented many major texts of Islamic philosophy and Sufism to the contemporary Islamic world as well as the West, the enterprise carried out indefatigably by Corbin with the collaboration of many Iranian scholars, such as the late M. Mo'in, S.J. Āshtiyānī, M. Mokri, S.H. Nasr, and M. Sarraf, as well as non-Persian scholars such as J. Aubin, M. Molé and O. Yahya.

From 1954 onward, the journey of Corbin to Iran became a regular affair until his death in 1978. He spent the fall semester regularly in Tehran, the winter one in Paris and the summer either in France or at Ascona in Switzerland where he became one of the main figures in the annual Eranos gatherings. Upon retirement, he was able to preserve this rhythm of life by becoming an active scholar and teacher at the Imperial Iranian Academy of Philosophy where he taught in the fall.

During his annual pilgrimage to Iran, Corbin became gradually acquainted with many of the leading traditional authorities of the country: with such theosophers and gnostics as 'Allāmah Sayyid Muhammad Ḥusayn Ṭabāṭabā'ī and Sayyid Muḥammad Kāẓim 'Aṣṣār, and with some of their younger students, such as Murtaḍā Muṭahharī and Sayyid Jalāl al-Dīn Āshtiyānī; with Sufi masters such as Javād Nourbakhsh, the supreme master of the Ni'matallāhī order; with such eminent traditional scholars as the late Badī' al-Zamān Furouzanfar and Jalāl Homā'ī; and also with many younger scholars, some of whom, like Isa Sepahbodi, translated some of his works into Persian.

During this same period, his courses in Paris revolved completely around the spiritual and philosophical works of Persian Islamic masters such as Suhrawardī, Sayyid Ḥaydar Āmulī, Mīr Dāmād and Mullā Ṣadrā, as well as with those of the great Andalusian gnostic, Ibn 'Arabī. Students from many countries came to his courses, including Persians and Arabs, and he opened up a new dimension in Islamic studies by unveiling fresh horizons in Islamic philosophy, Sufism and Shi'ism.

Corbin also participated in numerous conferences in Western Europe and expounded teachings ranging from the study of Western esotericism to modern philosophy, from the doctrines of Zoroaster to those of the great Islamic sages. But the Eranos meetings at Ascona occupied a central position in Corbin's intellectual life. He was a continuous presence in these meetings for three decades and, along with a few close friends, such as M. Eliade and E. Benz, in a sense set the tone for these conferences. Much of Corbin's most important writings, which were discussed in Tehran and Paris with circles of friends and students, found their first expression in various volumes of the *Eranos-Jahrbuch* and only later appeared in more developed book form.[4]

Endowed with great physical stamina and mental energy, with a singular devotion to his subject and aided by a wife who was totally dedicated to him, Corbin was able for many years to continue a heavily-charged program of teaching, research and writing which took him annually from Paris to Tehran, back to Paris and from there to Ascona. Throughout his life from the time of his youth, he worked throughout the night and slept only with the appearance of the dawn. His teaching and research activities began at noon in a day which was often spent, like the long night, in deciphering difficult Arabic and Persian manuscripts and in interpreting the wisdom contained therein for the modern world. The result of his perseverance in this strenuous schedule over long years is the remarkable corpus of work which Corbin produced and which stands as one of the most impressive achievements of Western orientalism in the domains of Islamic philosophy and of traditional Islamic thought in general.

Corbin also taught in Tehran University, conducting advanced seminars with me upon various themes of Islamic philosophy and examining them in confrontation with different problems posed by the West and various forces of modernization. Over the years there also took place regular sessions with ‘Allāmah Ṭabāṭabā’ī and several leading Persian scholars in which some of the most profound dialogues between East and West were carried out, the task of making the commentary and translation usually being left in my hands. Two widely popular volumes in Persian have resulted from this exchange between Corbin and ‘Allāmah Ṭabāṭabā’ī, one of the foremost traditional authorities of Shi‘ism and master of both the esoteric and exoteric sciences, who died shortly after Corbin.

The works of Corbin are so numerous and concern so many diverse fields that it is not possible to analyze them in any detail here. They would require a separate study to do justice to all the themes contained in them.[5] But they can be described in brief by considering them under several main categories. There are first of all his essays dealing with esoteric currents in the Occident, with such figures as the *Fedeli d'amore*, Joachim of Flora, the Renaissance alchemists, Böhme, Swedenborg, Goethe and others to whom Corbin was devoted both intellectually and spiritually. Moreover, he often compared the ideas and doctrines connected with this intellectual current with Islamic and occasionally Mazdaean themes, so that there is a greater concern with the Western esoteric schools as well as the spiritual and intellectual malaise of the modern West in the writings of Corbin than the titles of his writings might suggest.

From his early years as a student, Corbin was interested in ancient Persia and its religious traditions; in Zoroaster, whose teachings even influenced the Greeks; in Mithraism and in Manichaeism, whose ‘gnostic’ cosmology and cosmogony he interpreted in a completely positive vein and not as seen by the early Christian theologians, who attacked it so bitterly because of its insistence on a dualism which is theologically unacceptable. Some of the earliest writings of Corbin were on ancient Persia and translations from Pahlavi, which he had mastered early in his student period. Later in life, he was to pursue his interests in this field through comparative studies, reflected in several of his discourses at Eranos; through his attraction to Suhrawardī, who saw both Plato and the ancient Persians as the source of true philosophy; by means of his appreciation of Gemisthos Plethon, who like Suhrawardī turned his gaze upon both Plato and Zoroaster; and by his attempt to trace the continuity of certain myths, symbols and doctrines of ancient Persia into the Islamic period. As far as this last theme is concerned, although many of Corbin's works return to it again and again, it is his *Terre céleste et corps de résurrection* which stands out as his most notable achievement in this domain.

The writings of Corbin on Shi'ism form another major category of his works, one which reflects his own inner life perhaps more than any other. Corbin was always attracted to Shi'ism, especially Shi'ite esotericism, not only mentally but also in his heart and soul. When speaking of Shi'ism, he usually spoke of 'us' and considered himself to be identified with Shi'ism in spirit as well as in mind. Whether it was in his pilgrimage to the mosque of the Twelfth Imam in Jāmkarān near Qum, or in talks with Shi'ite spiritual and religious authorities, Corbin displayed an attachment to Shi'ism which was not only that of the usual Western scholar engaged in the subject of his research. Rather, it was participation in a spiritual world in which it can be said that Corbin possessed faith.

It is of interest to note how Corbin even interpreted his own philosophical position from the Shi'ite perspective. Corbin called himself a phenomenologist. Yet when I once asked him how he would translate 'phenomenology' into Persian, he told me that 'phenomenology' means *kashf-al-maḥjūb*, the 'casting aside of the veil,' which is a fundamental method of expounding the truth in Sufism and is also the title of one of the greatest classics of Sufism, by Hujwīrī. For Corbin, the fundamental distinction made in Islamic esotericism in general and Shi'ism in particular between the outward (*al-ẓāhir*) and the inward (*al-bāṭin*), and the process of relating the outward to the inward (*ta'wīl*) which, with an eye to the original sense of the word, he translated as 'hermeneutics', is the *only* correct method of reaching the truth and the real meaning of phenomenology. He called himself by this epithet, ignoring the fact that there are other philosophers in the West who call themselves phenomenologists but who do not even accept the reality of the noumenal world, much less the possibility of relating the phenomenal to the noumenal, the outward to the inward. It was characteristic of Corbin's immersion in the intellectual world of Shi'ism that he interpreted phenomenology itself from the Shi'ite point of view and considered himself a phenomonologist in the sense of one who 'unveils' the hidden and esoteric truth, who participates in the process of *kashf al-maḥjūb*.

The contributions of Corbin to Shi'ite studies have been numerous and profound and have left an indelible mark upon Islamic studies in the West, precisely because they have revealed so much that was completely neglected before him. They are particularly precious now that strong political interests have, in one way or another, colored most of the more recent studies in Shi'ism. Corbin has shown how important the inner aspects of both Ismā'īlī and Twelve-Imam Shi'ism are as integral parts of Islamic esotericism, and their philosophies and theologies as essential aspects of the intellectual life of the Islamic peoples.

As far as Ismā'īlism is concerned, Corbin has made so many contributions to it that he has completely changed the views that scholars had held before him about intellectual history. His edition of the works of Nāṣir-i Khusraw, Abū Ya'qūb al-Sijistānī and other Ismā'īlī theosophers and philosophers, his analysis of the teachings of the Fāṭimid as well as post-Fāṭimid schools of Ismā'īlī thought, his discovery and publication of later Ismā'īlī works belonging to the post-Alamut period in Persia, or the very different school in the Yemen, all represent pioneering efforts in the field of Ismā'īlī studies. Besides elucidating the teachings of the Ismā'īlīs and showing their relation with various other schools of thought, Corbin has been able to establish Ismā'īlī philosophy as one of the important schools of Islamic thought. Thanks most of all to his research, it is no longer possible to speak of early Islamic philosophy and neglect completely such figures as Abū Ḥātim al-Rāzī, Ḥamīd al-Dīn al-Kirmānī and Nāṣir-i Khusraw as if they had not even existed.

As far as Twelve-Imam Shi'ism is concerned, the contributions of Corbin have been of even more far-reaching consequence since in the field of Ismā'īlism there had been at least some notable research carried out in European languages in earlier days, whereas before Corbin's writings appeared, the spiritual and intellectual aspects of Twelve-Imam Shi'ism were practically a closed book for those solely acquainted with Western courses. Corbin devoted numerous studies over the years to the Shi'ite Imams and the question of what he calls '*imāmologie*,' to Shi'ite *Ḥadīth*, especially the *Uṣūl al-kāfī* of Kulaynī, to specifically Shi'ite gnosis (*'irfān-i shī'ī*) found in the works of such authors as Sayyid Ḥaydar Amulī and Qāḍī Sa'īd Qummī and to later schools which have grown out of Twelve-Imam

Shi'ism such as Shaykhism. Moreover, certain themes of 'Shi'ite gnosis' have affected many of his other studies, even those concerning Christology and certain esoteric movements in the medieval and Renaissance periods in the West.

Corbin's devotion to Sufism has paralleled his interest in Shi'ism, the two comprising Islamic esotericism, which from the beginning was the main dimension of Islam that attracted Corbin to the study of this tradition. Unlike his teacher, Massignon, whose studies of Sufism concerned mostly early masters such as al-Ḥallāj, Corbin was especially interested in later manifestations of Sufism and the metaphysical and cosmological doctrines issuing from the school of Ibn 'Arabī and other later masters of Islamic gnosis. Besides numerous studies on various Sufi figures, some of whom like 'Alā' al-Dawlah Simnānī were introduced in a serious manner to the West for the first time by him, Corbin produced several volumes on Sufism revolving around two major figures, Ibn 'Arabī, the sage of Andalusia, and Rūzbahān Baqlī, the master of the *Fedeli d'amore* of Persia. The *Bibliothèque iranienne*, directed by him, contains the first critical editions of the *'Abhar al-'āshiqīn* and *Sharḥ al-shaṭḥiyyāt* of Rūzbahān, as well as two volumes of Sayyid Ḥaydar Amūlī, which are commentaries and extensions of the works and teachings of Ibn 'Arabī, these last having been edited with the aid of 'Uthmān Yaḥyā. In fact, Corbin's contribution to the study of the Andalusian visionary and seer is based not only on his own works, which in this field are crowned by his celebrated *L'Imagination créatrice dans le soufisme d'Ibn 'Arabī*, but also in interesting the Syrian scholar, 'Uthmān Yaḥyā, in Ibn 'Arabī's works. The two-volume work on the classification of the writings of Ibn 'Arabī by 'Uthmān Yaḥyā, as well as the new edition of the *Futūḥāt al-makkiyyah* currently being brought out by him in Cairo, owe a great deal to Corbin both for their scholarly and intellectual inspiration and for their material realization.

It is in the nature of Corbin's definition of philosophy that he considered all the activities mentioned so far as belonging to the domain of his 'philosophical' works, which meant that for him the term 'philosophy' implied traditional wisdom or *sophia*, rather than what passes for philosophy in modern European parlance. But even in the more strict sense of philosophy (*al-falsafah*), and also theosophy (*al-ḥikmat al-ilāhiyyah*) as used in the Islamic tradition (namely, a particular branch of traditional wisdom distinct from, let us say, gnosis (*'irfān*) or theology (*kalām*)) Corbin has made an enormous contribution and must in fact be considered the first European scholar and thinker who has written on Islamic philosophy with a knowledge of its total history rather than according to the usual truncated version which ends with Ibn Rushd, a version which the West had accepted as unquestionable truth until a few years ago.

Corbin's numerous studies of the more particularly philosophical dimension of the Islamic intellectual tradition during the past few centuries, a dimension which has survived mostly in Persia, has opened new horizons and revealed that Islamic philosophy, far from being a short-lived activity among Muslims from al-Kindī to Ibn Rushd and endowed with the sole historical function of handing down the sciences and philosophy of Antiquity to the Latin West, has had a continuous and independent existence to the present day. His *Histoire de la philosophie islamique* (vol. I), written in collaboration with S.H. Nasr and O. Yahya, prepared the ground for a complete exposition of Islamic philosophy based, not only upon the Peripatetic school and the first few centuries of Islamic history, but on all the different schools of traditional Islamic thought and covering the whole of Islamic history down to the present day. Although the other volumes of this history have never been completed as first planned, Corbin himself produced a long sequel in the *Encyclopédie de la Pléiade* which completes this integral history of Islamic philosophy.

Corbin's interest in Islamic philosophy begins with Ibn Sīnā. He has written little on the earlier philosophers such as al-Kindī and al-Fārābī. But by means of a thorough re-examination of Ibn Sīnā and the brilliant reconstruction of his 'Oriental philosophy' (*al-ḥikmat al-mashriqiyyah*), Corbin was able to recreate the image of an Ibn Sīnā who has been alive in Persia for over a thousand years, who was meditated upon by such figures as Suhrawardī and Naṣīr al-Dīn Ṭūsī, an Ibn Sīnā who is very different from the exclusively Peripatetic master of the Scholastic texts. Corbin's *Avicenne et le récit visionnaire* is a landmark in Avicennan studies in the Occident. It also prepared the ground for Corbin's exposition of later Islamic philosophy, which depends, not only upon the Ibn Sīnā who wrote the *Shifā'*, but also upon the Ibn Sīnā who was seeking the 'Orient' of knowledge and to whom Suhrawardī was to refer a century and a half later in his recital concerning the 'Occidental Exile' (*Qiṣṣat al-ghurbat al-gharbiyyah*).

However, without doubt the figure who most occupied the attention of Corbin and who may be considered Corbin's intellectual guide was Shaykh al-ishrāq Shihāb al-Dīn Suhrawardī. He, as has already been mentioned, took Corbin by the hand and guided him from the libraries of Istanbul to his own homeland in Persia. Corbin's attachment to the doctrines of Suhrawardī, especially to his belief in the importance of both ratiocination and spiritual vision as 'instruments' for attaining knowledge, was something deeply personal; he felt a devotion to Suhrawardī which somehow embraced all his spiritual and intellectual interests and activities. Corbin was essentially the hermeneutic interpreter of the angelic world, and he saw in the 'Theosophy of the Orient of Light' (*ḥikmat al-ishrāq*) of Suhrawardī a complete science of the angelic world expressed in terms of the symbolism of light. We recall how once when going over certain pages of Suhrawardī with Corbin, he told us in a rather categorical fashion that all this discussion concerning existence and quiddity was not really of central interest to him; what excited him most of all in Suhrawardī was his magisterial discussion of the longitudinal and latitudinal hierarchies of lights or angels.

In recent times, Corbin has, without doubt, done more than anyone else, outside – or even inside – Persia, to revive the teachings of Suhrawardī and to make available critical editions of his works. His two-volume edition of Suhrawardī's *Opera Metaphysica et Mystica*, including the metaphysics of the *Talwīḥāt*, *Muqāwamāt* and *Muṭāraḥāt*, several shorter Arabic treatises, and the all-important *Ḥikmat al-ishrāq* and his encouraging me in the edition of the Persian works of Suhrawardī as volume III of the *Opera* have made it possible to have access to more writings of the master of *ishrāq* in a critically-edited form than to those of any other major Islamic philosopher. Moreover, Corbin has written numerous monographs and articles on Suhrawardī, beginning with his still-valuable *Sohrawardī, fondateur de la doctrine illuminative* (*ishrāqī*) and culminating in his monumental treatment of the master in his *En Islam iranien*. He has also translated into elegant French the Persian treatises of Suhrawardī under the title of one of the most intriguing of the treatises, namely, *'Aql-i surkh*, (*L'Archange empourprée*) and has prepared a French translation of the *Ḥikmat al-ishrāq*, which is now being prepared by Stella Corbin for publication. His lifelong work on Suhrawardī, which includes also the editions of several of the still unpublished works, most important among them being the *al-Wāridāt wa'l-taqdīsāt*, have opened a new chapter in Islamic philosophy, which is not only important for scholarship in general but is of special concern in the revival of interest among the Persians in their own intellectual and spiritual tradition, a revival which revolves most of all around the figures of Suhrawardī and Ṣadr al-Dīn Shīrazī.

Corbin himself was led to the discovery of Mullā Ṣadrā through the works of Suhrawardī and made his journey to Persia in an attempt to discover the heritage of the master in the land of his birth. Through the commentators of Suhrawardī, Corbin was led to such lesser-known but important figures as Ibn Turkah Iṣfahanī, whose works and ideas he made known to the West and finally to the great revival of Islamic philosophy during the Safavid period. The study of the very rich intellectual life of this period led Corbin to the correct belief that a new school was born at this time, one which he named the School of Isfahan. During the last two decades of his life, the works of Corbin dealt increasingly with this school, with such figures as Mīr Dāmād, who was its founder, and especially with Ṣadr al-Dīn Shīrāzī. Corbin has done much to make Mullā Ṣadrā known to the West and his edition and French translation of the Safavid sage's *Kitāb al-mashā'ir* as *Le Livre des pénétrations métaphysiques* which, as already mentioned, contains an important introduction comparing the destiny of the study of being in both East and West, and which is without doubt one of his most important philosophical contributions.

The discovery of the intellectual richness of the Safavid period led Corbin to seek the aid of a Persian scholar to prepare an anthology of the works of this period and its heritage down to the present day. He was to find an incomparable collaborator in Sayyid Jalāl al-Dīn Āshtiyānī who, with unbounded energy, combed through numerous public and private libraries and made many new discoveries which were startling even to Persian specialists of the period. The series, *Anthologie des philosophes iraniens*, has already altered the history of Islamic philosophy in Persia and has also posed a major problem for those in the West who have thought until now that only in their own quarter has there been intellectual activity worthy of attention since the end of the European Middle

Ages. It is hardly possible to study the wealth of material contained in these volumes and still think that the Muslims stopped their intellectual activity with Ibn Rushd or with the Mongol invasion.

Besides philosophy, Corbin also showed much interest in the traditional Islamic sciences of a cosmological and even physical nature. He made a profound study of Jābirean alchemy and the doctrine of the balance, of cosmic cycles, of sacred geography, of the symbolism of geometric figures as reflected in the Holy Ka'bah, of the symbolism of colors and many other related themes. His contributions to the study of the Islamic sciences, and especially their symbolic meaning, should not be underestimated, although Corbin always viewed these sciences in the light of the general metaphysical and philosophical perspectives which were his central concern.

In many ways, Corbin's life's work is summarized by the monumental *En Islam iranien*, in which over forty years of research and meditation upon Shi'ism, Sufism, Islamic philosophy, the relation between Islamic esoteric tradition and estoericism in the West (as manifested in such forms as the legend of the Holy Grail), and many other concerns are brought together. Without doubt this work is one of the most outstanding achievements of Western scholarship concerning the Islamic and particularly Persian worlds, a study which has already exercised much influence and is bound to remain one of Corbin's most enduring achievements. Many of the themes discussed in his numerous earlier works have found their most mature orchestration in this four-volume magnum opus.

If one were to summarize the contributions of Corbin to the world of scholarship, philosophy and thought, one could say that he transformed scholarship in nearly every field of Islamic thought and in Persian studies in particular. Corbin made clear once and for all the significance of the non-Sufi mode of Islamic esotericism as contained in Twelve-Imam and Ismā'īlī Shi'ism; of the vast metaphysical and theosophical teachings of the school of Ibn 'Arabī; of the school of the illumination of Suhrawardī and its role in remolding the very concept of philosophy in Persia and other eastern lands of Islam; of the continuous and living nature of Islamic philosophy stretching over the centuries after Ibn Rushd to the present day – and many other subjects of fundamental importance. He also remolded the concept of the intellectual and spiritual history of

Persia, highlighting many salient features of pre-Islamic Persian culture, its fecundity and richness in the fields of metaphysics, cosmology, cosmogony, etc., and the continuity of the life of many of the myths and symbols of pre-Islamic Persia into the Islamic period itself. Without doubt there have been very few Western scholars who have left such an extensive influence upon so many fields of Islamic and Persian scholarship.

As far as philosophy is concerned, there is no doubt that the writings of Corbin have presented a 'new' and, at the same time, ancient – even in fact perennial – world of wisdom in the contemporary language of Western thought for those concerned with the profoundest questions facing man today, just as they have faced men of all ages. Corbin's concern with 'prophetology,' 'imamology,' 'gnoseology' and other themes which seem to be related to Islamic thought are actually as much connected with the deepest questions facing Western man today as they are with Islam. The same may be said of Corbin's defense of the 'cyclic' concept of time and his virulent attack against historicism, which he considered as one of the most deadly maladies from which Western thought suffers today. Likewise, the repeated study and treatment by him of the 'imaginal world' (*mundis imaginalis*) in the works of Mullā Ṣadrā and others were carried out with one eye on the necessity of resuscitating the knowledge of this long-forgotten 'world' in the West. His profound studies of the angelic world were achieved with the aim of bringing back the attention of Western philosophers, who since Leibnitz had banished the angels from the cosmos, to the vital importance of the angelic domain in any serious cosmology and anthropology. Finally, it must be added that Corbin's often repeated concern with spiritual hermeneutics (*ta'wīl*) was as much related to his intention to revive spirituality and 'interiority' in Western religious circles as to the understanding of the inner meaning of Islamic texts. Altogether Corbin's concern with the living nature of this traditional philosophy, and its application to the contemporary philosophical and spiritual predicament of Western man caused by the forgetting of perennial wisdom complements his profound study of Islamic philosophy as the last major crystallization of this wisdom in human history and the sole surviving repository of much of the wisdom of the ancient world. Corbin must be seen, not only as an Islamicist, but also as a Western philosopher drawn toward tradition. Through him, for the first time since the

Middle Ages the Islamic philosophical tradition penetrated into certain European philosophical circles concerned with charting a new path and surmounting the debilitating obstacles by which modern Western thought is now beset.

The influence of Corbin has been extensive in both the Occident and the Islamic world, and especially in Persia itself. In the West, Corbin trained numerous students in the field of Islamic thought and, as already mentioned, transformed many branches of Islamic studies. His writings have also affected the wider public interested in spiritual and intellectual matters. Figures with as widely different backgrounds as G. Berger and J. Daniélou were attracted to Corbin's writings, and some of the philosophers who have now gained eminence in France, such as G. Durand and A. Faivre, have also been influenced by him as have many of the new *philosophes*, such as Christian Jambet. Through the meetings at Eranos, moreover, many well-known intellectual figures who have been concerned with other fields, such as the biologist A. Portmann and the outstanding scholar of Jewish mysticism, G. Scholem, came face to face with some of the more profound aspects of the Islamic tradition. Corbin's poetic translations of Sufi and Islamic philosophical texts have also affected many of the younger French writers questing to rediscover the traditional cosmos and its resplendent symbolism.

As far as the Arab world is concerned, the influence of Corbin has been confined mostly to the training of a small but competent number of advanced students, who in fact hailed mostly from the French-speaking countries of North Africa and who are now mostly professors and teachers of Islamic philosophy. Some of these men, such as M. Arkoun, are now themselves well-known scholars of Islamic thought.

In Persia, the influence of Corbin has been much more extensive. As a result of his regular visits there over the years, he was able to create numerous personal associations and have contact with groups far beyond the circle of professional scholars and students. Besides establishing close rapport with professors and students in various universities, religious scholars in Qum, Tehran, Mashhad, etc. and Sufi masters in various cities, Corbin was able to draw the attention of a large number of Persians in other walks of life to their own traditions. For many Persians who have studied in the West and who are more at home in French than in their mother tongue, especially as far as intellectual matters are concerned, the writings of Corbin have become the chief means of rediscovering a Suhrawardī or a Mullā Ṣadrā. Corbin's influence and aid in the recovery of awareness of the spiritual and intellectual traditions of Persia by modern Persians themselves can be seen in figures as different as the late cinematographer F. Rahnema, the miniaturist A. Tajvidi and the designer M. Ebrahimian, not to speak of many scholars in the field of Islamic and Persian thought. Corbin was also an important channel through which some men of action in various positions of responsibility in Persia were drawn to the study of the writings of their own great sages and seers.

For forty years, Corbin worked with incredible energy and enthusiasm to interpret the 'Orient of Light' to an Occident which, during this same period, became geographically much more widespread and has now practically banished the 'Orient' from the seven climates altogether. His work in Paris and Tehran, whether it was teaching or writing, was able to preserve its intensity and reign over three decades. This occidental exile, who found his true home in the 'Orient of Light', continued to strive to present to his contemporaries a whole intellectual world which had been practically neglected before him. He accomplished a great deal, but the task he set himself was vast and therefore there is still much to be accomplished before traditional wisdom is presented to the contemporary world in all its fullness, in its depth and breadth. In this crucial task of reinterpreting the intellectual patrimony of various traditions to the contemporary world, Corbin was one of the most productive and active figures and one of the foremost expositors of certain aspects of traditional wisdom.

In 1978, Corbin died after a short illness in Paris. It seems as if one of the angels to whose study he had devoted his life snatched him away from this earthly plane just in time to prevent him from witnessing the eruptions which transformed both Iran and the interpretation of Shiʿism – in at least certain circles – in such a drastic manner.

Notes

1. 'Humanisme actif', in *Mélanges d'art et de littérature offerts à Julien Cairn*, Paris, 1968, p. 310.
2. In his *Le Livre des pénétrations métaphysiques*, Tehran-Paris, 1964.
3. All three were reprinted by the Imperial Iranian Academy of Philosophy in 1976–77.
4. Some of these have been published since his death thanks to the indefatigable efforts of his wife, Stella Corbin.
5. Such a study is in fact being prepared by D. Shayegan.

Chapter Seventeen

With Titus Burckhardt at the Tomb of Muḥyī al-Dīn ibn ʿArabī

While Massignon was a Catholic thinker who possessed sympathy for and a universal knowledge of Islam, especially Sufism, and Corbin a Catholic turned Protestant who likewise spent years in the mastery of the disciplines associated with Islamic studies and particularly Shiʿism, Burckhardt was a Swiss of Protestant background who left Western academic circles to embrace Islam both intellectually and 'existentially'. He was not a Western scholar of Islam in the usual sense but a person of exceptional intellectual and spiritual gifts who went to the Islamic world as a young man to master the Islamic disciplines from within at the feet of masters of both the exoteric and esoteric sciences. He was providentially chosen to express the truths of the Islamic tradition, and in fact tradition in its universal sense, to the modern world and in a language comprehensible to contemporary man. His writings in fact represent one of the major formulations and statements of traditional Islam in the modern world.

In the fall of 1966, the occasion of the 100th anniversary of the founding of the American University of Beirut provided the opportunity for me to meet Titus Burckhardt, not on the soil of Europe as had happened often before, but for the first time within the boundaries of the Arab world. Hearing the *adhān*, despite the din and noise of the modern and Westernized city of Beirut, caused him to remark that the presence of Islam was to be felt even in this corner of the Islamic world which had been earmarked as the beachhead for the spread of modernization and Westernization. It was possible for us to visit the few old mosques near by together and to read and contemplate before the azure expanses of the Mediterranean and in the clear light of the Middle Eastern sky, certain Maryamian litanies which had just been composed and to meditate over the role of the Virgin in the religious life of the whole Mediterranean world. Moreover, we were able to visit together the saintly Yashruṭī Sufi woman, Sayyidah Fāṭimah, who recounted to us how it was impossible for her to choose a title for her famous Arabic work on Sufism, *al-Riḥlah ila'l-Ḥaqq*, until she had seen Ibn 'Arabī in a dream and received the title from him. The daughter of the founder of the Yashruṭiyyah Order was in fact so impressed by Titus Burckhardt's spiritual presence and radiant character that she devoted a most beautiful page to this encounter and to him in her autobiography, *Masīratī ila'l-Ḥaqq*.

Burckhardt was, however, anxious to visit the more traditional Islamic sites of the Arab Near East which provided more of traditional Islamic life and art than it was possible to encounter in Beirut. Therefore, after some consultation, we decided to visit Damascus together. During the two-hour drive across the beautiful mountains and valleys, which at that time conveyed a wonderful sense of peace and tranquility, he commented upon many aspects of Islamic culture and tradition in general, upon such subjects as the ecological and geographical resemblance of the region to Andalusia and the Maghrib, which he knew so well, and the complementarity between the mountains and the deserts which surround so many Islamic cities, such as Damascus and Marrakesh. His comments brought joy and freshness to the experience of scenery which I had seen so often and brought about an interiorization of the experience of the countryside which could result only from the spiritual effect of the companionship of a sage.

Upon arriving in Damascus, we decided to spend the day visiting the tomb or 'place of residence' (*maqām*)[1] of the granddaughter of the Blessed Prophet, Sayyidah Zaynab, the tomb of Ibn 'Arabī and, of course, the Umayyad Mosque, in that order. For Titus Burckhardt mentioned that traditional courtesy or *adab* required that we pay our respects first to the daughter of 'Alī and the granddaughter of the founder of Islam. Usually 'Sit Zaynab', as Damascenes call it, is full of pilgrims, but strangely enough on that morning we were the only pilgrims present. The only other people there were a number of Persian craftsmen from Isfahan who were reconstructing the dome and placing tiles upon the walls of the edifice. After prayers and a long period of quiet meditation, we turned to the craftsmen, whose activity obviously attracted the author of the most outstanding works on Islamic art to appear in the contemporary world. Burckhardt commented upon the deep piety of the craftsmen and their humility before their work. We reminisced about Fez and discussed further plans we had made together for him to write a book on Isfahan in the collection of *Stätten des Geistes* ('Homesteads of the Spirit'), which he was then editing for Urs Graf Verlag. It was my intense wish to have a book like *Fes – Stadt des Islam* written on the beautiful city of Isfahan, which he also wanted to visit. What a tragedy that this work was never realized and the world could not benefit from seeing the delicate and almost ethereal edifices of the Safavid capital through the eyes of the master interpreter of Islamic art that Burckhardt was.

It was after this pilgrimage and brief encounter with Persian art in the person and art of the Persian craftsmen working at Sayyidah Zaynab, that Titus Burckhardt and I set out from the southern fields where her *maqām* is located for the slopes of the mountains north of Damascus where Ibn 'Arabī lies buried. We entered the sanctuary reverentially and, after offering prayers, sat down by the tomb of the great metaphysician and saint, which was surrounded by an atmosphere of contemplative tranquility and calm. The peace and serenity of this atmosphere were accentuated by the fact that, at that moment, Burckhardt and I again happened to be alone in that sacred space, which, like every veritable sacred space, is the echo of the Center and a reflection of Eternity upon the moving image of peripheral existence.

While meditating upon the verities or the *Ḥaqīqah* at the heart of Sufism, I occasionally glanced at the contemplative face of my companion, whose closed eyes seemed to gaze inwardly upon the heart and whose face reflected the light of the Intellect before which his mind and soul were transparent. I thought at that time about Burckhardt's significance in making Ibn 'Arabī known to the Western world. I recalled his *La Sagesse des prophètes* ('The Wisdom of the Prophets'), *Von Sufitum* written also in French as *Introduction aux doctrines ésotériques de l'Islam* ('An Introduction to Sufi Doctrine'), *Clé spirituel de l'astrologie musulmane* ('Mystical Astrology according to ibn 'Arabī') and *De l'homme universel* ('Universal Man') with its incomparable introduction, all of which I had read as a graduate student at Harvard. How *essential* were these writings in the sense of expounding the essence of the teachings of Ibn 'Arabī and his school in a metaphysical language of great power and clarity, formulated first by Guénon, perfected in an amazing way by Schuon and applied in an ingenious manner to the teachings of Shaykh al-Akbar by Burckhardt.

During the years, as I plunged further into studying the texts of Ibn 'Arabī and their numerous Arabic and Persian commentaries with traditional masters in Persia, as well as discussing them extensively with H. Corbin and T. Izutsu (whose study of Ibn 'Arabī was deeply appreciated by Burckhardt), I realized fully the significance of Burckhardt's achievement. He had succeeded in reaching the heart of Akbarian metaphysics and making it known in contemporary language without divorcing it from the *barakah* of Sufism or the rest of that tradition. His translations and commentaries, which are at once traditional and full of living wisdom and light, differ markedly from those pedantic and dry translations by some claiming to adhere to the traditionalist school. Some of these would reduce the whole of Sufism to Ibn 'Arabī alone, and Ibn 'Arabī himself to a cerebral presentation of theoretical metaphysics far removed from the living presence that emanates from his teachings and which can be seen both in the writings of Burckhardt and the traditional masters of his school, whom I had the privilege to meet in Persia.

Later contacts with the school of Ibn 'Arabī have brought back often the memory of those moments when I sat with Titus Burckhardt at the tomb of the great master in Damascus. To have beheld Burckhardt there, lost in the contemplation of that Truth which lies at the heart of all traditional metaphysics and of course of Sufism itself; to have witnessed his humility before the Divine Presence and transparency before the Truth which manifests Itself in a mysterious fashion in certain *loci* determined by sacred geography and usually identified with tombs or *maqāms* of great saints – to have done this was fully to realize the incredible chasm which separates theoretical understanding of wisdom or *al-ḥikmah* from its realization. In contrast to many who write of Ibn 'Arabī and claim strict traditional orthodoxy without, however, having realized the truth of Sufism, Burckhardt lived the truth of which he wrote. The exceptional light of intelligence which emanated from him pierced to the heart of the texts that he studied and illuminated their meaning in a manner which is possible only for a person in whom the truth has descended from the place of the mind to the center of the heart and become fully realized. At the tomb of Ibn 'Arabī, Burckhardt manifested the qualities of a saintly man possessing a penetrating intelligence of extraordinary lucidity, combined with virtue and a luminous soul transmuted by the presence of that Truth whose doctrinal aspects he studied with such depth and understanding.

We left the tomb of the saint feeling a special proximity to the quintessential metaphysics of Sufism which Ibn 'Arabī had been destined to formulate and which are intertwined with many of the less central teachings in a vast tapestry which remains unique in the history of Sufism. Titus Burckhardt departed for Jerusalem with the aim of visiting not only the site of the Nocturnal Ascent (*al-mi'rāj*) of the Blessed Prophet, of which Ibn 'Arabī had written so eloquently, but also the tomb of the patriarch of monotheism, Abraham, after whom Burckhardt himself was named. He asked me to accompany him on this leg of the journey but unfortunately other demands forced me to return to Tehran. Little did we know that in a few months the status of both Jerusalem and al-Khalīl, or Hebron, would be changed so drastically. Later, he wrote me of the exceptional blessings of this pilgrimage and how this blessing was a continuation of what we had received from Heaven during that incredible day in Damascus at the tombs of Sayyidah Zaynab and Ibn 'Arabī. And again years later, as we circumambulated the Ka'bah, the reality of the nexus between the *barakah* of the Center and the secondary centers which reflect and echo the Center were discussed, and the blessedness of the visit to the tomb of the author of the *Makkan Revelations* evoked. Titus Ibrāhīm Burckhardt has now left this plane of ephemerality for the empyrean of the Spirit, but his works, which are the fruit of realized knowledge, continue in a unique fashion to illuminate the path of those seriously interested in Sufism in general and in the teachings of Ibn 'Arabī in particular. They are in fact among the most significant formulations of the essence of the teachings of traditional Islam in the modern world. May God shower His choicest blessing upon him. *Raḥimahu Allāh*.

Notes

1. There is some debate between scholars as to whether Sayyidah Zaynab is buried outside Damascus or in Cairo. In each of those cities there is in fact a tomb identified with her and both are sites of pilgrimage by vast multitudes coming from near and far. Whatever the historical reality, they are both her *maqāms*, where she resided, and are *loci* of the emanation of great *barakah* associated with the saint.

Part Five
Postscript

Chapter Eighteen

The Islamic World – Present Tendencies, Future Trends

The survival of traditional Islam in the modern world, the intrusion of modernism into *dār al-islām* and the recent resurgence of forces associated in either name or reality with Islam, added to the global significance of events which have occurred in the Middle East during the past few years all of these have helped to create, not a few, but a flood of works on Islam and its future, some of them being by the very people who but a few years ago rejected the very possibility of Islam being a force to be reckoned with in the future. This veritable new industry, often based on either passing political currents or on conclusions hastily drawn from incomplete data, has already made many predictions for the Islamic world, ranging in style from melodrama to science fiction, with a few more balanced judgements thrown in between. Our aim here is certainly not to add one more scenario to the already existing ones, especially since, according to a belief strongly held by all Muslims, the future lies in God's Hand and only He is aware of its content, as the Quran repeats in many of its verses. Our goal, rather, is to delve beyond the surface in order to bring out the nature of some of the more profound issues, ideas and forces at work within contemporary Islamic religious thought as well as in the Islamic world; also to cast an eye upon how these elements seem to be interacting with each other and with the world about them and how they are likely to do so in the near future. At the same time, we must remain fully aware of the unreliability of all futuristic projections based on present tendencies.

In carrying out this discussion, it is important to distinguish between Islam and the Islamic world. There are currents of thought, movements, affirmations and rejections within the world of Islamic religious thought. There are also, needless to say, very complex forces and movements at play in that part of the world which is called Islamic. The two are not by any means identical and should not be confused with each other for the purpose of any scholarly analysis. Nor should they be totally separated, either. That part of the globe called the Islamic world is Islamic in the most profound sense, in that, over the centuries, the laws, culture, social structures and, in fact, the whole world-view of the people inhabiting it have been molded in depth by Islam. Moreover, after over a century of retreat and sometimes recapitulation before the West, many people of that world called Islamic are again seeking in various ways and modes to turn to Islam, so that there is without doubt a 'revival' of one kind or another associated with Islam in many Muslim lands, although, as already discussed, the form and even content of this 'revival' is far from being the same everywhere. It is also essential to repeat that not all the movements using the name, symbols and language of Islam are of an authentically Islamic character.

There are, then, Islam and the Islamic world to consider; and there is the link between the two in the light of the pertinence of Islam, however it is understood and interpreted by different parties to that world. The future trends of the two, namely, Islam seen as a religion and the Islamic world, will most likely not be the same, but they cannot be totally unrelated either. To study the various current schools of thought and perspectives within Islam and in the circles of Muslim thinkers will therefore certainly cast some light upon what is likely to happen in the Islamic world itself, while remembering that without doubt forces and events from outside the Islamic world are likely to have the most profound effect upon that world without being in any way related to the internal religious and theological forces of Islam. Speculation about this second type of future intrusion into the Islamic world and the role of these external forces in changing the destinies of the Islamic peoples, as everyone has witnessed in several Islamic countries during the past few years, cannot be the concern of this study. Our task, rather, will be to study the trends associated with Islamic thought itself as it might influence and affect the future of the Islamic world. The influence of a particular form of Islamic thought on this or that segment of Islamic society is one thing; invasions by foreign troops or less overt manipulation and interference quite another. Of necessity it is only with the former category that we can be concerned here.

To summarize what has been discussed extensively in previous chapters: within the Islamic religious universe one can discern, not one but a large number of forces and forms of activity which can be classified into four categories, although within each category one can discern a wide spectrum of diversity. These general categories, as already stated, may be enumerated as follows: modernism, messianism, 'fundamentalism' and traditional Islam. Moreover, these categories are of such a nature that, despite their divergence and often inner opposition, they are likely to continue at least into the immediate future.

Modernism, which is the most nebulous of these terms, continues to undergo a change of content from one decade to another. The Muslim modernists of the late 19th century, or even of forty years ago, were not defending the same theses as those of today because of the transient nature of the modern world itself. But they are all called modernists because they place value and some degree of trust in one aspect or another of that post-medieval development in the West which is called modernism; and also because they have tried and continue to try to interpret Islam, or some of its features, according to the ideas, values and norms drawn from the modern outlook, with its own wide range of diversity.

The modernist schools range from those which wish to reinterpret Islam in the light of the humanistic and rationalistic trends of Western thought and which ally themselves with the prevailing paradigm of liberalism in the West, to others which are drawn to the

Marxist world-view and which have become much more numerous during the decades following the Second World War. The Islamic modernists range from serious scholars and thinkers like Fazlur Rahman and Muhammad Arkoun to journalistic popularizers, from those attracted to French existentialism and personalism, such as Muḥammad Lahbabi, to others who have been deeply influenced by Marxist thought, such as 'Alī Sharī'atī and 'Abdallāh Laroui. This class of modernists has usually been deeply concerned at the same time with the social aspect of Islam and often a kind of 'Third World philosophy', which has been a hallmark of French intellectual circles since the Second World War, circles within which most of this type of Muslim 'reformist' thinkers have been nurtured.

Altogether, the impact of the Islamic modernists of the older generations has decreased in most Muslim countries. Based often on a sense of inferiority *vis-à-vis* the West and anxious to emulate everything Western, the earlier reformers were a strong force as long as the Western model itself seemed viable and, in fact, world-dominating. With the gradual weakening of the prevailing Western paradigm in the West itself, combined with the tragedies which continue to occur in the Islamic world in such a manner that they are associated in the eyes of the populace with the West, there has been a decrease in the impact of the 'liberal', Western-oriented Muslim thinker. This trend is likely to continue as long as the forces at play, especially in the Arab-Israeli issue, continue to be what they are.

The second type of modernist, however, who substitutes Marx for Locke and some form of socialism for Western capitalism, and who tries to appear as a hero of the Third World and a champion of the 'down-trodden masses', might be a latecomer to the Islamic world, but his influence is far from being on the wane. On the contrary, there is every reason to think that it is on the rise in many parts of the Islamic world, being abetted materially and financially by certain sources both within and outside that world. Its force will diminish only if traditional Muslim thinkers confront the tenets of this kind of crypto-Marxism head on, as has happened once or twice (for example by 'Allāmah S.M.H. Ṭabāṭabā'ī in his *Principles of the Philosophy of Realism*) rather than circumventing it and refusing to consider its implications, as in fact has usually been the case with so many contemporary Muslim figures.

Messianism has always been present in Islam and has manifested itself whenever the Islamic community has felt an imminent danger to its world of value and meaning. The European invasion of the Islamic world in the 19th century was witness to one such wave of messianism ranging from West Africa to the Sudan, from Persia to India. This wave took very different forms in contexts of diverse nature producing the Mahdi in the Sudan as well as the Bāb in Persia. But the basis of the phenomenon was everywhere nearly the same. It was one of the appearance of a charismatic figure claiming to be the Mahdi or his representative in direct contact with God and his Agents in the Universe and representing a divine intervention in history with eschatological overtones. The last few years have been witness to the revival of this type of religious phenomenon. The early stages of the upheavals in Iran in 1978 definitely had a messianic dimension, not to speak of the capturing of the Grand Mosque in Mecca in 1979, where, strangely enough, messianic tendencies were mixed with a brand of Wahhabism. In this context one can also mention the recent messianic movements in northern Nigeria.

There is every reason to expect such forms of messianism to continue into the future. As a billion people become ever more frustrated in failing to achieve the goals which they believe themselves to be legitimately entitled to realize, one reaction is certainly some kind of a politico-social eruption or upheaval. Another possible reaction, however, is a messianism which promises victory with divine help but on the basis of the destruction of the existing order. Messianism cannot but posses a 'revolutionary' character. That is why traditional Muslims believe that only the Mahdi himself, who will come before the end of history, will be able to carry out a veritable religious revolution signifying nothing less than the establishment of the Divine Order on earth, all other revolutions being forms of subversion and further destruction of what remains of the religious tradition. To the extent that the world becomes a more dangerous place in which to live, and especially while the Muslim peoples see themselves as confronted by alien forces on all sides which threaten their very existence, the wave of messianism is bound to increase in accordance, in fact, with some of the sayings of the Prophet of Islam about the signs of the latter days.

As far as 'fundamentalism' is concerned, as pointed out in previous chapters, its use by journalists and even scholars in reference to a wide variety of phenomena in the Islamic world and to currents of Islamic thought, is most unfortunate and misleading because the term is drawn from the Christian context where it has quite a different connotation. 'Fundamentalism' in Christian religious circles, especially in America, refers to conservative forms of Protestantism, usually anti-modernist, with a rather narrow and literalist interpretation of the Bible and with strong emphasis upon traditional Christian ethics. These characteristics have little to do with most of what is classified today under the name of 'fundamentalism' in Islam, although some of the excessively exoteric but traditional currents of Islamic thought also called 'fundamentalist' do share a few common features with fundamentalism as generally understood in English. The differences, however, are much greater than the similarities, especially in the more violently anti-Western and 'revolutionary' currents which, despite their outward anti-Western attitude, now also refer to themselves as 'fundamentalist', having to invent this word for this particular context since such a term has not existed traditionally in the various Islamic languages (for example, *bunyāngarā'ī* in Persian).

The term *intégrisme*, used in French to describe the same set of phenomena as 'fundamentalism', might appear as more appropriate because it refers to the views of those traditional Catholics who wish to integrate all of life into their religion and, conversely, their religion into all aspects of life. Seen in this light, it might be said that traditional Islam is also *intégriste* and has never ceased to be so. But to use the term for what is now becoming known in English as 'fundamentalism' is a subversion of its meaning and the destruction of the basic distinction which exists between much that is called 'fundamentalism' and traditional Islam, a distinction upon which we have insisted throughout this book as well as in this discussion of contemporary Islam and its future trends. Be that as it may, not only the use of the terms *intégrisme* and 'fundamentalism', but also the classification of a widely diverse set of phenomena and tendencies under such names, is a misleading feature of many of the current studies of Islam and helps to hide the more profound realities involved, including the essential fact that much that is called 'fundamentalist Islam' is not traditional but counter-traditional and opposed to both the spirit and letter of the Islamic tradition as understood and practiced over the centuries since the descent of the Quranic revelation.

It needs to be repeated that under the category of 'fundamentalist' are included both organizations which hope to Islamicize society fully through the application of the *Sharīʿah*, but in a peaceful manner, and those which speak of 'revolution', using all the ideologies and even techniques belonging to the revolutionary movements of modern European history, but with an Islamic coloring. They include movements based on the idea of the rule of the *'ulamā'*, as in Iran, to those which try to eliminate the influence of the *'ulamā'* and, for all practical purposes, their existence, as in Libya. They embrace organizations as different as the Jamāʿat-i islāmī of Pakistan and the Ikhwān al-muslimīn, and governments as diametrically opposed in structure as those of Saudi Arabia and present-day Iran.

To gain a deeper understanding of the forces at play which are bound to determine trends in the near future, it is important to distinguish clearly between much of what is called 'fundamentalist Islam' by Western scholarship and traditional Islam. What the various movements described as 'fundamentalist' have in common is a cultural and religious frustration before the onslaught of Western culture and the desire to reassert themselves in the name of Islam. But their common ground stops at this point, because in trying to achieve their ends some have had recourse to revolutionary jargon drawn from the West, others to a puritanical and rationalistic interpretation of Islam which would do away with the whole Islamic intellectual and spiritual tradition in the name of a primordial purity no longer attainable. This latter group, although limited in its understanding and appreciation of the Islamic tradition, at least accepts a part of that tradition, namely the *Sharīʿah* which is the part of 'fundamentalism' closest to traditional Islam, while the former is counter-traditional in its nature and methods, despite all appearances. Moreover, in many of these so-called 'fundamentalist' movements, leftist ideology has simply replaced that of the classical, liberal schools of the West emulated by an earlier generation of Westernized Muslims. Also hatred, a sense of revenge, constant agitation and blind fury have come to characterize many of these movements, in place of the peace, tranquillity, harmony, and objectivity which have usually characterized authentic manifestations of Islam from the beginning and which are found reflected in both the Quran and the personality of the Prophet. In trying to render back to Islam its power on the stage of history, many of these movements have disfigured the nature of Islam itself. Rather than being a genuine revival of Islam, a revival which is in fact trying to take place in many quarters, they are in reality another form of modernism, but of a much more dangerous kind than the earlier forms because they make use of the language and certain popular symbols of the Islamic religion while adopting some of the most negative and spiritually devastating aspects of the modern West, including Marxism. Furthermore, in the name of religious fervor, they close the door to all intellectual efforts and logical deliberations about the problems and dangers which really confront the Islamic world.

If the hopes and aspirations of the Islamic world continue to be shattered by the force of current events, there is no doubt that the revolutionary type of 'fundamentalist' movements will continue to manifest themselves and even to spread. One must not forget the fact that many of these movements are supported and aggrandized not only by internal forces but also by both the Communist world and certain forces in the West itself, each providing support for its own reasons. Yet once an ideology of this kind is tried, it cannot continue to survive for long unless it is able to achieve the goals that it has promised. Islam is still strong enough in the Islamic world to be able to judge in the long run the Islamicity of all the movements and ideologies which use its name. Most likely, with the passage of time, the rigor of this test by the religious conscience of the community will be felt more strongly by all movements, forces and governments which speak of 'Islamic ideology'. Whatever the actual political implications of this sifting and testing of such forces by the Islamic population might be, there seems to be little doubt that on the level of religious thought, or of Islam itself considered as a religion, there is bound to be a greater discernment within Islamic society concerning all those movements which are dubbed as 'fundamentalist' today. Ideology is a Western concept hardly translatable into Arabic and Persian. Once Islam itself is interpreted, not as an all-embracing religion or *al-dīn*, but as an ideology which serves a particular movement or regime as its ideological prop in the modern sense, then the failure of that movement or regime reflects upon Islam itself. In this case, either people lose their faith or begin to scrutinize the actual nature of the forces that have presented themselves as Islamic. Both of these tendencies are bound to occur to the extent that the 'fundamentalist' movements are able to wield actual power and to affect the everyday lives of human beings.

Finally, there is traditional Islam itself to consider, which, as stated, is often mistaken for 'fundamentalism' as the term is currently used. Despite waves of modernism, puritanical reactions, messianism and the violent and revolutionary or theologically limitative forms of 'fundamentalism', traditional Islam continues to survive. Most Muslims still live in a world in which the equilibrium promulgated by the *Sharī'ah* and the serenity of Islamic spirituality are to be found to some extent, despite the experiences of European colonialism, a certain degree of decadence within the Islamic world (which became noticeable in the 18th century and increased during the 19th century), the constant political turmoils and the numerous economic problems which many Muslim countries face. Most of the interpreters of the *Sharī'ah* are still traditional *'ulamā'*. The Sufi orders, far from being dead, still possess an inner vitality; one can also find a few great spiritual masters within them. And the traditional intellectual and theological sciences are not by any means dead. Moreover, as already mentioned, during the past few decades a new class of scholars and thinkers has appeared in the Islamic world who are traditional in their adherence to and defense of the whole and integral Islamic tradition, but who also know the Western world in depth and are able to provide intellectual answers from the Islamic point of view to the problems posed by the modern world rather than having recourse to either blind faith or simple sloganeering and rhetoric.

Traditional Islam is bound to survive in the future, especially since the very structure of the Islamic tradition, with its emphasis upon the direct link between man and God and lack of a central religious authority, contains the maximum protection for survival in a world such as that of today. Moreover, the newly created class of traditional Muslim scholars and thinkers who are also fully cognizant of the nature of the modern world, its school of thought, philosophies and sciences, is bound to increase and is in fact doing so now. This trend is likely to spread, moreover, to the extent that various attempts made by different groups within the 'fundamentalist' camp to Islamicize society, knowledge and education without the full support of the Islamic intellectual tradition fails to deliver the results expected of it. The decay in the quality of traditional life is also likely to continue, but traditional Islam is bound to survive in its various dimensions and aspects and will ultimately be the judge and criterion of exactly how Islamic are all those revivals and resurgent movements which claim an Islamic character.

For several centuries the predominant form of theology in the Sunni part of the Islamic world has been Ash'arite, based on an all-encompassing voluntarism and resulting in a more or less fideist position in which knowledge is made subservient to faith. Moreover, the rise of such movements as Wahhabism, the Salafiyyah and the like has only helped strengthen this tendency. Even in the Shi'ite world, where the prevalent theology has been more conducive to the intellectual aspects of the Islamic tradition, the *akhbārī-uṣūlī* debates and the predominance of the exoteric element at the end of the Safavid period onward led what are traditionally called the 'intellectual sciences' (*al-'ulūm al-'aqliyyah*) to be eclipsed to a certain degree. Therefore, by and large, and despite the survival of centers of activity of the intellectual sciences in certain areas, especially in Persia and the Indian subcontinent, when those Islamic thinkers affected by this fideism confronted the West, they did so mostly from a perspective which was helpless before the specifically intellectual and rational challenges of the modern world and which had to have recourse to either an opposition based on fanaticism or refuge in the emotional aspect of faith alone. The result could not have but been catastrophic because the main challenge of the modern West to Islam, in contrast, let us say, to the Mongol invasion, is not primarily military, although the military dimension is certainly present even after the apparent end of the colonial period. Nor is it primarily religious, as it was in the encounter of Islam with Hinduism. The challenge, rather, concerns mainly the domain of the mind and requires a response suitable to its nature, whereas until recently the response of the Islamic world was not like that of the early Islamic centuries in the face of the Graceo-Alexandrian sciences and learning. The world of Islamic religious scholars has not produced its Ibn Sīnās, al-Bīrūnīs or even its al-Ghazzālīs. The response has echoed for the most part the fideism and voluntarism that have dominated the religious centers of learning.

During the past few years, Islamic thinkers have begun to confront this problem more fully and to come to terms with, not only the social, but also the intellectual and cultural challenges of the West. Numerous authorities throughout the Islamic world have come to realize the importance of the re-Islamicization of the educational system and the integration of the modern sciences into the Islamic world-view. Many educational conferences dealing with these problems have been held and are being planned for the future. There is little doubt that this trend will continue to grow in coming years and not lose its momentum so easily. Attempts will most likely continue to be made to create a single educational system in various Islamic countries to replace the two contending ones (the traditional Islamic and the modern) which dominate the scene in most Islamic lands at present. Likewise, efforts will continue to be expended to try to 'Islamicize' various sciences ranging from the humanities to the social and even the natural sciences.

The main question is whether, while making use of only one dimension of the Islamic tradition, namely the *Sharī'ah*, yet neglecting the other dimensions and the whole intellectual and spiritual tradition of Islam, it is possible to carry out such an enterprise. Is it in fact possible to integrate the sciences of nature into the Islamic perspective by limiting oneself only to the Islamic sciences of law and the literal meaning of the verses of the Quran; or by replacing an intellectual response by piety, no matter how sincere that piety might be? At the present moment there are two forces at play in this endeavor to Islamicize education and the sciences. One is closely allied to certain segments of that spectrum called 'fundamentalism' and sees the success of this process as being nothing more than the result and consequence of the re-establishment of the *Sharī'ah* in society. This group more or less follows the voluntarist-fideist theological position to which is added the rejection of the integral intellectual and spiritual tradition of Islam and a puritanical-rationalistic tendency going back to the so-called 'reform' movements of the 19th century.

The second group, which is traditional rather than 'fundamentalist', seeks to achieve the same goal of Islamicization, but through recourse to the complete Islamic intellectual tradition combined with a critique in depth of the modern world itself based on traditional principles. While agreeing with the first group upon the importance of the implementation of the *Sharī'ah*, it believes that the intellectual challenges posed by the modern world can only be answered by, first of all, understanding the nature of these challenges in depth and, secondly, by applying the intellectual principles of the Islamic tradition to counter these challenges and the premises of the modern world-view which oppose the sacred universe of Islam, not in this or that detail but in principle. Furthermore, this latter group believes that the challenge of modernism cannot be answered until the Islamic intellectual and spiritual tradition is resuscitated and revived in all its totality. It maintains that only the spiritual, inward and esoteric aspects of religion are able to provide the remedy for certain cracks which appear in the wall of exoteric religion as a result of the attacks of secularized and anti-traditional forces. The case of Islam cannot be an exception to this rule.

Both of these groups, as well as their ideas and goals, are bound to continue in the near future. Moreover, the degree of success which each school has will influence the course of Islamic theology and religious thought itself. Of course, the secularizing forces opposed to the educational aim of both groups are also alive and active in many lands and are bound to influence events in this domain to an appreciable degree, at least in some of the major Islamic countries. Their influence through educational channels upon Islamic thought itself is, however, bound to be less than that of the first two groups mentioned above. Where the secularists in educational theory and practice will wield their influence most visibly will be in helping to continue the existing dual system of education in the Islamic world, with the obvious results that such a system has in training members of a single society who hold opposing views on crucial issues and who cannot unite with their fellow countrymen in creating an integrated social order.

In this realm, even those who wish to Islamicize the educational system often help unwillingly in its further secularization by their wish to sweep the already century-old 'modern' educational institutions aside completely, in many of which generations of devout Muslims have sought to create some kind of bridge between the traditional schools and new ones and have even sought to mold the classical Islamic scientific vocabulary of such languages as Arabic and Persian to become suitable vehicles for the expression of contemporary scientific disciplines. In years to come, there will most likely be rivalry between those who wish to Islamicize the already existing educational institutions, thereby removing the present dichotomy which exists even despite efforts by a number of dedicated Muslim teachers and thinkers over the past century, and those who would do away with the existing modern institutions completely in the name of model 'new' institutions of an Islamic nature. The present-day effort to create Islamic universities throughout the Muslim world and their minor successes outside the field of the specifically religious disciplines (such as Sacred Law and hermeneutics) when set against the immense obstacles they face reveal both the enormity of the task involved and the crucial role that the whole presently ongoing process of Islamicization in education and the sciences will have for the future of both Islamic thought and the Islamic world.

The increase in awareness of the Islamic world as a single entity is itself one of the important trends to be observed in that world, a trend which is bound to continue. Both the traditionalists and the 'fundamentalists' cherish the ideal of the unity of the Islamic world, although they envisage its realization in very different ways. Messianism, on the other hand, has always had the unification of the Islamic world as an intrinsic part of its perspective and program. According to tradition, it is the Mahdi who will finally reunify the Islamic world at the end of time. The rise of greater awareness of the Islamic ethos and reactions to the onslaught of the West have in fact made the unity of the Islamic world a motto for political and religious forces of nearly every color and persuasion, save of course for the secularists. This strong Islamic sentiment has also been manipulated by some of the 'fundamentalist' forces, and regimes have even been established, the immediate political ends of which are none other than the creation of this unity, but usually without any result save the further weakening of the Islamic world.

The desire to achieve this unity manifests itself also in a strong inclination in theological circles to have closer co-operation and better understanding between Sunnism and Shi'ism. This tendency, which is several decades old and which was highlighted by the declaration a generation ago by Shaykh al-Shalṭūt, then rector of al-Azhar University, that Twelve-Imam Shi'ite (Ja'farī) Law would be taught as one of the orthodox schools of law in that venerable institution, is bound to continue. Also intra-Islamic dialogue between Sunni and Shi'ite thinkers will most likely increase on the legal, theological and philosophical levels. Parallel with these religious developments, however, political use of Sunni-Shi'ite differences not only continues but becomes aggravated to the extent that Islam is used as a political instrument by one group or regime against another. These differences also provide an ideal opportunity for all the external forces which reap their own benefits from the weakening of the Islamic world and the creation of chaos and disorder – not to speak of open warfare – therein. The disturbances and even wars of the past few years related to Sunni-Shi'ite differences are unlikely to disappear in the presence of the political forces active particularly in the central areas of the Islamic world, while the tendency among Islamic thinkers and the traditional *'ulamā'* in both camps to benefit from dialogue with each other and rapprochement on many theological and even legal matters is also likely to increase.

Against this strong desire toward 'unification' and the awareness of the Islamic peoples as a single people, or *ummah*, as mentioned in the Quran, stands not only the force of nationalism in its secular sense as derived from the French Revolution or various forms or ethnic provincialism, but also a more moderate and sober form which might be called 'Islamic nationalism'. Since the 19th century the forces that have been called Arab nationalism, Turkish nationalism, Iranian nationalism and the like have been most powerful in the Middle East region of the Islamic world. Now, there are revolutionary pan-Islamic movements which oppose all such forces in the name of the political unity of the Islamic world. These two contending forces are bound to struggle against each other in the years ahead. It is difficult to imagine that the forces for the unification of Islam will succeed in achieving a goal which, according to Prophetic tradition (*ḥadīth*) is to be accomplished by the Mahdi himself, although greater co-operation, communication and exchange are likely to take place among various Islamic nations and peoples in many fields, ranging from the economic and political to the cultural. Nor are the forces of nationalism likely to die out. In fact, there are now tendencies for fanning the fire of even manifestations of more local nationalism, which, if successful, would not only *not* lead to a single Islamic world but would cause the creation of small but helpless states at the mercy of outside forces which could manipulate them even more easily than they do now.

There is, however, a third type of force to consider, namely traditional 'Islamic nationalism' in the sense of the famous *ḥadīth*, 'The love of one's nation comes from faith'. Long before the French Revolution, the Arabs knew that they were not Persians or Turks and vice-versa, although an Arab could travel from Tangiers and settle in Delhi without any difficulty or a Persian migrate to Istanbul or Hyderabad and make it his second home. Many analysts confuse this traditional awareness of an Egyptian being an Egyptian or a

Persian a Persian with the more recent forms of the European type of nationalism. Between the extremes of the utopian idea of a single Islamic state covering the whole Islamic world and small warring states which continue to weaken internally as a result of constant enmity and rivalry, one can envisage the possibility of the rise, once again, of a trend in the future towards a kind of Islamic political thought which combines the ideal of the unity of the Islamic world based on culture, Divine Law, intellectual life, etc., with separate political units which embrace the major peoples and cultural zones of the Islamic world, such as the Arabic, the Persian, the Turkish, etc. It is most difficult to predict trends in such a domain where, in a world in chaos, political factors are so diverse and where one stands on shifting sand. But certainly this combining of a sense of religion with patriotism in a more traditional sense cannot be at all dismissed as a possibility, especially among peoples already scorched by the fires of fanaticism and extremism forced upon them in the name of Islam and for the sake of an elusive and as yet non-existent international order which, for the masses, cannot replace their natural love for their own homeland, language and people, and which, in certain cases, even creates the danger of their centuries-old love of Islam itself decreasing, a love that has always been combined in their eyes with their attachment to their homeland.

There is little doubt that what has been called the 'defiance of Islam' before the modern world will continue in future years, but it is likely to take new forms in addition to already existing ones. While political upheavals, using the name of Islam, are bound to continue in a world in which Islamic forces do not enjoy complete freedom of action but where instead external powers have access to and may manipulate such forces, other reactions not based simply upon sentiments and fanaticism are also likely to occur. As current forces working for revival use radio and television to attack the West, with their representatives standing in buildings emulating Western architecture and driving through streets designed according to modern ideas of urbanization, other forces are likely to come forward to examine the science and technology, the social theories and ideas of urban development which the Islamic world has been copying blindly, as if they had nothing to do with religion, while attacking the civilization of which they are the products. There is likely to be a greater battle with modernism than ever before in the fields of the arts, of architecture, of literature, of science and of philosophy. The recent interest in the revival of Islamic architecture and city planning as well as the arts and crafts is a sign of this important tendency, which only complements the revival of the intellectual and spiritual tradition of Islam. The battle is likely to be a bitter one, carried out directly with intellectual tools in fields ranging from historiography, the social sciences, language and literature, the arts and sciences to the study of other religions. These intellectual battles will, moreover, affect the religious thought of Islam itself and the mentality of Muslims and therefore influence the whole course of future events in the Islamic world.

As various waves of Mahdiism and 'fundamentalism' fail to solve the problems of the Islamic world until the Mahdi does in reality arrive, and as the hitherto current types of modernism display their bankruptcy in a world in which the civilization that gave birth to modernism is itself facing its greatest crises, the central reality in the Islamic world will most likely become the battle, not between traditional Islam and openly declared secularism and modernism as was the case until recently, but between traditional Islam and various counter-traditional and leftist ideologies parading as Islam. It is one of the characteristics of the life of the late 20th century, seen also fully in Christianity, that the forces opposed to religion no longer function only outside the citadel of religion but try to destroy it from within by penetrating that citadel and masquerading as part of religion. There is a great difference between the time when Jamāl al-Dīn Astrābādī, known as Afghānī, wrote his *Refutation of the Materialists*, attacking the modern West as being materialistic and agnostic, or the scholars of al-Azhar attacking Communism as being godless, and the recent exchange between traditional Muslims and those who espouse all the causes of the Communist world but who also call themselves Islamic. The main battle of the future in the Islamic world will most likely be between these two forces and the central problem will be the subversion of Islam from within by forces claiming to speak in its name.

In years to come, likewise, the debate between those who would interpret Islam as religion in its traditional sense, as against those who speak of it as ideology, is bound to continue, as are discussions between those who seek to revive ethics by reforming Islamic society from within as against those for whom reform can only come by violent change of the norms and structures of a society from without. There will be those who will seek to blend Islam with every aspect of society, standing against those who are not necessarily irreligious (often quite the contrary), but who believe that, in order to preserve the purity of their religion, its sacred name should not be used in the politico-economic arena where the very nature of the forces involved can only sully it. One will continue to see a strong opposition between those who have a triumphalistic and often sentimental view of Islam, according to which everything of value is 'Islamic' and even the West is successful because of its heritage of Islamic science, and others who do not at all wish to identify Islam with the modern West and its triumphs but who see Islam rather as an ally of the other traditional religions, including Christianity and Judaism, against the modern world which opposes not only Islam but religion as such.

Finally, there will continue to be contention between those who wish to revive the Islamic tradition in its wholeness and those who undermine the possibility of this revival by either misusing the name of Islam to serve ideas of a completely different nature, or, as a result of a sense of inferiority toward the modern world, which is often veiled by an emotional triumphalism. In all these cases, there will be the desire, at least outwardly, to revive Islamic society and the ethical norms which govern it. This element will remain the common denominator, while all the differences here stated concerning, not only the manner of implementing such a program of revival, but all the other factors of both an intellectual and political nature already mentioned, will most likely continue.

As the Quran states, the future is in God's Hands and His alone. All the tendencies mentioned above exist and can be projected into trends for the near future but only in a provisional way, for, from the Islamic point of view, there is no determinism in history. A single unforeseen event or the appearance of a single figure could change the entire texture of forces and tendencies which comprise the Islamic world. What can be said with certainty is that, despite becoming weakened, the Islamic tradition is still very much alive in both its outer and inner dimensions and that, at this point in its history, it has to react to a multiplicity of forces from both without and within, some of which are openly opposed to it and others, though they bear its name, are in reality of quite another nature. In any case, the vitality of the Islamic tradition will continue to the end of days, as promised by the Prophet. As to which of the trends cited will gain the upper hand, what plans the outside world hides behind veils of secrecy as it conspires to manipulate these trends and tendencies, and *how these* forces will affect the Islamic world itself, it is not possible to say with certitude. In this domain more than in all others, one can best conclude with the traditional Islamic dictum, God knows best (*wa'Llāhu a'lam*).

Index